ALSO BY ANN KAISER STEARNS

Living Through Personal Crisis

Coming Back—Rebuilding Lives After Crisis and Loss

LIVING THROUGH JOB LOSS

Coping with the Emotional Effects of Job Loss and Rebuilding Your Future

ANN KAISER STEARNS, PH. D.
with Rick Lamplugh

A FIRESIDE BOOK
Published by Simon & Schuster
New York   London   Toronto   Sydney   Tokyo   Singapore

FIRESIDE
Rockefeller Center
1230 Avenue of the Americas
New York, NY 10020

FIRESIDE and colophon are registered trademarks
of Simon & Schuster Inc.

Designed by Irving Perkins Associates

Manufactured in the United States of America

10   9   8   7   6   5   4   3   2   1

Library of Congress Cataloging-in-Publication Data

Stearns, Ann Kaiser
Living through job loss : coping with the emotional effects of job loss and rebuild-
ing your future / Ann Kaiser Stearns with Rick Lamplugh.
p.   cm.
"A Fireside book."
Includes bibliographical references and index.
1 Unemployment—Psychological aspects. 2. Unemployed—Life skills guides. I.
Lamplugh, Rick. II. Title.
HD5708.S72   1995
158.7—dc20   95-24740
                                                      CIP
ISBN 0-684-81045-X

The author gratefully acknowledges permission from the following sources to quote
material in the text:

Minding the Body, Mending the Mind (excerpted from pp. 23–26), © 1987, by Joan
Borysenko, Ph.D. Reprinted by permission of Addison-Wesley Publishing Co., Inc.

"The White-Collar Layoffs That We're Seeing Are Permanent and Structural. These
Jobs Are Gone Forever," pp. 34–39, *Time,* Nov. 22, 1993, by George Church. © 1993
Time Inc., reprinted by permission.

"Career Moves for Ages 20–70," *Psychology Today,* Nov.–Dec. 1992, by Peter Drucker.
Reprinted with permission from *Psychology Today,* copyright © 1992 (Sussex Publish-
ers, Inc.).

Additional permissions at back of book.

To my dear daughters Amanda and Ashley

Author's Note

This book includes dozens of true stories told to me and to Rick Lamplugh in hundreds of hours of interviews or obtained from researching the literature. In many instances certain identifying information of the people we interviewed has been changed to ensure confidentiality. While to the best of my knowledge each story is true, the names of many characters in the book are fictitious, including Mr. Lee, Roger, Marie Christopher, Dave Elway, the Jacksons, Ben, Oscar, Michael, Paul Burton, Angie Roberts, Susan, Ed Drexel, Doug Sweeny, and Ken Stack. Those we interviewed whose actual names are used have given us their permission to identify them. Where names are disguised, so are places and the names of certain employers or businesses.

Acknowledgments

My children were loving and helpful to me as I worked on this project for nearly three years and mourned the loss of three close friends. Amanda and Ashley have added to my life so many smiles and hugs, so much curiosity, shared meaningfulness, liveliness, and fun—and I'm thankful. Ilene McGrath is a wise and gifted freelance editor whose contributions here and to my three earlier publications are greatly valued. Joel Wattenbarger, one of two beloved godsons, contributed considerably as a research assistant while he was studying at Yale. Marian Wattenbarger, a dear friend for more than thirty years, read every word of the manuscript and provided helpful feedback and emotional support, as did my friend Linda J. Walter, who copyedited and offered valuable suggestions and encouragement. These good people and others—Eleanor and Frank Fink, Bob Fisher, Joanne Munden, Jack and Peggy Compton, and a woman psychologist friend—helped me heal in the aftermath of Dr. Al Marshello's death and the other losses. Mariann DePaulo assisted with some research, and her father, Dr. J. Raymond DePaulo, gave valuable guidance on certain medical segments of the book. My friend Beth DePaulo lent her loving support even as she was fighting cancer and facing death. Dr. Blake L. Wattenbarger, Gaylene and Elton Perry, Norma and Jack Danz, and Dr. Donald J. Slowinski played important informative or supportive roles, too. And Barbara Diehl, intelligent and capable, worked very hard and faithfully as she word-processed this work from start to finish. My part-time personal secretary, Jean Blickenstaff, gave generously of her time, too. Finally, I appreciate Rick Lamplugh, whose invitation to appear on his radio program sparked the idea in my mind of writing this book. Rick's extensive experience as a vocational counselor helped me begin to learn what I needed to know about the changing North American workplace. He also contributed as my consultant by conscientiously interviewing scores of unemployed and reemployed people. I thank every one of these special people for their contributions.

*"That which does not kill me
makes me stronger,"* wrote
*Friedrich Nietzsche a century ago.
These words have lasting value
but are true in our lives
only if we decide
to make them so.*

—ANN KAISER STEARNS

Contents

Preface

This book is not like any you've seen before. What you'll read about here is how to overcome the troublesome feelings and specific problems you've had since losing your job, and how to be at peace with yourself and more likely to succeed when reemployed. Other books will tell you how to improve your résumé or give a more impressive interview. My goal is to help you learn about the normal psychological adjustment process in response to job loss so you'll understand what you're going through, sleep better at night, and feel more like getting up in the morning. I will also help you have more confidence and hope as you build your future. You will be strengthened as you gain a clearer picture of the mental barriers you need to overcome and the new workplace realities you need to understand.

Living Through Job Loss is written for blue- and white-collar workers, for men and women who are or soon will be unemployed, indefinitely laid off, or downsized. It is also written for family members and professionals in a position to help.

You probably wouldn't expect yourself just to go right on with life after suffering the death of a loved one or enduring a difficult divorce. Remarkably, most people do expect themselves simply to find another job as soon as possible and carry on as usual after being thrown out of the workplace that defined and sustained them. In reality, you need time for reflection whether you've lost a loved one, seen the end of a marriage, or lost a job that has meant something to you. A bereavement process involving depression, disappointment, anger, self-doubt, and other common reactions is usually necessary for healing in *all* situations of loss.

Job loss plunges most people into a painful period of adjustment and significantly increases their risk of becoming ill. There is an increased risk of child abuse associated with unemployment, and a profound increase in family problems. Help is available and will be described here to enable you to avoid or overcome many such health, financial, or family concerns.

Because we have interviewed or surveyed scores of unemployed people for this book and studied their circumstances, personal strengths, and healing strategies, you can learn from the stories told here. You can discover how to cope with resentments, difficulties with relationships, the stress of job search, and other burdens. You can come to recognize the signs of severe depression and find out where and how to get help. You can develop your own healing strategies and buffer the stress in your life.

In *Living Through Job Loss* you will also learn about the changing North American workplace and what you need to know about your next job. You'll see the traits of the people I call "triumphant survivors" and you'll recognize many of their characteristic strengths as your own. You'll become better able to hold your head up in the face of adversity and become clearer about how to seize new opportunities for personal growth and a better life.

I

Job Loss:
A Personal Crisis

Work is the closest thing to sanity.

—SIGMUND FREUD

Surviving job loss is difficult for almost everyone, but most people can and do survive. You can move beyond unhappiness, worry, anger, and discouragement but first you must go through a recovery process. Healing begins with recognizing and then learning how to manage your symptoms of distress.

Sleeplessness or excessive sleep, depression, aches and pains, irritability, self-doubt, even thoughts of suicide or fantasies of harming someone else: These and many other reactions to job loss can be disturbing.

You probably find yourself having more arguments with loved ones and less patience with people in general, including strangers. Perhaps the pleasure has gone out of many of the activities you once enjoyed.

You may be avoiding certain friends or relatives who are important to you, people who might now keep asking whether you've found another job. Or maybe you are unhappily reemployed—in a part-time, temporary, or lower-status job with less pay—and you don't want to have to talk about it. Sometimes it's hard to share our pain with people who knew us in better times.

Perhaps you worry constantly about financial matters, or you may do the opposite, keeping yourself busy in an effort to avoid your problems. Like many others trying to cope with the anxieties of job loss, you may be spending numerous hours watching television, consequently growing all the more discouraged and depressed. Both worrying incessantly and working hard not to worry take enormous energy. You probably feel weary.

Most people aren't leaving their jobs these days under happy conditions. Except for lucky lottery winners and the truly blessed who get a generous retirement package and a party, the process of becoming unemployed is not much fun. It's devastating. "They brought me in and shot me," said one recently jobless person interviewed for this book.

"I felt raped," a burly blue-collar worker complained, describing the humiliating circumstances of his being fired and the degrading way he was treated by someone in authority at the unemployment office. Loyal to his employer for nearly twenty years, a hard worker, highly skilled, this man felt used, abused, and discarded. He knows he is a good person whose life will eventually get on track again. Millions like him have lost their jobs too. But overcoming such a setback requires time, emotional support from others, and strategies for survival.

"They said they were going to eliminate my job, but after I was gone they didn't," protested a sixty-three-year-old office manager, probably the victim of age discrimination. "I felt like I wasn't worth anything, like an old shoe," she said. "My arms aren't strong enough for me to be a waitress. I can't take the abuse of being a barmaid. Accounting is what I know and nobody will hire a woman my age." This mother of two sons, grandmother, and great-grandmother felt "alone and bitter and cried a lot" in the seven months it took to find a satisfying new job as a physician's business manager. She is happier at work now than she has ever been and sees her former employer as having done her a favor by dismissing her. But for many months she despaired and felt defeated.

Scores of people have reported that it took them a year or more to find acceptable new employment and even longer to turn the crisis of job loss into opportunity and a rewarding new life.

An experienced, highly successful sales manager—making $80,000 a year and having the perk of driving a late-model luxury car—came to work one Monday morning to be met at the door by his boss, who handed him a plastic bag containing the belongings from his desk. The company soon hired a younger man to replace him who would make half the money and have expanded responsibilities. After a period of excessive use of alcohol and related family problems, the former manager, along with his wife, received several months of counseling and strengthened their marriage. He is earning considerably less now in a promising new career but is enjoying greater satisfaction as a husband and father. Sometimes he still feels bitter.

In today's workplace, writes Dartmouth professor Leonard Greenhalgh, "unneeded human capital is written off in much the same way that plants and equipment are written off. The workforce reduction process is conceptualized as a *disposal* problem."[1] Discarded, rendered useless, not worth saving—that's how many men and women feel they have been treated when their jobs are taken away. In such a situation, even the strongest person will struggle with powerful feelings of hurt, anger, and dismay.

You may be ruminating daily over grievances carried in your head from your former workplace, replaying last events, or thinking hostile thoughts about individuals who you feel have betrayed you. You may have lost weight under duress or gained weight from compulsive eating as a result of stress. If you drink alcohol, you may be drinking more frequently, or in greater quantities.

Whatever the specific circumstances of your job loss, almost certainly your self-confidence has diminished. In today's changing world economy, you may also be struggling with feelings of disillusionment. Hard work, talent, productivity, longevity, and loyalty no longer seem to provide security at the workplace. "Where now is the American Dream?" many ask. "Can the dream still have reality for me?"

Preparing for Job Loss

If you haven't yet lost your job but soon will, you can develop your coping strategy in advance. In their book *Parting Company,* William Morin and James Cabrera suggest putting into motion some of the following, which I have quoted or paraphrased,* along with one suggestion from another author. Take the actions as words of advice as they are applicable to you:

- Don't vent your emotions on the spot when getting the bad news. It's a good idea to say you need some time to think things over, and make an appointment for the next day. If you wait much longer than that, however, the company may start to lose interest in you and become more difficult to deal with. This delay will enable you to come to terms with your emotions and think about what you need from the company.
- Go home. Don't have a drink. Don't phone everyone you know. Don't start to make contacts for another job right away. Getting a new job is a systematic process which must be done in the proper sequence.
- Find someone with whom you can let off steam before you meet again with the boss. This should be someone who is not in the same predicament as you are; co-workers losing their jobs too are probably equally upset, so choose someone else.
- Talk over your feelings and your options at length with a good listener, someone you trust. If you can't speak in person, use the phone—even several hours of phone calls with breaks in between.
- Remember that your goal is to work through your intense feelings and ultimately compose yourself so that you can decide what is the best thing for you to do for yourself.
- Take some notes in preparation for your meeting with your boss so that you can ask questions as you figure out what he or she is willing to do for you.
- Find out if the company has a severance plan. Try to have payments made in installments rather than as a lump sum. Receiving regular paychecks will reduce your stress. However, if your company is in

danger of bankruptcy or you are planning to retire, a lump sum is better. If you do take the full amount, you need to see a qualified financial planner. Don't try to make important financial or other decisions while in your current state of mind.

- Find out if medical coverage, a life insurance policy, or other benefits will continue while you are receiving severance pay. If not, see if you can pay to have them continue.
- Ask if the company will help you in finding another job. Will they offer career counseling; an office where you can use a desk, telephone, and word processor; or secretarial help?
- Ask your supervisor to write down an explanation of why your job is being eliminated. Also ask for a copy of your personnel records. While as few as one person in twenty may have a strong antidiscrimination case, this is a possibility. For example, if you are forty or more and no younger employees were laid off, you may be the victim of age discrimination. The letter from your employer, your personnel record, and the employee handbook may come in handy if you later decide to consult a legal expert.†
- Think about family needs. If a vacation was being planned, for example, consider how canceling it might affect all of you. Unless you're in dire financial straits, take the vacation. It will reduce the stress for everyone.

*William J. Morin and James C. Cabrera, *Parting Company: How to Survive the Loss of a Job and Find Another Successfully* (New York: Harcourt Brace Jovanovich, 1991).
†This suggestion is from Dan Moreau, "If You Lose Your Job," *Changing Times*, March 1991, 62–63.

A GRIEF AND HEALING PROCESS

Somehow it must be possible to approach the future with a calmed heart, new confidence, and hope. That's a tough assignment, however, for a person who is grieving. Job loss is an experience in bereavement. Shock, sadness, insomnia, an appetite problem, anger, self-doubt or self-blame, anxiety, and depression are all symptoms of the grief and healing process in response to a personal crisis. These are normal reactions and emotions which you can understand, work through, and move beyond.

Many people see bereavement as stages of sorrow, remembrance, and reflection that we all go through when a loved one dies. What isn't commonly understood is that bereavement is a natural response to many other kinds of loss or crisis events as well—including unemployment and any economic downsizing that may accompany reemployment.

Mary Jo Purcell, whose job was eliminated, wrote in *Newsweek* that "the unemployed haven't 'lost' their jobs; they know where they are. The jobs are now overseas or they are one of the balls juggled and dropped in union-contract negotiations. Very often these lost jobs can be found listed proudly as 'efficiency accomplishments' in the résumés of corporate executives. . . . So I haven't 'lost' my job," she explains. "My job *died*."[2]

Friends and acquaintances who want to help but don't know how, continues Purcell, should "avoid clichés" such as "'When God closes a door, He opens a window'" and "'Behind every cloud. . . .'" Nor does the unemployed person want to hear depressing stories about a neighbor who finally found work after nearly two years of unemployment. Gloomy comments such as these are "too much like the warnings of three days of unrelenting labor that women, facing their first childbirth, are forced to endure." It is far better to "treat the unemployed as if there were a death in the family" and to be available as a good listener when the person needs to talk.[3]

Healing takes far longer than most people expect. Generally speaking, bereavement lasts at least a year. Some especially difficult losses including job loss often involve a grief and recovery process that lasts several years. Even your doctor or spiritual leader may not understand that you are struggling with normal bereavement reactions. You aren't "crazy" or "weak" because it is taking you a long time to adjust to changed circumstances.

DENIAL

Especially in the early weeks and months of a personal crisis, people often deny the full impact of a loss, not allowing even themselves to know how much hurt, anger, or concern lies within.

Stephen Fineman, in his book *White Collar Unemployment and Stress,* reported findings from a four-year study of 100 unemployed managers and professionals ranging in age from the early twenties to late fifties. Writes Fineman, "Someone who has been made suddenly unemployed might aimlessly drift, doing nothing in particular for weeks, avoiding the problem as much as possible. Rather different avoidant behavior would be to become actively involved in anything but job hunting (holidays, sports, hobbies) and evading discussions about unemployment. These sorts of reactions are perhaps most likely during an early 'shock' phase of unemployment."[4] Experiencing a threat to their self-image, competence, and status, many of the white-collar workers in this study used denial as a coping mechanism, Fineman found. "Inactivity and avoidance are both . . . special forms of defense under threat," he explained. "They . . . are usually automatic processes which protect us from acute levels of anxiety by blocking the tension build-up."[5]

According to Fineman, although the mechanisms of inaction and avoidance may protect someone from such threats, these devices do not actually deal with the problem. "Unless somehow the problem 'goes away by itself' (for example, despite inaction, an individual is reinstated or is offered another job) then the problem which threatens constantly lurks behind the defenses."[6]

Keeping up these defenses requires a lot of energy, explains Fineman. Increasingly tired, the individual can become severely tense and anxious.[7] This is true for blue-collar workers as well as white-collar workers, women as well as men.

In the lives of hundreds of people I have encountered as a teacher, counselor, and author, as well as in my own life, I have seen what Fineman saw in studying unemployed people: Clearly the burdensome stress we experience is the result of a "failure to master threatening problems."[8] If we face our difficulties with honesty and courage, we can find solutions to seemingly unresolvable problems and conflicts. As we confront and examine our emotions, we can release ourselves from the burden of stress caused by anxiety and tension. We can learn new ways to cope with specific concerns and problems, one at a time.

WHAT YOU'VE LOST

Leonard Fagin and Martin Little examined the psychological meaning of work on the basis of various unemployment studies in Britain. In their book *The Forsaken Families,* they describe seven key meanings of work that explain why job loss commonly produces significant levels of anxiety and distress: Work enables us to structure our time, it provides a source of identity, it gives us relationships outside the nuclear family, it is a source of obligatory activity, it enables us to develop skills and creativity, it provides a sense of purpose, and it gives us a source of income so we can exercise control in our lives.[9]

Recently I've been teaching "Surviving Job Loss" seminars at the college in Baltimore where I've been a psychology professor for more than twenty years. When I asked men and women of a wide variety of ages and occupations what their former jobs provided, here's what they said:

"A paycheck."
"My identity, a sense of who I am."
"Financial support for my family."
"A sense of accomplishment."
"Security."
"Self-confidence."
"A place where I fit in."
"Enjoyment."
"A challenge."
"Medical benefits."
"Money for the things I need or want."
"Self-respect."
"Friendships."

"Recognition."

"Time structure."

"A sense of purpose."

"Mental stimulation."

"Opportunities for new learning."

"More control over my life."

"The knowledge that I'm needed."

"Validation."

"Self-expression."

"The ability to make a positive contribution."

"A future I can plan for."

Like these jobless or unhappily reemployed people who sign up for my seminars, you, too, may feel relieved to recognize that your symptoms of distress are understandable and inevitable given what work has meant to you.

A DISQUIETING ORDEAL FOR ALMOST EVERYONE

"Who falls hardest in response to job loss?" Rick Lamplugh and I often asked ourselves as we worked together. White-collar or blue-collar workers? Women or men? African Americans? Hispanics? White males? Young adults, baby boomers, or older workers? People who fall from high incomes or the working poor? Injured workers? Parents with young children? Single people?

As I researched the literature and we interviewed scores of men and women across a wide spectrum of ages, socioeconomic groups, and occupations, it soon became clear that job loss is a difficult life crisis experience for almost everyone. According to one study approximately 8 percent are healthier and happier because they've left workplace stress behind,[10] but the overwhelming majority show symptoms of depression and anxiety. Many become physically ill. Others develop family or relationship problems. Among unemployed men there is an increased risk of violence against women, substance abuse, and child abuse.

While the financially well-off and a lot of other people may temporarily enjoy a period of unemployment—as if it were an "extended vacation"—most of the people we talked with said job loss was an "ordeal." In most cases, the longer the unemployment or un-satisfactory reemployment lasted, the more disquieting and disrup-tive the ordeal.

Managers and professionals find unemployment devastating be-cause they "define their social identity through occupation more than anyone else in today's marketplace," write the authors of a re-cent *Business Week* article on downward mobility. "Many simply don't know where they fit in or where they are anymore."[11]

Blue-collar workers also suffer a tremendous loss of status when they lose their jobs. For example, because of the hierarchy within the logging trade, an injured timber faller who can no longer cut down giant trees feels a profound ego loss. The "head sawyer" at a mill and others who had been in positions of high skill or responsi-bility have fallen hard in the declining timber industry. Blue-collar workers representing many occupations feel less respected in their communities or at home as a result of becoming unemployed.

Men who are primary breadwinners and women who are single parents, and people who were financially stretched even while em-ployed, often experience job loss as a catastrophe, as do those who endure a dramatic income plunge. Members of racial or ethnic mi-nority groups, women, significantly overweight people, and older or disabled workers commonly find themselves at the mercy of po-tential employers with prejudiced and stereotypical ways of think-ing. Many middle-aged white males feel disadvantaged because of hiring practices that favor younger men or affirmative action pro-grams that can make it harder to land a specific job.

Men and women who find their work fulfilling and challenging are especially shattered when much of the meaning in their lives vanishes with their job. One study "found that the young people at greatest risk of developing problems after losing a job were those with the highest commitment or motivation to work."[12] Perhaps, however, it is the "already alienated" who suffer most, workers in low-status jobs who were already feeling unappreciated and unaf-firmed by their labors.[13] These individuals fall further into the cellar of despair when losing what little dignity work did provide.

Some experts believe that being fired or laid off troubles men far more than women because of society's long-standing gender roles and expectations. Most Western men have internalized the notion that any man who is worth anything is a working man. In addition, there is a far greater tendency among men to define themselves primarily with reference to occupation; women, on the other hand, tend to define their value and purpose in life more broadly and according to multiple roles. Men of all ages can find job loss extremely stressful: They may even face an increased risk of heart attack unless they develop some effective ways of alleviating stress.[14]

Yet job loss has a harsh impact on women as well. While many women experience motherhood as deeply fulfilling, a lot of women feel more respected and overtly affirmed at the salaried workplace than in their homemaker roles. And "a woman [who] finds her family role unsatisfactory" is even more vulnerable because "she may have no alternative sources of gratification."[15] Similarly, many single women rely on work not only to support themselves but also as a means of defining themselves and gaining satisfaction in their lives.

Employment provides clear health benefits for women: In the United Kingdom and North America women who work outside the home are treated less often for mental illnesses than their age-matched counterparts who are full-time housewives.[16] According to authors Gove and Geerken, "The data indicate that married men who work are in the best mental health, married women who are unemployed are in the worst mental health, and the mental health of employed housewives falls in between."[17]

In another landmark study, lack of employment was seen as a major factor in explaining why working-class women with young children at home were five times more likely to become depressed than middle-income women.[18] Work outside the home was found to have a positive impact on the health of many women "by improving economic status, increasing self-esteem and social contacts, and alleviating boredom."[19]

Swedish studies have shown that even when a country provides a protective social service net for those who lose their jobs, most unemployed women show symptoms of depression. With universal welfare benefits and a guaranteed 90 percent of their previous paychecks for a one-year period, unemployed Swedish women still had significantly increased rates of depression.[20]

One authority has written that Ph.D.'s and others who have invested a great deal of money and energy in becoming well educated are among the most vulnerable to the stress of job loss. In

Professionals in Search of Work, H. G. Kaufman writes that "two-thirds of professionals who completed at least a Master's degree reported high stress resulting from unemployment, [a rate more than twice as high as the stress levels seen in those] without any graduate work."[21] When individuals with advanced degrees lose their jobs, Kaufman explains, they begin to doubt whether their efforts were worthwhile, they struggle with life's unfairness given the professional rewards they had expected, and they feel deprived of "work that provides great ego satisfaction" and "deprived of an essential part of their very identity."[22]

On the other hand, highly educated professionals often are better equipped, in the long run, to face the challenges ahead. They have had an opportunity to internalize an attitude of positive self-regard. They have seen themselves as resourceful, capable people and have been regarded as such by others. While initially these individuals may experience self-doubt, eventually they can rebuild their lives with the knowledge that in the past their abilities led to achievement.

By contrast, many factory workers, clerical staff, and others who previously may have done well with only high school diplomas now find that their skills are becoming obsolete. Without sufficient confidence in their capabilities and economic resources, it is difficult for them to face a demanding new workplace. Without the advantages of education and a sturdy self-concept, they may have great difficulty coping. It is important for blue-collar workers to remember, however, that they, too, have worked hard, been resourceful, and made important contributions at the workplace. While lacking in formal education, many blue-collar workers have demonstrated as much determination and ability to learn as workers with graduate degrees.

ONE STEP AT A TIME

Well-meaning but annoying friends and family members may say, "You just have to get out there and find another job!" What most people don't understand is how hard it can be to get out of bed. How do you get motivated when you find yourself mesmerized by mindless hours of television watching or other diversions? How does a person set aside self-doubt and despair in a highly competitive job market? Is it possible to job search successfully while you're feeling so negative?

Unless you can somehow get another good job almost immediately, you are apt to be more successful at finding satisfactory work if you take some time for psychic repair. You will almost surely have a more positive attitude, be happier, and be more productive at your next place of work if you can first sort through your job loss experience. You can begin to make some sense out of recent events and examine how your life may have permanently changed. People invariably face the future with greater equanimity once negatives from the past are named and begin to lose their grip.

Promise yourself that you will discover how job loss can lead to better things. It is important to decide now that you are going to become a wiser and stronger person. Commit yourself to making a better life for yourself and your loved ones.

Be patient with the healing process. After all, you aren't just saying goodbye to a lost job and looking for an acceptable new one. You're rebuilding your life.

II

Struggling with Anger and Fatigue

When you're dancing with a bear you can't sit down when you're tired. You have to wait until the bear gets tired.

—JOYCELYN ELDERS, M.D.

Mr. Lee is a forty-year-old taxi driver in the Midwest, a handsome, well-educated husband and father, barely making sufficient income to support his family. Six months ago he was a production control specialist for a defense industry, making $53,000 a year. He was diagnosed with colon cancer, had surgery, and three weeks after returning to work was told that his position was being eliminated. Because a dozen others lost their job on the same day, Mr. Lee does not feel that he can prove in court the credible suspicion that his company saw him as an expensive medical liability and dumped him.

He came to the United States from Korea as a young college graduate eighteen years ago, became an American citizen, enlisted and served in the U. S. Army, worked his way into a management position as a civilian, and saw himself as a full participant in the American Dream. Certain thoughts consume him now: What if the cancer comes back? Where would the money come from for a medical emergency? When and where can he find a job with medical benefits, some vacation days, and perhaps even a pension? Why were there no interview offers in response to the 200 résumés he mailed out to prospective employers?

EXHAUSTION

Currently Mr. Lee works twelve to fifteen hours a day, rarely sees his young daughters, falls into bed in the early morning hours, and starts again the next day. For the privilege of picking up airport passengers, he must pay a taxi driver's "standing fee" of $145 each week, fifty-two weeks a year, regardless of any time that he might be required to take off for illness or emergency. However, the high fee is a small price to pay for safety: Taxi drivers on the job in America have a higher risk of being murdered on the job than do workers in any other occupation,[1] and airport work subjects him to less danger.

Mr. Lee yearns to make a change but feels so mentally and physically tired most of the time that he lacks the energy to think through any major decisions that could lead to a new life. He desperately needs to take some time off so he can rest, get some distance from his dilemma, and think about the future with a clear mind. Recording his thoughts and occupational dreams in a journal; confiding in his wife, a close friend, or a religious advisor; and talking to a vocational counselor could help him too. Mr. Lee is not going to be able to develop a vocational strategy for himself and an economic survival plan for his family until he gets some free time.

Like Mr. Lee, you also may feel that you're dancing with a bear and simply can't risk the consequences of stopping to rest or reflect. Perhaps you're working hard at one or more temporary jobs or otherwise staying almost frantically busy. Possibly you aren't yet working anywhere but instead are stuck in the doldrums of fatigue and discouragement.

Even a day or two of a change in scenery can begin the process of putting your life on a new path. Time off doesn't have to be expensive. You could visit some friends out of town, go to a campground, or take some day trips into the countryside. It is important that you find a setting where you can begin to think about your problems in some entirely new ways.

Facing the decisions now confronting you and mastering the problems ahead will take a good deal of time. You may as well begin somewhere, and a good place to start is with self-care.

ANGER

In twenty years of studying crisis and bereavement, I have seen more anger and dismay in people suffering job loss than in almost any other group of grieving individuals. Except for senseless violence and other acts of human cruelty, including incest, ugly divorces, child custody fights, and the damages wrought by drunken drivers—job loss seems to produce the most anger. Especially in an era when finding another job with comparable pay is so difficult, when dreams and security can be shattered, many struggle with bitterness.

Of course the fury over a loved one's death or suffering because of a perpetrator's cruelty or recklessness is by far more anguishing and infuriating than job loss. But most people eventually get through life's worst nightmares by returning to the jobs which support and sustain them. When you are feeling angry in the aftermath of job loss, there is no immediate workplace to which you can escape for respite, to lose yourself in responsibility, or somehow to redirect your anger toward productive ends.

When people become unemployed, not only do they lose the place where much of their healing has occurred in the past, they also tend to lose a familiar and necessary time structure. The structure that automatically organizes daily activity, the tasks that typically keep us mortals from overly ruminating on our sorrows, and the routine relationships with people that fill considerably our need for human contact are lost when we are taken away from work.

LIFE'S UNFAIRNESS

There is anger at the unfairness of it all. Even though life often doesn't work this way, in our heart of hearts most of us believe in a just-world theory: "If I work hard and live a good life," we reason, "things will work out for me."

Even if we continue to believe that there is justice and goodness in the scheme of things, when we or our loved ones suffer, our beliefs are challenged. It takes time to rethink these basic assumptions and arrive at a reconstructed but still positive view of life. It's not easy to incorporate into our worldview the reality that "bad things happen to good people," including us.[2]

Part of what confuses and angers people is echoed in statements such as these:

"I was a good worker."
"I was loyal."
"I was productive."
"They've cheated me out of my pension!"
"I'm a good person. I don't deserve this."
"I sacrificed my family time, did what they asked me to do, worked weekends and overtime—and they still got rid of me!"
"Our family needs this job and its benefits."
"This will hurt the people I love."
"I hate trying to cope with all these changes!"
"What if we lose everything?"
"It used to be that if you worked hard and contributed, you'd have a middle-class life, the basic pleasures, and then some. . . ."
"I never thought I'd be treated this way after all these years of service."
"When I try to talk about losing my job, some people act like I've got leprosy and it's contagious."
"I never knew how degrading an unemployment office could be."
"It is *infuriating* to have to start life all over again at my age!"

Anger is virtually inevitable in the presence of human adversity. Whenever life slams us up against a wall—for whatever reason—typically we experience frustration, disappointment, pressures of various kinds bearing down upon us, the reality of life's fundamental unpredictability, and our own vulnerability. All that stirs within us some degree of fury.

People are often mistreated in the process of termination. After one layoff that eliminated 600 jobs, a job developer with a dislocated worker program told me that discharged company employees believed they were misled. "There was evidence that the company knew these jobs would be lost to overseas contracts," said the spokeswoman, "yet management continually reassured many of the workers that their jobs were stable by offering training programs on upgraded industrial procedures that they never intended to implement. Workers . . . were convinced that the expensive training was 'proof' that their employment would continue."

A 1993 U. S. Government Accounting Office document, as reported by the *New York Times* News Service, revealed that "half of the employers who are required by federal law to give employees notice of impending layoffs are not complying with the law. The 1988 Worker Adjustment and Retraining Act requires employers with 100 or more full-time employees to give 60 days' warning of closure or layoff. Closures affecting 50 or more employees trigger the notification requirement."[3] When employers mislead employees in this way, life is more difficult for the displaced workers because they are emotionally unprepared for the loss and unable to make prudent financial decisions prior to the layoff.

In America—and apparently in other countries as well—many bosses and supervisors don't know how to say goodbye. Countless men and women describe ill-timed, insensitive, and otherwise horribly handled layoffs and firings. One man suffered the humiliation of being fired unexpectedly in front of his offspring on Take Your Daughter to Work day! And in view of a recent *USA Today* piece, a special award for clumsiness and cruelty might go to someone at General Dynamics, the company that fired Dean Farness of Santee, California, just after he returned from bereavement leave following the sudden death of his six-year-old son. He was fired on March 15, the day his little boy would have turned seven, a date already almost unbearably painful. Farness explained, "They just called me in and said, 'It's hard for us to do this, but we've got to do it.'"[4]

While it is true that the company was laying off 1,600 of 4,200 workers, the Farness family pastor spoke a higher truth: "Holding off a bit would not have made a significant dent in [the company's] profit-loss margin, but it would have been compassionate."[5] At a later time, Farness was rehired.

In the presence of crisis or loss, we are apt to feel angry at God or life's unfairness; angry at those who seem at fault for our distress; angry at co-workers, friends, or family who fail us when we need them most; angry at ourselves; and angry at certain groups of people such as business or government leaders. Often, in our resentment, we behave angrily toward our innocent loved ones at home.

FATIGUE AND OTHER CONSEQUENCES OF HOSTILITY

Fatigue and anger are often related reactions to a personal crisis. More than any other emotion—including joy, sorrow, love, and fear—anger consumes and controls us. When we work hard to deny our angry feelings, we grow tired from the energy it takes to keep the anger under wraps.

When we release unbridled anger on those with whom we have a grievance or when we displace it on others, we stir within ourselves a hornet's nest of still more anger and fatigue. Dumping anger on others also burdens us with the weary consequences of our actions—guilt, retribution from others, family crisis, and potential legal problems.

Child abuse statistics range from three to six times higher for men who are unemployed than among men who are working.[6] Not only are fathers who have lost their jobs within the previous year more likely to strike their children, to a lesser extent they are also more likely to use violence against the women in their lives.[7] Getting in charge of one's anger can be a matter of great urgency.

There is also no doubt that anger can be injurious to your health. Redford Williams of Duke University, through many years of scientific research, has demonstrated that anger and hostility can significantly increase one's risk of having a heart attack. The so-called Type A traits of competitiveness, perfectionism, and time urgency, once believed to be culprits in early cardiovascular disease and mortality, are no longer seen as primary villains. Now implicated in cardiovascular disease are the biological effects of chronic hostility. "Indeed," writes Dr. Williams, "it is likely that the hormones—epinephrine, norepinephrine, and cortisol—poured out during these anger episodes produce long-term biological consequences, leading over time to disease."[8] According to Dr. Williams, hostility can be fatal.

In his wonderfully readable and useful book, *The Trusting Heart*, Williams describes the telltale signs and symptoms he has observed:

> The driving force behind hostility is a cynical mistrust of others. Expecting that others will mistreat us, we are on the lookout for their bad behavior—and we can usually find it. This generates the frequent anger to which the hostile person is prone, and that anger, combined

with a lack of empathy for others . . . leads us to express our hostility overtly, in the form of aggressive acts toward others. . . .

When expressed toward loved ones, cynical mistrust can have especially undesirable effects. Even if you don't utter a word, the anger or disgust you feel is written on your face. The message you give to your husband, wife, or child is that he or she is incompetent, that he or she did [something you're angry about] on purpose, and that he or she is in danger of being rejected by you.[9]

Other symptoms of hostility are described by Dr. Williams: a racing heartbeat, tightness of the arm and leg muscles, and a feeling of being "'charged up,' ready for intense action."[10] Clearly, he continues, "the most important thing you can do to decrease your coronary risk if you are a Type A person is to learn to reduce your hostility and anger."[11]

Professor M. H. Brenner of the Johns Hopkins School of Public Health reviewed the correlation between cardiovascular disease mortality rates and unemployment rates in nine industrialized countries over a twenty-four-year period, report authors Nick Kates, Barrie Greiff, and Duane Hagen in *The Psychosocial Impact of Job Loss*.[12] Using a statistical analysis that controlled "for the effects of smoking and animal fat consumption, both of which increase the risk of heart disease," Brenner found a positive association between unemployment and increased heart disease mortality in all nine countries. There exists apparently a two- to three-year lag period between an increase in unemployment and in cardiovascular death rates, the authors explain, "because it may take a number of years for stress-induced effects to lead to pathological changes."[13]

Since it takes some time to become ill from chronic hostility, the good news is that changes in attitude and behavior can make a difference. In Williams's words, one can learn "to have a more trusting heart." It's not easy, he says, but with effort it is possible to reduce the cynical mistrust of others' motives, "the frequency and intensity with which you experience negative emotions of anger, irritation, frustration, rage, and the like," and to "learn to treat others with kindness and consideration."[14]

WHAT NOT TO DO

"'DON'T GET MAD, GET EVEN' is a popular saying and, if you've just lost your job, a terrible piece of advice," say William Morin and James Cabrera in *Parting Company.*[15]

If you sabotage a computer program, jam up some machinery, or steal something before you leave a job, not only can you end up in trouble with the law but you'll have to live with the loss of some self-respect and the possibility of having permanently impaired your reputation and chances of future success. Cursing, threatening, or assassinating the character of the boss, or writing an ugly letter to a former supervisor or the newspaper damning the company can come back to haunt you.

Most angry feelings are a normal response to personal crisis, but the problem with unrestrained anger is that it ruins lives. Anger misdirected can irreversibly injure your personal relationships; lead to alcohol or drug abuse; make you ill or accident prone; be a contributing factor in depression, anxiety, and suicide; or put you in jail.[16]

A growing problem in America is violence at the workplace. "Frequently the perpetrator of workplace violence is male, age 35 or older, with a history of violence toward women, children or animals, owns a gun and [is a person] whose self-esteem is closely tied to his job," according to a study published in 1993 by Joseph Kinney and Dennis Johnson of The Workplace Institute.[17]

A report from Northwestern Life Insurance indicates that 2 million Americans were physically attacked on the job in 1993 while 6 million others were threatened.[18] In 44 percent of the cases the attacker was a customer, in 20 percent a co-worker, and in just 3 percent of the cases a former employee. Professor James Fox, dean of the College of Criminal Justice at Northeastern University, told Susan Stamberg on National Public Radio that "the really bad news is that this is nothing compared to what we might see in the rest of this decade, where more and more angry workers, particularly middle-aged white men, are facing job loss and they just want to get even with all the people they think have hurt them."[19]

If you are a person with fantasies of hurting someone, *don't do it.* Nothing good ever comes to those who act out violently in response to job loss—only regret, sorrow to loved ones, death, or a prison term. Violence will only ruin your own life and cause others to lose respect for you.

If you need help in working through a serious problem with anger, ask your family doctor, clergyperson, or a friend to recommend a good therapist, and talk it out frankly. It is also important to avoid drinking alcohol, since alcohol disinhibits, often leads to aggression, and is involved in more than half of all fatal accidents, suicides, and homicides. When sober you may not think you're angry enough to hurt yourself or someone else, but drugs and alcohol cloud a person's perspective and judgment.

Whether you realize it or not, potential employers will see the chip on your shoulder in job interviews unless you take some steps to get those bitter feelings resolved or under control. One supervisor told us that he makes it a practice never to hire someone who has critical things to say about a previous job, company, or boss in the initial interviews. But it's not just what you say that gives you away; anger is an energy that finds expression both subtly and overtly until you find positive ways to channel and redirect it.

Finally, it is important to develop strategies for releasing your anger in healthy and productive ways and to make peace with the past—because leftover resentments have a way of contaminating even the most potentially rewarding new situation. Just as it's a mistake to start a new love relationship immediately after ending a marriage or love affair that has left you bitter and angry, so it is unwise to try to build a new occupational life without first making some peace with your resentments.

Old anger breaks down new relationships in love and at work; sometimes the old resentments wreck the relationships and sabotage the dreams we cherish most.

LAWSUITS: WARRANTED? WORTH IT?

Janice Goodman, a New York lawyer who has handled many job discrimination cases, says that businesses mistakenly assume they can push women aside because the women won't care. Goodman is quoted in a January 1993 *New York Times* editorial called "Women, Children and Work." The editorial describes an Ohio Civil Rights Commission study revealing that "a woman on pregnancy leave is 10 times more likely to lose her job than one on medical leave for other reasons." While The Family and Medical Leave Act allows American workers in companies with fifty or more employees to take as many as three months of unpaid child care leave, the act does not protect women employed in smaller businesses, which represent the majority.[20]

Bernadette Lorestani was simply a woman "on the wrong side of The Mommy Track," according to a 1993 *Baltimore Sun* article written by Michele Morris. Ms. Lorestani "never dreamed that having a baby would cost her her job. But three days before she was scheduled to return from maternity leave" to her $26,000-a-year job, she was fired. "'I felt thrown away like a piece of garbage,'" she recalled.[21]

The firing—as so often happens—was clumsy and hurtful. "On the Friday before she was to return to her . . . job, she stopped by the office with her infant son.

"'A few minutes after I arrived, the controller asked me to come to his office,' Ms. Lorestani says. 'I told him how happy I was to be returning to work on Monday. He shut the door and told me that they no longer had a place for me, that everything was running smoothly without me.'"[22]

Shocked and in tears, Ms. Lorestani scooped up her baby in his infant seat, left the controller's office, and fled from the building. She felt "'humiliated, as if everyone else knew.'" Later co-workers confided that the controller came out of his office and told the staff that she had just resigned.[23]

Says Joan Bertin, associate director of the Women's Rights Project of the American Civil Liberties Union, "'Pregnancy is the moment in a woman's life when discrimination is most likely to occur,'" whether blatantly or subtly.[24] But finding a new job is often a higher priority than filing a claim, according to attorney Ellen Vargyas of the National Women's Law Center. "'You can't expect a woman to be Joan of Arc if there's nothing to be gained,'" she says.[25]

Bernadette Lorestani's story had a happy ending: Four years and nine months after being fired, she and another woman fired after a pregnancy leave won a sex discrimination award totaling $935,000 in compensatory and punitive damages. Their former employer in New Jersey, the president of Pantzer Management Company, vowed to "'vigorously pursue all appeals and other remedies available to the company in order to rectify this miscarriage of justice.'"[26]

Because lawsuits typically are emotionally draining and involve years of uncertainty and expense, many people decide to forgo the courts and work through their anger in alternative ways. Generally, displaced workers are said by some authorities to become reemployed sooner when not pursuing a lawsuit, presumably because their energies are channeled more into job search.[27] On the other hand, for some people who sue and win, there are sweet financial or moral victories, albeit emotionally expensive ones.

If you believe that you are the victim of job loss discrimination on the basis of race, age, disability, sex, religion, or ethnicity, you should seek good advice first from the Equal Employment Opportunity Commission (see Appendix A) and then from a trusted lawyer who has no personal stake in your decision whether or not to sue. Ask a lawyer whom you know as a neighbor, friend, or acquaintance at your church or synagogue for a personal reference. Employment law is very complex, so it is important to choose a specialist in order to receive the best advice.[28]

FINDING SOLUTIONS

Redirecting Anger's Energy

A University of Sussex professor in England who has studied the process of adaptation to unemployment, Ian Miles, has found that many people experience involuntary job loss as *abandonment*. According to Miles, "'Being left on the scrapheap' is one of the most common phrases used by unemployed people to describe their situation."[29]

If you have been wronged in some way—accused falsely, misled, discriminated against, cheated out of a fair settlement or pension, or otherwise mistreated by your former employer—there are certain healing strategies that can give you back your energy, optimism, and faith in other people. Anger can be put to good use and can drive you forward in building a new life. Redirecting anger's energy is the key to survival.

"The Turkeys Won't Change"

Between 1989 and 1991, 40 percent of the architects in Maryland lost their jobs.[30] One of these representatives of the real estate sector's most devastated professions was Roger, a man who signed up for my first "Surviving Job Loss" seminar. When I met him, Roger had been laid off for more than two years. He was feeling bitter and had grown cynical, it seemed to me, as a result of having one discouraging experience after another in job search.

Roger applied for many jobs including one as a housing inspector, thinking his expertise in construction would serve him well. No luck. He applied for a job as a marine electrician with a waterfront company, assuming his graduation from Electrician's Mate Class A School at the Great Lakes Naval Training Center (twenty-five years earlier) would mean something. He was not offered the job. "How much can the theory of electricity have changed?" he wondered.

Since Roger had had two years' experience working in a lumber yard before attending college, he applied to work as an inside sales clerk at a wholesale lumber store. "The prospective boss on the phone was rude and impatient," Roger told me. "I explained my situation as briefly as I could and attempted to explain how my background could be of great benefit to the position he needed filled. Then bang, the guy slammed the phone down in my ear!

"Angry at not being shown a little common courtesy, I wanted to go down to the lumber yard where this rude S.O.B. was and adjust his attitude with a length of his own 2-by-4!" Roger exclaimed. "But when you have been an architect for twenty years, you know an ignorant S.O.B. will always be the same no matter how bad you whip him."

Roger had the wisdom to know that there are a certain number of obnoxious people in this world who will never be any different. We take the best care of ourselves and our long-term interests when we refuse to allow such persons to provoke us into some action we will later regret.

"Don't let the turkeys get you down" is good advice. As you recover from job loss and pursue the often discouraging tasks of job search, decide in advance on some strategies to stay in control of your emotions. Walk away. Get some exercise. Call a friend and let off steam. Do some deep breathing along with relaxation techniques. Write an angry letter and tear it up. Use prayer or whatever works to calm you down.

Physical Activity

Medical science has established that regular physical exercise such as aerobic walking affects brain chemistries. A change in our neurotransmitters lifts many of us out of depression. Exercise truly does go far to alleviate frustration, stress, worry, anger, and other burdens.

Exercise also improves circulation, reduces cholesterol levels, controls blood pressure, and lowers the risk of heart disease, explains Gary Scheiner, an exercise physiologist. Exercise is a "drug," he says, that "reduces body fat, enhances muscle function, instills a sense of control and self-esteem, and provides some fun and excitement to boot."[31]

If your friends' or relatives' reactions to the changes in your life have been less than helpful or even annoying, if you've been treated poorly at the unemployment office or in job interviews, if you've been the victim of a scam or otherwise been taken advantage of in this time of crisis, if other losses have hit you hard just when you're vulnerable because of job loss—regular, daily exercise is all the more necessary.

It is important, says Scheiner, to treat exercise with the same respect that you give to your prescription or other medications. A person who is new to exercise shouldn't "overdose"[32]; it's best at first to take short walks (fifteen or twenty minutes, several times a week) and gradually build up to thirty or forty minutes of increasing intensity. The American College of Sports Medicine recommends a thirty-minute session three times a week as a good, average workout.[33] If you have cardiovascular disease, high blood pressure, elevated cholesterol levels, or a family history of heart disease, or if you are over age forty or are a smoker, you should have a medical exam before starting an exercise program.[34]

Choose an activity that you enjoy—walking, swimming, biking, dancing, or playing a sport—and find a friend to exercise with on a regular basis. The advantages to walking are that you can find a neighbor, friend, or family member to walk with; it's cost free; it's the most aerobically beneficial and injury-free form of exercise; and it is readily available in that you can always go walking, even in a mall in bad weather. Furthermore, no expensive equipment is needed, only a good pair of walking shoes.

Harold Kohl, an epidemiologist at the Cooper Institute for Aero-
bics Research in Dallas, in a 1989 study he co-authored, reported
that a daily thirty-minute walk can reduce a person's risk of dying
from heart disease or cancer almost as much as training for a
marathon would.[35] And Carol Tavris, a psychologist who has written
frequently on the topic of anger, says that "the best cure for consistent anger is to improve self-regard."[36] Regular exercise reduces tension and improves fitness—both of which will help you feel better
about yourself.

Other physical activities can be beneficial as well, such as cleaning out some closets or the garage, washing windows or the car,
painting a room, building something, or working in the yard. While
the last thing you may want to do when feeling depressed is clean
up some clutter or exercise, you can start with just ten-minute periods of activity and gradually mobilize yourself for more. Whenever
you can take an action that brings more order or pleasure to your
life—and burns some energy in the process—you help yourself to
manage your emotions and be productive at the same time.

Activity is also beneficial as you work through what psychologists
call "the task of intellectual acceptance" in grieving a loss, which is
"the need expressed by newly unemployed people to develop an
account of why the loss [has] happened."[37] There is a lot to figure
out and I believe that many people get their thinking done more
successfully with a paint brush, scrub brush, or broom in their
hands. Walking or jogging often produces similar effects: There is
something about the rhythm of the activity that facilitates clearer
reasoning.

As you find physical outlets for releasing stress, you will experience a significant reduction in fatigue. You'll also gain a renewed
feeling of energy every time you clarify a specific feeling or problem that is troubling you.

Talking It Out

Most people carrying troublesome feelings need a human "sounding board." Often we have to hear ourselves express anger or other
negative feelings in order to realize how we are actually experiencing a loss. Without knowing it, we may be stuck somewhere in the
grief and healing process. Talking with a trusted friend or family

member, confiding in a professional counselor or religious advisor, can be an unburdening and empowering experience.

Find someone to confide in who is supportive and not competitive or judgmental. In a strong marriage or other relationship, opening up is a good idea. If your partner or friend has his or her own problems right now, however, and can't be a help to you, or the relationship is in trouble lately, look elsewhere for the emotional support you need.

Professional help is needed if your troubles are disturbing your sleep, appetite, and relationships with loved ones and if your depression sometimes feels overwhelming. Get help if you can't seem to shake feelings of hopelessness or anger, thoughts of death or revenge. Your family doctor, clergyperson, or someone else you trust can recommend a good psychiatrist, psychologist, pastoral counselor, social worker, or mental health counselor. If you have no insurance and are low on funds, many such professionals are willing to work at a reduced rate or can recommend someone affordable. Ask them. There are also good clinics that have sliding fee scales, where people pay according to level of income. When you reach out for help, you can respect yourself for making a decision to work through your problems and not to remain a victim.

As you talk over your situation with whomever you have chosen, keep in mind that ventilating emotion is especially beneficial when you make an effort to be as specific as possible in naming your feelings. Try to put into words *why* you are anxious, angry, worried, or saddened. If you are blaming yourself for some reason, explain the circumstances and say why you feel at fault. If you feel angry at your former boss or someone else, try to describe exactly why. If there is something you regret—such as a career path you followed or that you never went to graduate school—unburden yourself. Even feelings that seem unreasonable or unjustified need to be explored.

So far as resentment is concerned, the point of unburdening is to allow angry feelings to surface so they'll be less likely to get in the way when you're looking for a job. You also will be surprised to see a fresh perspective on your situation once your personal reactions are shared with someone who understands. Life is often not as it seems.

A "Going Away" Party

Retirement—at the end of a long and productive life of work—does not produce the same turmoil that involuntary job loss and premature retirement cause. For one thing, the goodbyes are different. Retirement will involve some major adjustments, but if somebody gives you a watch or a wall plaque, a party, or an envelope full of money, and co-workers gather around to send you off with their good wishes, then the changes won't seem brutal. When the process of job separation is kindly and in its proper season, people cope well with transition.

Deprived by circumstances of a comfortable way of separating from your last workplace, you may want to consider having your own party. You could invite your favorite former co-workers, celebrate and toast your many good times together, and even throw wads of paper at an enlarged photograph of the company's overpaid chief executive or its new buildings on foreign soil.

Deborah Lindemon, a successful small business owner in California, for fourteen years, couldn't believe how fast her business died. Within two months of the passing of a new state law, referrals to her business dried up. She began struggling to decide which one of her employees she would keep. A short time later, a business that once had seven employees and three offices closed two offices, moved to less expensive quarters, and had just one employee. Having created the business, Deborah grieved as she watched it die.

The new state rules hurt other companies as well as Deborah's, forcing downsizing and industry closings. Owners and employees were in shock. People who had worked together for many years found that relationships with co-workers and customers were ending as the jobs they held in common disappeared.

People in the industry talked to Deborah about their feelings of anger, frustration, and fear. Realizing she wasn't alone in her grief, Deborah felt that she and others could benefit from a ritual of sharing. She researched several alternatives and decided to hold an Irish type of wake. Deborah liked the idea of music, dancing, and a sense of celebration as well as a ritual of mourning.

Celebrating the positive was important to Deborah Lindemon. "What happens when businesses are dying," she explained, "is that you feel the grief so much that you forget to look at some of the positive memories."

She invited people to the party who had been open with their feelings about the loss of a job or business—co-workers, customers, and even competitors. The competitors were the hardest to invite. "We came out of an era where businesses are so competitive," she said, "you're not supposed to be a feeling person because it takes away the killer instinct." But Deborah responded to a different inner drive. She felt a strong desire to help others with their loss.

The wake was held at the office that had housed Deborah's business for the past fourteen years. Ironically this would be her last night in that space before moving to less expensive quarters. Two-thirds of the people who were invited showed up.

Upon entering the office, two dozen "mourners" found a wall covered with photographs of themselves either at work or enjoying various social activities. The photos prompted people to reminisce, sharing many warm memories. There was food, followed by Irish music and dancing. Before long, people were comfortable and ready to open up. At Deborah's encouragement, they all pulled their chairs into a large circle and some began to offer "eulogies." Deborah told the group that she wanted to connect with the people in the room and affirm that "we've done a good job; we can be proud; we've worked hard."

Some people recalled fun-filled moments shared with co-workers or competitors over the years. Others talked about present concerns, how difficult some of the changes had been or soon would be. There was a lot of laughter and some tears during a forty-five-minute period of sharing. "We were honoring what we've done," Deborah explained. "Even when it's not your fault, when a company goes out of business there is a negative feeling, a feeling of failure. People second-guess themselves and wonder, 'Has my business failed because I've done something wrong, or could have done something better, or worked harder?'"

Having the wake/party for a dying industry and downsizing business left Deborah Lindemon and the others with a sense of "validation," she explained. "We felt validated for all the work we've done in the last fourteen years."

Deborah's "going away" party accomplished what she had hoped it would, probably because everyone's expectations were clear when the invitations were handed out. Many people came prepared not only to dance and have a good time but also to talk about the loss of their job and what their job had meant to them. When people left Lindemon's office that evening, they still faced joblessness or job insecurity, but something important had begun, a process of acceptance. Through a ritual of healing and sharing in community, a group of men and women were able to gain strength and perspective toward creating a new work life.

Sorting Out Problems on Paper

A group of researchers led by psychologist Stefanie Spera of the consulting firm of Drake Beam Morin, Inc., in Dallas, has found that writing eases the pain of job loss and "boosts new job prospects."[38] Studying forty-one unemployed, middle-aged professionals, most of them engineers, Dr. Spera and her colleagues found that those who wrote about their job loss in a journal—even though they did not more actively search for a job than did those in a nonwriting control group—were twice as likely to have a full-time job eight months later and four times more likely to be employed![39]

Therapists frequently recommend that their clients keep a diary or journal as a means of releasing tension, gaining perspective, and achieving increased control over their own destiny. Says psychologist James Pennebaker, "Not only is the pen mightier than the sword, it can be mightier than the army of anxieties that keep us captive to stress." Pennebaker, the author of *Opening Up: The Healing Power of Confiding in Others,* explains that writing is "a way of putting our problems into more manageable form which can make them more understandable and . . . easier to solve."[40] He recommends setting a time limit of twenty to thirty minutes, writing for the entire time even if you're repeating yourself, stating specifically what is troubling you (not just recording day-to-day events), and writing with the assurance of privacy.

Marilynn Knowles of Muskegon, Michigan, began journal writing as a way of coping with arthritis and the fear of losing her job following five major surgeries in four years. Knowles remembers the first few months as being mostly "moaning and groaning" about her condition. In an *Arthritis* magazine article written by psychiatric nurse Gayle Brown, Knowles recalls that, after a time, something changed: "'I found that once I put my negative emotions down, they seemed to dissipate.'"[41]

It is important to date your journal entries, so you can come back later and track your progress. Most people are surprised and encouraged, as the months go by, to observe the peace they are making with painful events. Advises Brown, "Don't hold yourself to writing every day. A strict timetable can inhibit and frustrate you. In the beginning, try to write a minimum of three times a week. Soon you'll find yourself reaching for your journal because you want to, not because you feel you should."[42]

It is a necessary part of healing to sort through the "whys" and "hows" of difficult life events, to try to make sense of things in our own minds. Pennebaker calls this "the need for completion and the search for meaning." Just as recurrent dreams can keep haunting us until some specific conflict is resolved, we aren't really free to go forward in the aftermath of upsetting events, says Dr. Pennebaker, until we achieve "a new understanding of the events."[43]

After two decades of bereavement work, it is clear to me that "resolution" of a personal crisis—the peace that enables someone once devastated by loss to rebuild a life—occurs because new insights are gained into the meaning of life. In the many years I worked as a therapist, I always knew that an individual's healing was well underway when he or she had learned something of lasting benefit from a loss. You also can decide that you'll learn valuable lessons from your loss and carry this wisdom, like a friend held in your arms, for the rest of your life.

Journal writing and confiding for a time in an understanding friend or therapist can be empowering experiences—if you open yourself to growth and change. Whatever discomfort or fury the turmoil of job loss has brought about, these events eventually can make you a wiser, kinder, more balanced, and happier human being. It is up to you to decide just how.

Recognizing Anger from Another Place and Time

If you were physically abused as a child or abused mentally with belittling, ridicule, mean threats, or hurtful teasing, you probably carry as an adult an understandable intolerance toward being mistreated. When feeling wronged by another person, you may be quick to anger and apt to fantasize about doing harm to the person who has hurt you. While your recent grievance may be genuine, your reactions to job loss are apt to go beyond what most people would feel in such a situation. Perhaps your intense feelings of fury are out of proportion with present events because you had your fill of mistreatment years ago.

I am convinced that when a fired employee "goes berserk"—lashing out verbally or physically against a former boss or co-worker—often he or she is really attacking someone in the past. Innocent people frequently become the victims of displaced rage when an individual in the past (usually a parent) was verbally or physically abusive.

Sometimes a person who becomes violent is mentally ill. More often, he or she has been psychologically scarred from past experience, usually at a young age. Alcohol or other substances frequently act as the torch that ignites the explosion.

If violence sometimes crosses your mind as an alternative to solving your problems or if you have an urge to verbally humiliate or punish someone to get revenge—it's important to stop and ask yourself a couple of questions. When have I felt this way before? When did I feel a similar anger and desire to hit back, strong feelings like those I'm having now?

Try to be honest with yourself and with someone you trust. Examine those long-ago hurts and your feelings of rage, which probably have far less to do with present problems than with the young and vulnerable child you once were. With professional help, your hurts from the past can lose their power over you. You can find the courage to track down exaggerated anger, identify its primary source, and make peace with the past.

Success and Happiness: The Sweetest "Revenge"

When you are wronged by someone, the most satisfying way to make things right is to make the most of your life now and in the future. The problem, of course, is how to get beyond the anger which is so inevitable and human.

Penny Harrington waged a fierce battle with anger after losing her job but refused to allow the anger to destroy her. In January 1985 Harrington had become the first woman in America to run a major police department, after a twenty-one-year fight to move up through the ranks in Portland, Oregon. She had become the Police

Bureau's first woman detective, then sergeant, lieutenant, and captain—after filing a sexual discrimination complaint in the 1960s to change the "patrolman" job into a "police officer" position so women could apply. Now she was chief of police in Portland—a woman of the year on *Ms.* magazine's cover and a guest on the "Today Show," "NBC Nightly News," and the "MacNeil/Lehrer News Hour."[44]

Unfortunately, there was trouble ahead. Two weeks after Harrington took office, an arbitrator awarded the police union a 10 percent raise—7 percent more than the city had budgeted. Chief Harrington was stuck with the mayor's decision to let the Portland Police Department take the full hit. Plans to hire sixty new officers had to be abandoned, and in addition Harrington had to lay off sixteen officers, the first layoffs in the city's history. As a result of the lost positions, some of the officers had to be demoted to fill lower positions. She tried to eliminate and combine some specialty units but all the changes, reshuffling, and demotions "upset officers and detectives who were used to the status quo."[45]

More trouble rumbled after a black man—a former Marine who was an off-duty security guard—got in a fight with another man and was accidentally killed in a choke hold by two white police officers. Harrington believed the officers had followed proper procedure, but she eventually banned this carotid-artery hold after reading national studies about its dangerous effects. She was accused by the head of the police association "of caving in to the public and not supporting the officers."[46] On the day of the young black man's funeral, two officers began selling T-shirts that read "Don't Choke 'Em, Smoke 'Em," implying that a gun was the only tool left for officers. Harrington, after an investigation, fired the officers. Several months later a police union arbitrator ordered the officers back to work, embarrassing the chief and infuriating the African American community.

One problem after another occurred pitting police union president Stan Peters against Chief Harrington—and putting her on the losing side. At one point, her police officer husband was accused of wrongdoing and the chief was accused of "defects of leadership." "'I should have built a political support network,' she said [later]. 'But I hated politics. . . . It never sunk in until the very end what a political job I had. I was too naive to see that my neck was on the block.'"[47]

Chief Penny Harrington was forced to resign seventeen months after her historic appointment. "Losing my job was a tremendous loss of face," she told me; "I felt used and abused." She was angry at the mayor's apparent lack of courage as shown in not supporting her and furious at the police union president for his obvious delight in gunning her down. She knew that the attacks on her competence and judgment were unwarranted as were the claims regarding the integrity of her husband. The Harringtons had a lot to be angry about.

For several months the former chief found it helpful to ventilate her fury in weekly sessions with an understanding psychiatrist. As for unburdening her feelings of fury with friends, "Some people disappeared who I had thought were my best friends," she remembered. "Others who I had seen as just acquaintances were highly supportive."

Rather early on, Harrington felt a necessity to get away and start thinking about making a fresh start. She and her husband spent the summer with her parents in Michigan at a simple cottage on a lake. It felt good to be anonymous and far away from Oregon. After a few days, she intentionally stopped talking about past events with her relatives, knowing that to do so would only stir up more angry emotion. "I can't relive these feelings every day," she realized.

Realizing also that getting away from Oregon was necessary to starting a new life, the couple moved to California. Penny's husband ran a plumbing supply place, and she recruited sales and management people for the electrical industry, but both were miserable in jobs so dramatically unrelated to what they had been trained for.

After about a year, Penny Harrington's husband felt that he had to return to Portland to rejoin the police department and reclaim his reputation as a "good cop." The couple thought they could maintain their marriage in separate states but their physical separation eventually led to an amiable but sad divorce.[48]

Still Penny Harrington was determined to go forward and build another life. Her "heart and soul," she says, are now focused in a rewarding new career as special assistant to the California State Bar's director of investigations. Working in a state with 130,000 lawyers, in the office responsible for all major investigations of lawyers accused of fraud and other offenses, Harrington heads up big investigations and also trains all of the staff members. She also has designed an innovative computer tracking system. "It's been so good for me to have someone appreciate my skills,"[49] she said. Harrington knows she has regained her credibility.

Plunging herself into meaningful work that draws extensively on a quarter century of law enforcement experience, Harrington also has found healing through new friendships and her hobbies of reading avidly and enjoying music.

"I was very angry for several years," Harrington told me in a recent interview. She believes she made the right decisions as Portland's chief of police and that her leadership would have been effective had she been given more time.

Finally, "I let the anger go," she explained. "I saw what happened in Portland as an old festering sore. Okay, it was unfair and it was awful. But it's over." She was determined not to become a bitter person for the rest of her life as she had seen other people do in such situations.

For Penny Harrington, "the most important thing was getting away from Portland," since "after a while, too much commiserating with certain people keeps the anger alive. I wanted to move on emotionally," she reflects. "I've been able to be happy somewhere else."

"What happened made me stronger," she told Tom Hallman, Jr., of *The Sunday Oregonian* staff. "I spent my entire career at the Police Bureau. And then one day it was all gone. I never thought I'd be happy again. I had to start over. A new dentist, a new hairdresser, you name it. Everything.

"But I'm no longer afraid of being unemployed, and I'm no longer afraid of starting over," she says, triumphantly. "I did it."[50]

After the 1994 California earthquake, a Portland police officer who had supported her phoned to see if she was all right. As they chatted, Harrington was aware that "I hardly ever think about Portland anymore. You know it seems so long ago [only eight years], and it's almost as if it didn't happen. But it was an interesting ride."

Like Penny Harrington, you'll probably have to work at finding a happier life, but you can resolve not to let negative expectations, past conflicts, and bitter feelings dog you as you try to move forward. You can make peace with the past by deciding—once you've had a good chance to ventilate and reflect on your angry feelings—that it's time to lay your anger down.

Penny Harrington's positive attitude reminded me of a message I included in one of the most difficult lectures I've ever presented, to an auditorium of people whose loved ones either were murdered or were killed by drunk drivers. "There is one thing that could be worse than what that killer or reckless drunk did to your loved one," I said. "And that would be if you allowed the killer to destroy your life too!"

Like Penny Harrington, you can turn away from the past and the urge to get even, and turn toward the future and opportunities to move ahead.

Accepting Personal Responsibility

John Hutchinson, a colleague and friend who teaches college sociology and has taught prison inmates, has an interesting perspective on anger and personal responsibility. Professor Hutchinson has seen certain criminals bring hope into their lives while serving time by changing their thinking about past events and future possibilities. Those who blame others for their unfortunate circumstances are "disempowered," says Hutchinson. On the other hand, continues the professor, "When people take responsibility for their lives they begin to have a life, to have the power to become the persons they are capable of becoming."

To blame someone or something else—parents who abandoned you; people who provoked you; friends who betrayed you; an employer who fired you; drugs, alcohol, divorce, or other ruinous events—for your unhappy plight, leads only to despair or futile rage. Yes, hurtful and horrible things happen and anger is an understandable response, says Hutchinson. "But anger devours. To blame someone else is to give them a consuming power over your life. When you accept the responsibility for making your life what you still can, then you give yourself that power."

Reframing Events: "It's Not Just Me"

While it is understandable that you feel cast out or abandoned, it is important for you to begin to place your job loss into its cultural, global, and historical context.

At the beginning of 1995, during a period of "economic recovery,"

7.2 million Americans still worried about finding a job. An additional 445,000 "discouraged workers" no longer believed they could find work and had recently stopped looking. Meanwhile, 1.4 million Canadians and 17 million Europeans were also unemployed (9.6 percent of the working population of Canada and more than 10 percent of the working population of most European countries). In the U.S. defense industry alone, 1.4 million of the 6 million Americans with defense-related jobs were expected to lose them.[51]

As the decade of the 1990s began, unprecedented turbulence came to the American workplace. IBM announced that it would lay off 85,000 people, up from its original estimates of 25,000.[52] General Motors laid off 80,000. A reduction of 252,000 positions in the federal workforce was proposed to make the U. S. government work better and cost less by 1998.[53] In addition, the following jobs were among those lost:

- Beginning with 5,000 layoffs in 1994, Xerox said it would eliminate 10 percent of its worldwide workforce—a total of 10,000 jobs—in the largest workforce cuts in the company's history.
- Entering 1994, RJR Nabisco announced that 6,000 of its 63,000 worldwide jobs would be cut, spread throughout the blue- and white-collar workplace.
- Philip Morris planned to eliminate 14,000 jobs, about 8 percent of its workforce.
- National Cash Register Corporation announced 7,500 job cuts, closing out 15 percent of its workforce.
- Scott Paper eliminated 8,300 jobs, 25 percent of its workforce.
- DuPont said it would trim 4,500 domestic jobs.
- Drug maker Warner-Lambert announced plans to cut its workforce by 2,800, as did Upjohn by 1,500, and Pfizer by 3,000.
- Boeing announced 30,000 job cuts; McDonnell Douglas more than 10,000; BankAmerica 10,000–12,000; Aetna Life and Casualty 4,800; Pratt and Whitney 10,600; American Express 4,800; Goodyear 1,000; Ames Department Stores 4,500; Compaq Computer 1,000; Ameritech Corporation 6,000; and Kodak 2,000.
- Sears, having earlier cut 48,000 jobs, announced plans to close 113 stores and terminate up to 50,000 more jobs, most of them part-time positions.[54]

- As part of the ongoing process of restructuring, Bell South Corporation fashioned 10,200 job cuts; Westinghouse 6,000; US West 9,000; and Bristol-Myers 5,000 through 1996.
- AT&T planned to lay off 14,000, half of them managers, and Dun and Bradstreet said that several thousand jobs would be cut.
- Airlines across the United States (Delta, Northwest, USAir, United, American, and Alaska Air) announced the elimination of 20,000 jobs.
- Bell Atlantic projected a loss of 5,600 jobs by 1997.[55]
- Procter and Gamble planned thirty plant closings between 1993 and 1997 to cut 13,000 jobs.[56]
- Nynex Corporation said it would eliminate 16,800 jobs by 1997.[57]

Virtually every household name in North America is on the ever-increasing list of downsized or downsizing companies: General Mills, Merrill Lynch, Alcoa, John Hancock, Mobil, Fleet Financial, Northrop, Tektronix, Pillsbury, Bethlehem Steel, Chrysler, Ford, Gillette, Westinghouse, and many more.[58] And hundreds of thousands of additional people have lost their jobs through small business downsizings, farm foreclosures, bankruptcies, and the restructuring which is occurring in every sector of the country including manufacturing, education, health care, real estate, insurance, banking, state and local government, publishing, entertainment, and countless others.

The bottom line is this: Yes, job loss is a stressful, disillusioning, frustrating, problem-causing, and infuriating experience. But in most cases—because of the economic and technological changes sweeping North America and the rest of the world—how can you take it personally? You have not failed. Someone is not out to "get" you. What has happened to you—although it is highly distressing—is not really anybody's "fault," any more than the industrial revolution that put craftsmen and skilled artisans out of work in another era was someone's fault. Time changes things and these are times of dramatic change.

You can take comfort in the fact that you are not alone. And you will transcend your fury and fatigue to rise to the challenges of a new age.

III

Overcoming Diminished Self-Esteem

No one can make you feel inferior without your consent.

—ELEANOR ROOSEVELT

Virtually every expert who has studied job loss has identified diminished self-esteem as a central problem. Interviews that we conducted with scores of men and women made it apparent that a person who suffers job loss typically feels as if he or she is "not a complete person anymore." "Over time," write authors Kates, Greiff, and Hagen, "being workless comes to be equated with being worthless."[1]

Many people experience job loss as a physical mutilation, say British psychologists John Archer and Valerie Rhodes, citing several studies. "A former plasterer said, 'It's like somebody cutting your throat'; an engineer . . . said that news of his job loss made him feel as if he had been 'kicked in the stomach'"; and an "unemployed managerial worker said he felt as though he had lost a leg."[2]

We live in a social context that so defines a person according to work that some unemployed people pretend to go out to work in order to maintain their status in the family or personal identity in the community. In Fagin and Little's book *The Forsaken Families,* the story is told of a thirty-seven-year-old design engineer who resigned, with his wife's encouragement, from a job in which he felt "used and unacknowledged" by his bosses. "I kept it from the children," he explained. "But I think they suspected something when they noticed the change of hours and when I returned the [company] car. I thought I would get a new car before the girls noticed.

In fact, at the time, I had an offer of a job, but that fell through." Eventually the engineer's stepdaughters "got very suspicious and started asking awkward questions. It suddenly came out at dinner one night."[3]

A fired sales representative in Utah, an Oklahoma banker, and others told us that they cried coming out of the unemployment office or telling a loved one about the lost job. A California woman whose husband lost an executive position told of driving many miles from her own community to buy groceries with the family's food stamps. Many families feel ashamed and embarrassed over their circumstances.

In an article in the *British Journal of Social Psychology,* Archer and Rhodes explain that while the stresses of work are considerable ("time pressures and job overload, physical exhaustion, humiliating social interactions with superiors, boredom, environmental stressors such as noise and air pollution, and role ambiguity and conflict"), the stresses of not working are greater. For most people unemployment causes a deprivation far greater than the financial consequences.[4]

After several months of searching actively for a job, many plunge to a low point in self-esteem, says William J. Morin, the chairman of a well-known consulting firm. "All of a sudden people don't call you back. Reject letters start coming in. The opportunities you thought early on were available, don't materialize. It happens to everybody: top executives, middle managers and hourly workers. You begin to feel forsaken."[5]

Mr. Morin goes on to say that the despondency and dip in self-esteem eventually end and that "out of all this mumbo-jumbo emerge three or four promising leads" and reemployment.[6] It's just hard to keep your spirits up, even when you know that you're having one of those predictable low points that professionals have observed.

ALAN BEAUCHAMP: "YOU'VE GOT TO FEEL GOOD ABOUT YOURSELF"

Alan Beauchamp had been a senior financial officer for a large computer company in Boston. Three months after he left his well-paying position to become the budget director of a high-tech corporation in Oregon, he realized that his new employer was "on financial quicksand." Indeed, six months later, Alan and 500 others lost their jobs. "It's amazing," said Alan after the layoff. "One day you're on top of the world and one afternoon, the next week, some secretary is looking at her watch, telling you that you have to leave the company-provided outplacement office because it's three o'clock and she has important things to do."

Alan went through a phase of lying in bed every day until noon. Then he started reading everything he could get his hands on about job loss and job search. He realized that putting structure back into his life would save him: "You've got to get up, shave, and have an agenda for the day," he decided.

His biggest loss was a sense of self-worth and personal well-being. A low point came one day in the unemployment office. Burdened by a $2,000 monthly mortgage and accustomed to an annual income in six figures, he was asked by the young man behind the desk whether he had applied for a bag-boy job at one of the supermarkets. Alan replied, "Excuse me? No, but that's a very good idea."

He left the unemployment office saying to himself, "I never thought I would sink this low." Alan did not apply for any bag-boy jobs, but he did teach some college courses to supplement his unemployment income. Teaching helped him feel valuable and kept him busy.

"You've got to look the old layoff devil in the eye and realize that you didn't screw up," says Alan. "What happened was out of your control and you've got to feel good about yourself."

Alan felt embarrassed that his wife had to take a job at a department store, just as she had done twenty-five years before to afford Christmas gifts. On the other hand, Alan found it touching that she wanted to go out and contribute.

They became more frugal and changed many aspects of their lifestyle. "I never thought we'd become coupon clippers or that I'd iron my own shirts," he says. "I'd never ironed a shirt before in my life."

He has begun to recognize a long-standing pattern in his work life of long hours away from home, at a great emotional cost to his family and himself. His periods of unemployment, lasting many months at a time, have been beneficial in causing a reevaluation of goals and priorities. "I'm not going to take another job with twelve-to fourteen-hour days," he says. "I'd rather work eight-hour days, make $40,000 a year, and have time for my family. Money isn't everything," Alan continues. "A walk in the woods with the old hound is more enjoyable than a hundred dollar dinner."

June Santa: Recognizing the Problem and Taking Steps to Raise Self-Esteem

June Santa was forty-two years old when she lost her midmanagement position as a computer analyst in North Carolina, the victim of corporate downsizing and the 1991 recession. She had been with the company for almost twenty-four years, and it was the only employer she had ever had.

She had been an excellent employee, "always going the extra mile for the company," she told us, "and this is the thanks I get, a pink slip." Even two years later it would distress her that some people who weren't doing their jobs well stayed on, while she was gone.

For the first several months June felt devastated. "You think it's the end of the world," she explained. "My identity, my everything is gone." Job loss "is like losing a loved one except it's not a person you lose. You've lost a part of yourself."

June found social situations difficult. She hated hearing the question "Where do you work?" She would describe herself as "between jobs right now," whereupon the other person usually seemed to just slip away. Perhaps others thought there was nothing more to discuss or that June's unemployment might be contagious. "It was very rare that someone would actually stay and talk to me or ask about my job loss," she said.

Out of work for eleven months, June used the outplacement services offered by her ex-employer. She and other displaced workers met once a week to talk about what they were going through and how they were feeling. Group members also helped each other with the nuts and bolts of job search: job listings, access to job lines, help with résumé writing, and brainstorming ideas.

After her severance pay lapsed, June found dealing with certain individuals at the unemployment office humiliating. During that time she managed to pay all of her bills by taking temporary work.

Because job loss brought up such a range of feelings and involved so much rejection by others, June decided to start a support group. About six months after the layoff, she created HIRE (Helping Individuals Regain Employment), a group in which people in this situation could help and understand each other. When she called the local newspaper to place an ad about her group, someone saw a story and sent a reporter. The result was a full-blown article with her picture. June started getting phone calls right away.

It seemed to June that it was harder for men to come to the HIRE group than for women. In fact, she found some women coming to talk about their husbands' job loss.

At the first meeting there were ten people. Each introduced himself or herself, described the details of the job loss, and told how they felt about it, both then and currently. As the weeks went by, the group grew larger. "People really wanted to talk," June explained. It was all right for group members to feel sorry for themselves for a little while but "you have to try and move on." Some people, she realized, "had a really hard time forgiving the company, after all their years of loyal service," and others "were so angry that they wouldn't even look for another job."

After listening to each other, group members would ask, "What are you going to do this week to motivate yourself?" This exercise was highly beneficial, June remembers, because "when you're unemployed, you don't have anyone telling you what to do. You have to be your own boss." Assigning tasks to yourself and carrying them out are difficult, however, when you don't know what the time frame is, how long your unemployment is going to last.

Some people found the open discussion helpful. Others left the group, feeling that they didn't want to sit around pitying themselves. So the membership changed from time to time. Still, the support group kept going for nearly two years. Every few weeks a speaker came in to describe services available to unemployed people or to discuss job search resources at the library or elsewhere. Group members began to network, sharing job leads and contacts, and people started getting jobs.

One of the rules of the group was that when a member landed a job, he or she had to leave the group. Those who were employed, however, returned as guest speakers, giving hope to the others by talking about their new jobs. "You see, you can do it, you can build a new life," former group members seemed to be saying. Eventually June, too, was able to become one of these speakers who came back to inspire those still struggling with job loss. Through network-ing and the job-seeking skills she gradually learned, June was able to find a new job in which she was happy.

June Santa helped herself through a difficult period of diminished self-esteem by giving and receiving emotional encouragement in a support group and by assigning herself daily tasks and carrying them out. "You know, when you work, you have projects to do and deadlines," she explained. "So I made a 'to-do' list. For example, I would decide to make six contact calls, write a cover letter and mail in a particular application. By the end of the day I would make cer-tain that I had finished my list." People who find ways to put struc-ture back into their lives, and who actively help themselves and others regain a feeling of wholeness.

Some people do volunteer work while unemployed and benefit from working with people whose needs and problems are greater than their own. Others help out at their children's school or do odd jobs around the house or in the community. Making yourself useful is an important way to regain self-respect.

In times of reduced self-esteem, often you can lift yourself out of the doldrums by getting regular exercise, reducing your intake of al-cohol and sugar, involving yourself in a hobby, joining a support group, listening to uplifting music, enjoying a sport, and staying away from negative or critical people who seem to cause you more grief. Maximize the time you spend with people who treat you well and respectfully; they are often themselves persons who have over-come feelings of diminished self-esteem.

Many find it helpful to make a list of personal strengths, talents, and accomplishments. You may want to make this part of your jour-nal work. If you try writing as a technique for raising self-esteem, be sure to record things you have done for other people, as well as work-related achievements. Make note of such contributions as helping out certain friends or neighbors. List specific tasks well done in a job you held, including acquiring computer skills and the ability to work with people or mastering difficult concepts or com-plex machines. Include major difficulties you have overcome, and try to recall, as specifically as possible, how you managed to con-quer them. Remind yourself often that the personal qualities that previously led to success can work for you again.

Self-esteem is inextricably connected to competency and meaningful work—but work is far too important to the sanity of all of us to be narrowly defined as a certain place or simply bringing home a paycheck. Work is being productive, it's an activity that fulfills you. Work is effort that you put out to better your life or to benefit someone else. The reward is a good feeling in your soul about your usefulness as a human being.

Although you may be missing the validation of co-workers and supervisors or longing for the satisfaction of earning or contributing financially as before, you can decide to learn something of value, build or create something someone will enjoy, or accomplish something else worthwhile.

YOU AREN'T WHAT YOU EARN AND YOU AREN'T WHAT YOU DO

A friend of mine and most of his relatives spent their adult lives working at Bethlehem Steel, in Baltimore, where there were once 30,000 employees and there are now fewer than 6,000. Since his high school graduation, and except for military service in Vietnam, Bob Fisher worked for the company—through countless layoffs—in the nail mill, at the brickyard, in refrigeration, and eventually with computers.

In social situations, when people ask the inevitable question, "What do you do?" Bob's response has always been: "I'm a father. I like having good times with my kids. I also like handball, softball, water sports, karaoke, card games, and taking college courses." He is a good friend to many and the kind of man who likes to fix things or otherwise help people out when he is needed. Since recently becoming a grandfather, he enjoys playing with his grandkids, too.

I have always admired the way Bob defines his life and personal worth in categories not related to money or job status. He was the same guy when he got his hands, clothes, and lungs dirty making a living as he was when he was making straight A's in college, or is now when he gives advice on computer software. Bob's values are straight in his own mind and his sense of self-worth is in clear focus: These are powerful tools for coping with vocational and economic uncertainty.

To whatever extent you have had a tendency in the past to think that your worth as a person is determined by the type of work that you do, how much money you make, or even if you have a job at all—it is time to reexamine these fundamental assumptions.

The people who really care don't love you for how much you have or don't have in the bank, how fancy or plain your office is or if you have one at all, how impressive your material acquisitions are or aren't, or whether or not your hands get greasy on a regular day. What others want to know is far more basic: Are you a good person? Do you care about people besides yourself? Are you loyal? A person of integrity? An understanding person? Do you enjoy life and cherish the good times with a thankful heart? Are you a positive, upbeat kind of person? Can you see the humor in life? Give as well as receive? Do you stand by people in times of need? All of these are the qualities that matter most and define you. And to whatever extent they are qualities that need more development, there is still time to grow and change for the better. Whether or not you soon find a decent job, there is still time to pursue and nurture the human qualities that are genuinely worthwhile.

A MATTER OF PERSPECTIVE

David Jacobson, who studied reactions to job loss among technical professionals, wrote that stress from an event does not result from the event itself but results from how the individual sees it. Jacobson found that the displaced workers who were the most vulnerable to stress were those who "allowed the market to define their abilities." Those who saw themselves as past their prime or no longer in control of their own vocational life were greatly affected by their own interpretations of events.[7]

A friend of mine lost her forty-six-year-old son to cancer last Thanksgiving Day. When I called her the following Saturday to give Dorris my condolences, she was just walking in the door, returning from the funeral. After we talked awhile, I told my friend how sorry I was that—of all days—her son had died on Thanksgiving. "No, it was okay," she replied. "We are so thankful for Mark's life that it was fitting that he died on that day." Life is so much a matter of perspective, I remember thinking.

Of course my friend, her husband, and their other children have to mourn the loss of a dear son and brother. Their healing will take a long time, will never be entirely complete, and their lives will never be the same. Yet Dorris's example offers a valuable lesson for anyone dealing with a loss: Soon after tragedy occurred, she started helping herself heal by choosing how to think about her loss and deciding what meaning she would assign to certain events.

What meaning will you assign to the circumstances of your job loss? How will you choose to interpret the timing of your unemployment or its potential impact? Are you willing to help yourself by looking for something positive to emerge from these events? Will you refuse to allow the circumstances of your loss to define your worth or abilities? Are you determined not to be robbed of a sense of personal control?

IV

Reducing Financial Worry

I lost the conviction that lights would always turn green for me.

—Joan Didion

Of course it is difficult to know how long your unemployment will last and, if you've taken a temporary lower-paying job, how long you may have a significantly reduced income. Economist Christopher Ruhm reports that "the vast majority of displaced workers are reemployed rather quickly and virtually all are reemployed two years later." The problem is that from one-half to two-thirds of such people earn lower wages once reemployed. According to Professor Ruhm, the average size of the income loss is from 10 percent to 15 percent.[1] At least one-fourth of today's displaced workers suffer reduced earnings of 25 percent or more.[2]

In a sobering *Newsweek* article, business columnist Jane Bryant Quinn explains that recessions come and go "but workers will be coping with layoffs and low pay for years."[3]

If regaining your full income or achieving greater prosperity is an unwavering goal, there is no reason why you shouldn't aim for that target. The other side of Professor Ruhm's statistics, after all, reveal that from one-third to one-half of displaced workers will earn the same or a larger income once reemployed. Just as cancer recurrence statistics do not predict for an individual—but only for groups of individuals—so the "cancer" at the workplace is unpredictable regarding its specific impact on you.

Moving into an economic survival mode makes good sense: You can both work toward attaining your desired level of income and you can establish financial security with considerably less income.

Almost everyone initially denies that lifestyle alterations will be needed. Many of us who are "baby boomers" have not had to cope with as much economic hardship as our parents experienced. Often we resist the idea of self-restraint. Americans in particular save less of their income than the people of any other industrialized nation. We are known worldwide as consumers and spenders, generally speaking, rather than as having lifestyles of moderation.

Change doesn't come easily. On the other hand, scores of individuals told Rick Lamplugh and me in interviews that losing their jobs caused them to rethink their values and that they have been living more happily ever since.

While most people use denial as a coping mechanism, at least temporarily, problems have a way of getting worse until we face them. Denying the need for making certain financial decisions intensifies anxiety, eats up energy that is needed for job search and personal relationships, and can put you into a position of great vulnerability. Not getting your financial house in order also makes you more likely to accept a job that you'll come to hate instead of waiting for something more satisfying.

But the best motivation for reexamining how you and the people you live with handle money is the immediate benefit: You'll all feel less stress once the wolf has been chased away from the door.

THINKING ABOUT MONEY IN NEW WAYS

It is important to see making changes not as a burden imposed by outside forces but as something you choose. You may later decide to return to your previous habits and lifestyle, but for now, think of cutting expenses as a decision made to render you and your family less vulnerable and to ease your mind somewhat. You'll feel less like yelling at people, getting drunk, or giving up, and you'll feel a lot less angry or depressed, once you can lay down the heavy load of constant worry over money.

Families probably argue as much or more about money as any other issue, so you'll want to have some strategies in mind for handling disagreements. It is a good idea to hold regular family meetings where parents and children can discuss the need for working together through a difficult period. The more democracy you practice in these meetings, the more successful they will be: Cost-cutting, money-earning, and money-saving ideas should be solicited from everyone, including children as young as elementary school age. Avoid creating an atmosphere in which the adult puts his or her foot down and gives pronouncements regarding changes to be made. If communication completely breaks down, you might restore peace through a few sessions of couple or family counseling with a trained counselor or social worker.

If money was a source of family conflict as we grew up, we often revert to childhood ways of thinking when it comes to financial constraints. As adults, we may feel like little kids being forced by our parents to behave a certain way in dealing with money matters. For example, even though you are the one who has decided to put away your credit cards, you may automatically rebel against your own rule because you had similarly rebelled against a parent's restrictions many years before. Our "inner child of the past," as Dr. Hugh Missildine has described it, walks along with us through life and especially interferes in times of crisis:

> Much friction between husbands and wives occurs over money. Many people are unreasonable about money as adults simply because in their childhood they were surrounded by persons who were anxious about money. To the "child of the past," money can mean security, a means of expressing individuality, a way of getting away from circumstances that are unpleasant, a promise of good things. Conversely, it may mean control, deprivation, withdrawal of love or status. These strong childhood reactions can easily obscure adult goals.[4]

I often recommend Missildine's book, *Your Inner Child of the Past,* to individuals and couples in conflict. Life is too short for any of us to let our relationships be sabotaged and our goals be thwarted by events that happened long ago.

THE PROBLEM WITH BORROWING FROM RELATIVES

It's a good idea not to approach family members for financial assistance until you carefully think through any potential problems.

When borrowing money from relatives, people naively believe that everything will work out because "this is family," says Dr. Jim

Gottfurch, a California psychologist whose specialty is helping those with money problems.[5] When family members have healthy adult relationships, treat each other with respect, and don't try to control or manipulate, borrowing and repaying money can be an acceptable solution to financial difficulties. The problem is that otherwise money issues can shatter family ties.

A married man who turns to his parents or siblings for help, or even worse, to his in-laws, for example, might be walking into an "emotional minefield," says Columbia University anthropologist Katherine Newman. His wife's family "can feel obligated to help, but resentful. Confusion and embarrassment can intensify over whether material help is a loan, a gift, a favor, or a right—self-abasement or a statement of love and sharing."[6]

"Impersonality is a buffer against embarrassment," continues Newman. Talking over financial problems with a bank officer is less difficult and awkward than approaching a friend or relative. And if a default should occur, the bank absorbs the loss instead of a loved one whose hard-earned funds could be lost.[7]

Anthropologists have long been interested in the ties created and broken between people as a result of gifts, indebtedness, or exchange, says Professor Newman, and she emphasizes that sudden financial distress can distort relationships with kinfolk. When obligations and expectations are clear and family members take turns giving and taking, she says, there is less ambiguity and more symmetry between the receiver and the giver.[8]

In a psychologically healthy family where money is not used to control people, induce guilt, or achieve other hidden goals, you won't have to pay an emotional price for borrowing money. Still, it is probably best to think of relatives as "your ace in the hole," says financial advisor Jane Bryant Quinn. Family members, she says, are "the only people who might be able to help you finance a new start in life. So try to tap them last, not first."[9]

REDUCE STRESS BY MAKING WISE FINANCIAL DECISIONS

The experts offer many valuable money management tips which can greatly reduce your financial and emotional distress. Because each individual and family situation is unique, some of these suggestions will help you and others may not apply:

- Apply right away for unemployment benefits to maximize the length of time you will receive compensation. Unless it is appropriate, don't use the word "fired" in making your application, as it implies wrongdoing and makes you ineligible for benefits. Says Dorian Burden, writing for *Executive Female* magazine, plan on spending an entire day applying for unemployment and take along: your last pay stub, W-2 form, any dismissal notice you may have received, your Social Security card, the company's business name, address, and IRS identification number, and *something to read*.[10]

- Look at any severance pay you receive as "bridge money" to be managed carefully until you find another job. Advises Dan Moreau in *Changing Times,* it is not a good idea to use a severance stipend to pay off a mortgage or credit cards, if doing so will cause you to end up broke.[11]

- Manage your debt. "Your job search may last longer than your resources," says Moreau. But the first step is immediately to "apply the brakes on borrowing"—eliminating credit card charges, new installment debt, and any new credit buying.[12]

- Seek the advice of a qualified financial advisor by paying an hourly fee to a certified financial planner (C.F.P.) in your area. This professional can help you decide what to do about credit card debt (including whether to get a home equity loan, if possible), how best to utilize severance pay, how to manage and protect your assets and savings, and so on. A consolidation loan, for instance, is not necessarily your best bet because it can get you into more trouble: While you pay less per month, the total amount that you pay may be far greater unless you shop around for a much lower interest rate. Ask your trusted financial advisor to help you find alternative solutions.

- Obtain free budget counseling and other valuable help from the National Consumer Credit Service. (For more information about this nonprofit group, and to locate offices in your region, see Appendix B.)

- Begin to redefine the good life. "Your best cost-cutting tool," says Lani Luciano in *Money* magazine, is "an open mind."[13] Ask yourself: Which lifestyle changes would enrich my life, reduce stress, *and* save money? What changes would provide for more family fun and closeness yet cut costs?

- Draw up a budget listing what you owe, your monthly expenses, all investments and savings, and your monthly income. Include everything necessary for a clear and accurate picture of your basic needs and resources. List separately important areas of personal spending (for each family member) and allow for these expenses. Ask yourself where you feel comfortable trying some cost cutting in various categories and discuss proposed cuts with your spouse to see where you agree. One person's necessity is often another person's idea of frivolity so it's important for family members to try to respect each other. Each person (including school-age children) can contribute in his or her own way to designing and implementing the savings strategy.

- Make it difficult to do impulse buying: Don't carry credit cards; stay away from malls and favorite stores; and don't grocery shop when you're hungry, more often than once a week, or without a list. Research indicates that people who use cash instead of credit spend 23 percent less.[14]

- "Try to bring in some extra income," writes Jane Bryant Quinn in *Executive Female* magazine. "Sign up with a temporary-help agency. Pitch for consulting jobs. Advertise your services in the neighborhood: typing, carpentry, accounting, daycare. If your spouse doesn't work, now is the time for him [or her] to start. Ask your teenagers to pitch in with after-school jobs." It's not easy, says Quinn, but "managing money without a paycheck" is possible.[15]

- Choose public colleges instead of expensive private ones for yourself or your children, saving thousands of dollars each year without compromising the quality of education.[16] You can also obtain valuable training in career programs or begin a college education at your local community college—where the tuition is more affordable and the faculty is usually more dedicated to teaching than to research. (Studies show that a higher proportion of community college graduates achieve academic excellence when they transfer to most state universities than do students who begin their education at the four-year institution.) Since there is an oversupply of Ph.D.'s in many fields, most two- and four-year colleges have been selective in choosing highly qualified faculty members.

- File early for college financial aid, writes Elizabeth Fenner in *Money* magazine. "The earlier you get started, the better your chance of getting a package with a higher ratio of grant dollars (which you don't have to repay) to loan dollars (which you do). That's because many colleges—particularly smaller, less wealthy ones—tend to dole out grants on a first come, first served basis. You must refile every year to maintain aid eligibility."[17]

- Choose carefully, if you are thinking about enrolling in a trade or vocational school. According to a 1991 U.S. Senate subcommittee investigating abuses in federal student loan programs, hundreds of thousands of students have been victimized by "unscrupulous, inept and dishonest trade school operators and were left with no training, no jobs and significant debts impossible to repay." In some trade schools around the country, cautions the Maryland Attorney General's Office, students get federal loans to cover tuition, get little or no training, and do not get the help that was promised to find a job. The student, poorly served, even cheated, still must repay the federal loan. Contact employers in the community and talk confidentially to current students and past graduates (ask the school for names) to help verify the school's integrity and track record for placing its graduates in jobs.[18]

- Don't sign anything on your first visit to a school. And don't be taken in by a common sales ploy: Someone tells you there is limited space in the next class and urges you to make a quick decision. You need to research the school to be sure

that the skills you'll learn there will be valued by the companies that do the hiring. As any good lawyer would caution
you, some applications are binding contracts, so read them
carefully before signing. Be sure to get a receipt for any payments you make and to keep a copy of the application, contract, and any other documents.[19]

- If the debt you already have makes it impossible to make installment payments, do something to take the pressure off, advises Moreau. It is usually best not to try to hide your financial
condition from creditors. Let them know that you've lost your
job, that you're seeking a new one, and that you wish to make
token payments until you can make up the difference.[20] If
your creditors accept new terms, be sure to get the new payment agreement in writing.

- Keep creditors informed, but "don't cave in, even if your account is turned over to a bill collector," says Quinn. "Your top
priorities are to husband cash, hold your life together and
keep your job search going. When you find a job—and you
will—you can work out a repayment plan."[21]

- Keep reminding yourself that it is best not to pay creditors
what you can't afford to pay, continues Quinn. A basic survival
rule is to "make no payments on postponable bills if doing so
means that you'll run out of money within a few months.
Don't worry about hurting your credit rating. You can repair it
later. It's far more important to conserve your savings in order
to keep the lights on, the telephone connected, gas in the car,
and food on the table."[22]

- Harassment or abuse from debt collectors is against the law,
explains the author of a helpful article in *Black Enterprise*
magazine. The federal Fair Debt Collection Practices Act (FD-
CPA) protects debtors and their families from "unfair, unreasonable or abusive actions from collection agencies and
attorneys." If threats of violence occur or are implied, if pro-
fane or abusive language is used against you, or if you are
badgered with annoying telephone calls, you can file a com-

plaint with the Federal Trade Commission. (See Appendix B for the number to call.)[23]

- Talk to your pharmacist and physician about generic drugs, free drug samples, needed tests at reduced rates, and partial payments. Often these professionals are flexible and kind when made aware of a person's circumstance.

- You can arrange for a "forbearance agreement"—with most mortgage holders—enabling you to pay nothing, or a partial payment, for a set period of time, says Moreau. The difference is made up later on, when you resume regular mortgage payments.[24]

- Consider moving to a more affordable apartment complex, a smaller house, or a less expensive community in your area. If you are a homeowner, you may be able to refinance at a lower interest rate or to find a house with one less bedroom. Explains Lani Luciano, in *Money* magazine: Since housing prices in most places are remaining the same or declining, and the average appreciation rate, according to housing analysts, is expected to be barely ahead of inflation until the end of the decade, trading down to a smaller house can greatly improve your financial situation. This is also a good way to avoid increasing property taxes. Unfortunately, unless you qualify for the one-time capital gains exclusion, you will owe taxes on any profit you make. And "if falling prices have wiped out your equity, trading down would be impractical since you'd have to [come up with] a down payment on your new home."[25]

- Consider moving to a different part of the United States, Luciano continues. "Although the cost of living varies as much as 90 percent from the most expensive parts of the country (California and the Northeast) to the least expensive (Florida and Texas), salaries seldom vary by more than 25 percent.[26]

- Try to "break decision deadlock by gathering more facts," advises housing expert Ellen James Martin. Often a difficult problem can be remedied once a few more pieces of information come together, she explains. Be sure to get your priorities in focus and examine the future as well as your current needs.[27]

- "Rethink your life from the ground up," writes Quinn in her book, *Making the Most of Your Money.* It is important to consider jobs at a lower salary.[28] Ask yourself: How can I change my thinking about how much money I have to earn in order to regain a positive attitude toward work and my future? Which lifestyle adjustments would enable me or my family to build a life that is emotionally rewarding despite less income?

- You can probably roll over your company retirement plan or Individual Retirement Account (IRA), if you had one at the last workplace, into a "no-risk IRA that can be tapped easily, like a bank money-market account," explains Quinn. As an emergency measure, you'll want to withdraw funds only as you need them. There are taxes to pay and you'll have to pay a penalty on the withdrawn money, so as soon as you find work, you should immediately stop the withdrawals.[29] It is preferable, of course, not to touch retirement savings.

- You can lower many of your everyday expenses without lowering your standard of living, according to Lee and Barbara Simmons in their paperback book, *Penny Pinching.* Buy generic products, shop through the mail, use unit pricing, find better buys on higher and lower store shelves, buy store brands, use coupons only for brands and products you normally would purchase, and avoid supermarkets for nonfood items much cheaper elsewhere. Also join a warehouse club such as Price, Costco, Pace, Sam's Wholesale Club, or Super-Saver. And avoid "convenience ripoffs, such as prepared produce and baby food, fancy packaging, and frozen dinners." *Penny Pinching* also shows how to save 20 percent on water and heating, how to get your own 800 number if your children are away at college, how to reduce insurance premiums and taxes, how to minimize car expenses, how to cut travel and clothing expenses, how to deal with banks, and much more.[30] See "For Further Reading" at the back of this book for other helpful materials on saving money.

- Shop at manufacturers' outlet stores and pay 20 percent to 60 percent less than retail prices.

- Take advantage of the Self-Help and Resource Exchange (SHARE). Through this program you can save 60 percent on food and help your community, too. SHARE-USA has twenty-five affiliates in local communities. As many as 500,000 American families each month take advantage of this wonderful opportunity to help themselves and their communities at the same time.

  In this program, a person pays $13 for a food package worth $25–$30 (enough food for a family of four for approximately two weeks), donates two hours of volunteer time in the community, and then picks up the food package on a designated day of the month. Six or eight hours of service in the community provide three or four packages of food. The volunteer work includes helping out at schools, local churches, synagogues, or nursing homes; helping elderly neighbors with yard work or taking them to doctor appointments; and writing letters to elected officials on unemployment or other issues of concern in the community. Volunteers can also help out at local libraries, volunteer at shelters for homeless people or battered women, work a few hours in a soup kitchen or for the Department of Aging, or bag the food and assist on food distribution days.

  A person does not have to be unemployed to participate; in fact, numerous people in families that have two paychecks still need this program. (For specific information on SHARE-USA programs in your region, you can call one of the numbers listed in the SHARE Directory at the back of this book in Appendix C.)

- For information or help finding any kind of public assistance, including food stamps, medical care, and fuel assistance, call the Department of Human Resources information and referral hotline in your area.

TAKE CARE OF YOURSELF FINANCIALLY: WATCH OUT FOR SCAMS

Most people, at least financially, want to get back to the place where they were before the loss of a job. It's tough trying to cope with a smaller income, dwindling savings, bills coming in, and less security. That kind of discomfort makes you vulnerable to the creeps of this world who take advantage of hurting, worried people.

Don Halferty, fifty-five years old, was a carpenter accustomed to earning $15 to $20 an hour, until the construction industry in his region fell on hard times. Suddenly he found himself applying for jobs paying $9 an hour and competing with more than sixty other applicants for the position. During one period of unemployment, the best job he could find paid $6 an hour. "It used to be," Don explained, "that an employer would hire you as a long-term employee. Now a contractor gets a bid to build a dozen apartment buildings, hires a crew, and when the apartments are finished, so are all the jobs."

Being in the predicament of never having a job longer than a year prompted Don to answer a couple of classified ads in *USA Today,* placed by companies that represented themselves as agencies in the business of helping people find work. He sent his résumé and $350 to a Florida address and $100 to a company in New England. Although a "ninety-day refund policy" was advertised, Don lost his money. He received nothing from Florida despite five follow-up calls (on the sixth call he was told the telephone was disconnected), and from New England he received nothing more than a dozen letters from companies saying they had no openings.

Don later saw an item in the classified section of the *Wall Street Journal* asking for up-front money from job seekers, but he was determined not to get burned again. Reputable and respected newspapers, he finally realized, are often used by those who prey on vulnerable people.

Don does subcontract work now, remodeling stores in malls around the country. He was unemployed for eight months when he responded to a help wanted ad in his local paper. Don and his grown son work three to six weeks at a time, staying together in a motel until the job is done. It is the first time that he has ever worked outside of his home state of Oregon. A company representative calls him up and says, "We've got a job worth $10,000. Load your truck and head to Indiana." And they go. Don is a good carpenter, likes the "fringe benefit" of working with his son, is making a "decent living," and is glad not to have the responsibilities and indebtedness of trying to run his own company as he did for a time.

One Illinois-based scam charged from $3,900 to $7,000, supposedly to help people find jobs in the $40,000 to $100,000 range. Explains Carol Kleiman in the *Chicago Tribune,* what the customers received was an outdated list of places to send their résumés.[31]

"Australia to U. S. Job Seekers: We Really Don't Need You," headlined a column in the *Miami Herald.* The article described a North Carolina sales manager, whose company was six months into bankruptcy, who had answered an "Australia Wants You" item in the newspaper. For $164.95 he had received a packet of information that he could have obtained from any public library. At the peak of the early 1990s recession, Australian embassy officials were flooded with sometimes as many as 400 calls a day, some from hopeful people who wanted visas, others from unhappy people who had been burned—at a time when the recession and unemployment figures were worse in Australia than in the United States.[32]

FBI agents in Atlanta raided and closed down Pro Career Services after it had victimized approximately a thousand people by promising, in newspaper advertisements around the country, "overseas jobs with high salaries, low or no taxes, and the good life in exotic locales." According to Gene Tharpe of the *Atlanta Journal/Atlanta Constitution,* the agency had operated for three months, was charging each customer $295, and was taking in $20,000 per week![33]

The Caribbean, Saudi Arabia, Mexico, Australia, Japan, and other foreign lands are often mentioned in advertisements as lands of promise and job opportunity.[34] One unemployed carpenter lost $675 after answering an ad, even though he checked the agency with the Better Business Bureau and found no complaints against it. When he called the firm he was told that an advance fee was needed to pay the cost of contacting employers overseas and revising his résumé. He was promised a refund if he did not find a job within a year. The company is no longer in business and, of course, the man received no refund.[35]

A variety of employment scams are operating today, according to Stuart Rado, a Miami Beach consumer advocate and consultant:

firms offering lists of jobs for an advance fee; firms offering overseas jobs for $150 to $1,000; and career marketing/counseling firms providing access to a hidden job market for $2,000 to $10,000.[36]

In a *USA Today* article entitled, "Job-Scam Artists Work Overtime," Julia Lawlor quotes Rado and other authorities and cautions the jobless to beware of advance fees.[37] "In 95 percent of legitimate cases, employers—not job seekers—pay hiring costs," Lawlor says, quoting Rick Kean, an official with the international placement firm Dunhill Personnel System. One should be leery of claims such as "We have access to the hidden job market"; and "Our clients average a 20 percent increase in starting salaries." It is equally important not to give out your credit card number.[38]

One should also be suspicious when an agency requires the advance fee to be sent by private delivery service such as Federal Express, continues Gene Tharpe of the *Atlanta Journal/Atlanta Constitution.* The agency could be trying to avoid mail-fraud charges. Also be suspicious if the agency refuses to identify the firm offering the job, even after you've accepted, and be wary if it guarantees that the job is yours. Only the employer can guarantee a job.[39]

There will always be an abundance of con artists trying to take advantage of vulnerable people. If you are having trouble getting a loan or are attracted to a newspaper or billboard ad for a "credit clearing kit," for example, you need to know that thousands of people have been victimized by scams involving loan offers or "fresh start" credit opportunities. The loan company asks the consumer for a "processing" or "application" fee, ranging from $50 to hundreds of dollars. Sometimes an 800 or 900 number is listed as a way to learn more about a particular advertisement. Often, the loan company promises to refund the money if a lender cannot be found, but the refund promise is just part of the scam.

"With Work-At-Home Scams, You're the One Who Pays," cautions a consumer protection bulletin issued by the Maryland Attorney General's Office. One out-of-work woman saw an ad for a company that promised to pay $3 for each envelope she stuffed and mailed from her home. She sent $25 for the starter packet and got nothing but information on how she could place ads like the one she'd answered. Another woman sent $45 to a company that promised to pay her to decorate picture frames in her home. Neither the starter kit nor a promised refund was ever received. Still another person sent $24.85 to a company that said it would send a list of businesses that hire freelance workers to proofread in their homes. Although she received a list of companies to contact, none was interested in hiring freelance proofreaders. In 1991, a period of high unemployment, such complaints filed with the Consumer Protection Division in Maryland against companies offering work-at-home plans more than doubled.[40]

Some states have laws that prohibit a company from requiring advance payments or deposits from people for work they will perform in their homes. Whether or not there is such a law where you live, you shouldn't pay for information about a work-at-home offer, advises the Maryland Attorney General's Office. "Be suspicious of companies that promise a regular market or steady salary. Use common sense. It is unlikely a company would pay several dollars for each envelope you stuff and mail. Before entering into any work-at-home agreement, call the Consumer Protection Division to see if complaints have been filed against the company you are considering doing business with . . . [but] don't assume a company is legitimate just because no one has registered a complaint." Many illegitimate companies advertise vigorously for a time, rake in the money, and move to another locale before any complaints are filed.[41]

One scam, reported by the CBS News program "48 Hours," targeted women who paid hundreds of dollars for an expensive portfolio of photographs after being assured of plentiful job opportunities as models. Older women and others who were told they had "beautiful hands for modeling" were among the victims. Some women spent as much as $800 and, of course, never got to be models and make back the money. In another scam, a fortune teller started out with a $28 fee and eventually took hundreds and even thousands of dollars from superstitious victims, promising to "remove an aura" or "fix a curse," supposedly to render the individual more employable. Obviously, some people will try to steal from you mentally and spiritually as well as financially.[42]

A person who wants to use the "powers of the universe" to get a new life would be better advised to see a qualified counselor or make good use of prayer. "I've learned that prayer might not change things, but it does change the person who prays," said one man, quoted in the little book, *Live and Learn and Pass It On*.[43]

There is also great healing power in relaxation techniques, exercise, music, friendship, journal writing, and a healthy diet.

In addition to promises of employment that are outright dishonest, many misleading money-making schemes that misrepresent the truth often appear in newspapers and on television and the radio. Offers that sound too good to be true should be approached with suspicion.

BE CAUTIOUS ABOUT GOODS OR SERVICES YOU BUY TO SELL

Multilevel marketing can also be risky for a person in financial straits. A multilevel distribution company is one that sells goods or services through independent agents or distributors, with different pricing or discount rates at different levels. If you are promised good money for selling a product and also convincing others to sell it, you should think carefully, even if it's a friend or family member who wants you to get involved. You may have to invest a lot of money to buy the product first and then find that you can't sell it. Instead of making money, you lose it—and you're stuck with the product.

A Milwaukee woman whose husband was out of work for many months borrowed from relatives and spent $1,300 on expensive beauty products which she was to sell at a profit. Several months later she had only sold $200 worth of the products and was unable to dispose of the rest. Soon after, the couple's bank threatened foreclosure on their home. People usually sell such products to their relatives and friends, many of whom have their own financial constraints or good-naturedly make a purchase once but never buy again.[44] If the program calls for getting others involved in sales, remember that that also is a task much more difficult than it sounds.

Before entering into any multilevel marketing program, be sure you have a contract that guarantees that the company will buy back all goods in a resellable condition (for at least 90 percent of the original purchase price) and talk to someone qualified to verify the company's integrity and track record in such matters. Be sure that you have the right to cancel your contract with a multilevel distribution company by notifying the company in writing of your desire to cancel after you receive the merchandise. In many states such company programs are not registered or preapproved by the government, so you'll need to protect yourself.

INVESTIGATE CAREER COUNSELING CENTERS

It is important for you to know that an "employment counseling service" or a "career consulting firm" is a career marketing agency and not an employment agency, regardless of what anyone tells you. While forty-two states prohibit employment agencies from charging advance fees, *Newsweek* reports that only ten states ban career marketing firms from seeking up-front fees.[45] Since seven states have no laws governing these matters, scam operators often set up their operations in the unregulated states and do a mail order business. (Florida has been an especially popular state for scam artists.)[46]

You can check out a firm by contacting the office of the attorney general in the state in which the agency is operating; the Federal Trade Commission in Washington, D.C.; and the Better Business Bureau. (If you've already been burned, be sure to report your experience to the agencies listed here and possibly to a newspaper reporter.)

It is also a good idea to ask for names of clients who have used the service and to call them. If the company hesitates to give you the phone numbers of satisfied ex-clients, you should be suspicious. You can also ask what professional associations the firm belongs to. Most of the reputable placement services are affiliated with the Society for Human Resource Managers, the American Management Association, National Association of Personnel Consultants, the National Association of Temporary Workers, or some similar association of the industry.[47]

A career counseling center can be helpful to you, especially if your former company hasn't helped with job search or career counseling. Just remember to investigate before you spend any money. Ask about your counselor's education and credentials, and whether you'll have the same counselor every time you visit the center. Find out in advance how much you will be charged for each visit and whether there are any other fees such as for aptitude tests.

Try to determine whether the staff sees you as an individual, listens carefully, and note whether they pressure you to sign a contract immediately. If the career counselor wants a percentage of your future paychecks, do not do business with that agency. Employment agencies operate this way, but not career counselors.

Get Wise Financial Advice

Kevin Shea was thirty-three years old and a New York City firefighter when he fell forty feet trying to rescue a victim of the terrorist bombing disaster at Manhattan's World Trade Center in February 1993. Three months after the accident, Kevin realized that his injuries might require him to give up his beloved job as a firefighter and $45,000 a year in income. "I thought I was going to be a fireman my entire life," Kevin explained. "Now I'm realizing that something can always happen to change your plans."[48]

While he was still unsure how lasting his injuries would be, Kevin began to consider other ways of making a living. "I've always been interested in holistic health," he decided. "I might look into becoming a physical therapist, a massage therapist, or a chiropractor."[49]

Making "such a career change would be costly of course," wrote Elizabeth Fenner in *Money* magazine. To become a physical therapist, he would need to add to the thirty community college credits he already had to receive the appropriate bachelor's degree. Fenner estimated that tuition at a public college would be about $8,400, two or three years of massage therapy training would cost $4,000 to $10,000, and becoming a chiropractor would cost about $45,000.[50]

Financial advisors Ron Rogé and Gideon Rothschild, on behalf of *Money* magazine, gave Kevin Shea and his wife the following advice: Wait until Kevin returns to work before buying the more expensive home they had been planning for; refinance their present home to a thirty-year fixed rate mortgage, cutting monthly payments significantly; adjust their income tax withholding to eliminate their typical $3,000 refund, so Kevin's wife can start contributing to her employer's tax-deferred savings plan; save and invest as much as possible while Kevin is still drawing his firefighter's pay on disability; sell off a bad real estate investment that has long had a negative cash flow; reconsider becoming a chiropractor because of the high cost of schooling and the need to save for their children's college education, only six years away; beef up their life insurance; and redo their will, which was never witnessed and isn't valid.[51]

You can benefit from reading money-related magazines such as *Kiplinger's Personal Finance Magazine* (formerly *Changing Times*), *Money, Worth,* and *Black Enterprise,* all generally available at the local library. Important information is available in such periodicals on making critical financial decisions.

But one of your most important tasks is to find a financial advisor who is both wise and honest. "You will need a professional person with lots of experience in a lot of disciplines, and this is damn hard to find," says John G. Danz, Jr., co-owner of an investment counseling firm in Baltimore, Oxford Capital Management. As with finding a good physician or therapist, your best bet is usually a personal referral: If someone you know has been well served and is satisfied, you can go to that person's financial advisor for advice. Your accountant or trusted attorney also can provide a personal recommendation.

You want to be certain, however, that the person is a certified financial planner (C.F.P.), trained to give financial advice and certified by the International Board of Financial Planners. This professional will be listed in the yellow pages.

"There are two kinds of financial advisors—the good ones and the crooks," says Danz. The best way to avoid trouble is to find a certified financial planner whose service is based on fees and not on commission. In other words, to ensure that you get objective advice, you will want a financial advisor who does not benefit from selling certain products (usually insurance policies or mutual funds).

"Many financial planners have come out of the insurance business and the stock brokerage industry," continues Danz, "and are selling annuities or mutual funds." A telltale sign of the kind of professional advisor you don't want is one who recommends an investment that would earn him or her a 7 percent to 8 percent commission instead of recommending no-load mutual funds that would cost you nothing. If you find that you are being pressured to purchase particular investments, find another C.F.P.

"Look for a person with plain common sense," advises Danz. It is a kind of wisdom that is not very common, he says. "You need help to get through this period of unemployment: A well-qualified person will sit down with you, ask the details of your situation, and come up with a specific financial plan." While you may feel that you don't want to pay $50 to $100 an hour for advice, it is well worth the money when you realize that a reputable C.F.P. can help solve your financial problems and alleviate your emotional distress.

In a study of engineers, scientists, and technical managers, Jacobson found that the stress they experienced was largely a result of the impact unemployment had on their financial resources. "All those with resources sufficient to meet their monthly expenses described themselves as 'in good shape' or as 'managing' and those without such resources described themselves as 'in trouble.'"[52] Likewise, M. Aiken, who studied blue-collar workers following an automobile plant closing in Michigan, found that "the availability of economic resources is the single most important factor affecting . . . morale and mental health."[53]

You can take charge of your life by thinking about money in new ways, keeping a clear head in relation to money matters and family members, reducing stress by reducing expenses, watching out for scams, and getting good financial advice. You will feel stronger, less stressed and vulnerable, and not nearly as angry once your job loss can no longer hurt you like a boxer's punches coming unexpectedly. With a well-developed strategy for fighting a good fight, you will prevail in the end.

V

Job Loss Can Be Harmful to Your Health

Life is filled with changes. It's whether we can cope with those changes or not that determines whether we will grow with the situation or be overcome by it, whether we will act helplessly or have hope.

—JOAN BORYSENKO

The stress of job loss can make you sick, physically and emotionally. Furthermore, if you are married or in a long-term relationship, your distress over time can affect your partner's health as well; wives especially are at an increased risk of illness when a husband's unemployment continues for more than a few months. The good news is that illness is not inevitable; you don't have to become a victim.

Before stress exacts too great a toll or even if you are already ill, there is much that you can do to feel better and live longer. Many physical symptoms are simply a normal part of a grieving process and diminish with time, usually ceasing entirely within three months after a loss. Most long-term health risks associated with job loss can be avoided entirely or overcome.

THE PHYSICAL AND EMOTIONAL TOLL

In an anonymous questionnaire routinely given to those who take my "Surviving Job Loss" seminars, the vast majority of these out-of-work men and women have told me that they suffer from depression, have had sleep problems, and are more irritable and fatigued. Half of them report headaches, digestive disturbances, backaches, or aching limbs. Nearly half say that, since losing their jobs, they have had increased colds, flu, infections, and other sicknesses; they say they are "worried" about their health. One in three report an increased use of prescription drugs and one in four say a new medical problem has been diagnosed since they lost their jobs. In response to stress, it is completely understandable and natural that your body would be exhibiting such symptoms.

In a study by Sara Arber, unemployed men and women were found to be more vulnerable to illness than the employed, even when social class differences were taken into account. (Since lower-income people tend to have generally poorer health than the rest of the population, most of the studies I discuss in this book were carefully controlled so the effects of unemployment are seen apart from the effects of poverty.) In Arber's British study, more than twice as many unemployed as employed reported that their health was not good.[1]

Stress can cause a chronic illness to worsen, trigger an episode of an illness you've had before, or cause a latent illness to emerge. Whether you are a blue- or white-collar worker, were working for someone else or were self-employed, owned a business or ran a farm—the effects of job loss, business failure, or bankruptcy are similar.[2] If you feel depressed, anxious, listless, unable to concentrate, irritable, and generally nervous, you are not unusual.[3] Sleep problems occur frequently. High blood pressure, alcohol abuse, increased smoking, bronchitis, some decrease in immune function, and even unhealthy cholesterol changes are other physical and emotional reactions that can occur.[4]

Typically, you can expect the strongest reactions to occur in the first year, beginning possibly in the uncertain last months of your employment, when you anxiously awaited the news about the future of your job. Many experience debilitating stress when their unemployment benefits have run out, after their savings are depleted, or if it becomes obvious that satisfactory reemployment will be difficult. After more than a year of unemployment, listlessness or hopelessness and apathy often set in, further evidence that the stress of job loss is taking its toll.[5]

Researchers in Austria studied the health consequences of long-term unemployment among the former employees of a furniture factory that closed in 1986. Those who were still unemployed after twelve months were found to be eight times likelier to report poor psychological health than those reemployed. Men, older workers, those in white-collar jobs, those already ill, and those who had been unemployed before seemed to show the most psychological distress.[6]

Some people become physically or mentally ill because the strain over time is too great. If you have a family history of depression, anxiety disorder, diabetes, arthritis, heart disease, or other medical problems, you might have a hereditary predisposition, and the stress of job loss may act as the triggering mechanism for an onset of the illness. Most people who have a close relative with diabetes or some other illness, however, *don't* come down with the same illness just because they lose their jobs.

In *The Forsaken Families,* Fagin and Little explain that in Western, industrialized nations, it is better to be sick and unemployed than healthy and unemployed, especially for a jobless man.[7] Society has different expectations of people who are unemployed than of those who are ill.

If you have lost your job, unfortunately most people think you can recover if you want to: You are expected to look for work energetically and if you somehow can't muster the necessary enthusiasm, something must be "wrong" with you. If you are the primary provider, you are also supposed to support your family or you risk being seen by society as a "bad person." These things are not expected of the sick or the injured. It is no wonder, then, that many people feel a sense of *relief* on becoming ill: Finally it is no longer necessary to deal with the immense stress of stringent social expectations.

I do not believe that people who lose their jobs deliberately scheme to acquire a sickness or be injured in an accident. Human beings, in my experience, are much braver than that, and not nearly so calculating. What does happen, as I see it and a number of scientific studies have demonstrated, is that stress contributes greatly to an individual's susceptibility to illness or injury. And who could blame you—after the fact—for being glad to have society's pressure lifted?

As I wrote in one of my earlier books, *Living Through Personal Crisis,* Americans tend to be compassionate and sympathetic toward themselves and others when dealing with health problems, and often impatient and even intolerant when it comes to bereavement. Thus you may be able to accept yourself as a person who is having difficulty finding another job while you are ill or injured, but not as a person having difficulty otherwise. You may realize that bodies take time to heal but expect your injured spirits to be revived immediately.

WHAT STUDIES SHOW ABOUT ILLNESS AND UNEMPLOYMENT

In a Swedish study of 354 blue-collar workers, Bengt Arnetz and associates found that the psychological stress of job loss caused accentuated biochemical and cardiovascular reactions during the first year of unemployment. "Systolic blood pressure and serum cholesterol tended to be higher among the unemployed even during the second year and HDL [high-density lipoprotein, the good cholesterol] remained consistently depressed among the unemployed." Independent of changes in financial conditions, the psychological stress of unemployment was "associated with increased risk for cardiovascular disease."[8]

Research scholar Carl D'Arcy, analyzing a Canada Health Survey of 32,000 individuals, found significant mental and physical health differences between the employed and unemployed. D'Arcy found that job loss has an adverse health impact on large numbers of men and women representing a wide variety of age and socioeconomic groups. His findings generally support an extensive body of research in North America and Europe.

Certain problems were said by D'Arcy to be more prevalent among those unemployed who held university degrees. Hypertension, for example, was more common among college graduates who lost their jobs. However, while no economic group is immune, unemployment has more adverse effects on blue-collar and poorer people. People with low incomes before becoming unemployed experienced more psychological distress in general, including more symptoms of anxiety and depression, especially principal family earners.[9]

D'Arcy's large Canadian study also showed that age and sex play an important role. Contrary to some findings reported earlier, this study found that women and older unemployed individuals had more health problems and physician visits, whereas those unemployed under age forty reported more psychological distress. People in the thirty to fifty age range showed more anxiety and depression than the unemployed who were younger or older, and men and women thirty to forty had the highest rates of anxiety and depression.[10]

K. A. Moser, who conducted a ten-year study of British men seeking work and of their wives, found a marked excess of suicides and an abnormally high mortality rate from heart disease among younger unemployed men. There was also a higher mortality rate among the wives of unemployed men.[11] A thirty-year study in Sweden as well as studies in Australia, Canada, the United States, Wales, Scotland, France, West Germany, Denmark, and Finland similarly found harmful health effects from unemployment.[12]

It is also believed that ailments resulting from unemployment are especially apt to affect certain vulnerable groups, including minorities. In America "the impact among blacks is about three times as great in general because they are more likely to lose their jobs and they are less healthy to begin with," M. Harvey Brenner of Johns Hopkins University told Lorraine Branham of the *Baltimore Sun*.[13]

WHY A STRATEGY IS NEEDED FOR DEALING WITH THE HEARTBREAK OF JOB LOSS

In 1991, when two aviation giants went under, 30,000 Eastern Airlines workers and 12,000 Pan Am employees lost their jobs. Many of these highly skilled and well-paid employees had been with their company for more than twenty years. A year and a half later, writer Barbara Koeppel reported in the *Washington Post* that suicide among these laid-off workers had reached epidemic proportions, and heart attacks also had surged. Men in their midforties to midfifties seemed especially at risk.[14]

One fifty-eight-year-old Eastern Airlines pilot, who seemed physically fit and jogged regularly, learned his pension would be 40 percent less than he had counted on. He had flown with the company for eighteen years. Three days after learning of the vastly reduced pension, the former pilot had a heart attack and died.[15]

Three months after losing his job, Richard Brooks, a former maintenance supervisor at Pan Am, told his *Washington Post* interviewer that he wasn't sleeping and was in a troubled state. After working for twenty-five years at John F. Kennedy Airport in New York City, he took a job with Northwest Airlines and moved his family to the Midwest. Like many others, Brooks had never held another job, having gone right to Pan Am from military service. Leaving Pan Am was like losing his family, he said, along with his job, income, prestige and way of life.[16]

"I felt very guilty, too," Brooks recalled, "because I'd finally gotten a job, and my friends hadn't. Just when I moved to Minneapolis to begin work [at Northwest Airlines], the heart attack happened. I remember crying like a baby in the hospital. All I could think of was that I would lose my new job."

As events transpired, Brooks was able to conceal his heart attack from his new employer but lost the job anyway, as did all the new hires from Eastern and Pan Am. There were layoffs at Northwest and, as usual, those last hired were the first to go.

Brooks believes that as a group the displaced airline workers would have suffered even more illnesses and deaths were it not for the support groups that formed almost immediately. Two days after the closing, several of them met for breakfast in a Long Island diner. Two months later the group had grown to 200 and moved to a Knights of Columbus hall.

Work is stressful, too, and no one will ever know whether Brooks would have suffered a heart attack had he not endured the emotional ordeal of job loss, a difficult lifestyle change, and a major geographical move. He was also removed from his friends and peer support group and was struggling with the powerful emotion of guilt when the heart attack occurred. Statistics always apply to groups and can almost never be used to predict whether a particular individual will fall ill.

Several hopeful findings in Arnetz's 1991 Swedish study (referred to in the preceding section), for example, show that those with high self-esteem have higher HDL levels, those in a state of mental well-being have lower systolic blood pressure readings, and coping style greatly influences how people react to unemployment.[17] Self-care strategies make a difference.

STRESS BUFFERING: YOU *CAN* HELP YOURSELF STAY HEALTHY

For at least twenty years a rich body of research has been accumulating in psychology and behavioral medicine, helping us to understand how stress can be harmful to our health and how it needn't be so. There are a number of behaviors and attitudes you can adopt that can "buffer" stress, counteracting its ill effects on your life. Of course, many illnesses and tragedies are beyond our control, but practicing certain healthy behaviors can make you decidedly less vulnerable.

Just as it makes sense to stop smoking, exercise regularly, and reduce fat intake to have a healthier cardiovascular system, similarly it makes sense to heed what medical and social scientists have discovered about coping skills and lifestyles that promote health.

The Healing Power of Emotional Support

Dr. Joan Borysenko, a cell biologist and psychologist from Harvard Medical School, details one scientific study after another to illustrate the powerful role that mental health plays in predicting physical health. Borysenko tells of Roseto, Pennsylvania, a little town of great interest to scientists because of the community's unusually low rate of death from heart disease. The epidemiologists who studied Roseto expected to find low rates of fat consumption, obesity, cigarette smoking, and sedentary lifestyle but were astonished to find the opposite.

The people of Roseto had terrible health habits, explained Borysenko, and were actually high in all of the usual risk categories. What was unique about the Rosetans was that they were an extraordinarily close-knit group of people whose extended families and friends tended to remain in the community throughout their lifetime. People knew each other well, knew each other's family histories, and were available to help one another in times of need. In Roseto the stress buffer of social support was so important in predicting good health that when people moved away from the town, their rate of heart attack rose to the predicted level.[18] We literally become hardier through our relationships with others, says Dr. Borysenko, "and come to believe in our own capabilities and inner goodness."

While the intricate physiological mechanisms of stress and the effects of stress buffers are still in the process of being studied by scientists, there is no question that chronic stress has an impact on your body chemistry and your central nervous system and can therefore affect every system of your body.

"We've always known that we can literally die of broken hearts and shattered dreams," says Borysenko. "Laboratory findings are now corroborating that intuitive sense." The critical question now becomes "how to reconnect with hope, faith, and love, and how to use these states for minding the body and mending the mind."[19]

Hundreds of studies have demonstrated that certain people do much better than others in a personal crisis because of the quality of emotional support they allow themselves to receive. Small children having tonsillectomies cry less and have fewer postoperative problems when they are well supported by their loved ones. Men who maintain a good human support network are less likely to suffer impotence after prostate surgery than those who lack such support. Women and men who have elective surgery of many types or are injured in automobile accidents request less pain medication and recover sooner when they have a strong network of supportive family members or friends.[20] Pregnant women who experience highly stressful events have one-third as many pregnancy and childbirth complications if they have strong social support, as compared with highly stressed women who have weak support systems.[21]

Professor Susan Gore, studying a group of laid-off factory workers, measured each worker's level of social support. She found that those who did not have a good support system had higher cholesterol levels, had more depression, and suffered from more physical illness than those who had strong social support. Gore even found that unemployed people who were emotionally well supported saw themselves as better off financially than poorly supported people in similar economic circumstances![22] Having a support system will definitely increase your coping ability.

Most psychologists define "social support" as a subjective feeling of belonging and of being cared about. We all need to feel accepted and valued for who we are and not simply for the work we can do.[23] Especially after losing a job, it's important for you to feel needed by others and to feel that you can count on certain friends or relatives to be there for you.

Support may be available in your daily life in simple ways so obvious and accessible that you can easily overlook it. Reach out to your children or grandchildren and to others you love with affection and warmth. Don't miss the simple truth that people usually give us back what we give to them.

Trips to the zoo, bike rides and movies, fun shared at home playing games or watching a special TV show, picnics, playgrounds, and silly times enjoyed as a family can be a source of strength. Long talks, card games, long walks on a regular basis, shared vacations, and other outings can provide good times and ultimately empower you.

Seek out those who have demonstrated in the past an ability not to judge, criticize, or second-guess you. Choose those who will safeguard the things you share that are confidential and who will trust you as an adult to solve your own problems. Good listeners often provide the best support.

Psychologist James Pennebaker has described the positive health effects of entrusting your problems to a confidant. When we hold back important thoughts and feelings about a loss or crisis event in our lives, says Pennebaker, we require our bodies to do greater physiological work, and over time this work of inhibition stresses the body cumulatively, making it more vulnerable to illness and other problems.

Not talking about a troubling event can also prevent you from understanding and assimilating the event. As a result, explains Pennebaker, "Significant experiences that are inhibited are likely to surface in the form of ruminations, dreams, and associated thought disturbances." On the other hand, when you confide in someone, you immediately reduce both the physiological work and the biological stress of inhibition.[24]

Research has shown that the lack of a confidant is associated with depression. People who have a decrease in the number of their social relationships—as typically happens when a person loses a job—are especially prone to depression, anxiety, and physical illness in the absence of having a confidant. Even if you maintain your social interactions but do not have someone to confide in, poor morale results.[25]

The person you confide in may be a professional therapist, your spouse or lover, or a dear friend. What matters is the ability to talk openly and share troublesome feelings honestly. The opportunity to ventilate and be accepted as the person one genuinely is brings healing. We all enjoy better health when good-quality emotional support is a regular part of our lives.

A "Transformational" Coping Style

Stresses don't have to be bad for you if you try to master them instead of feeling overwhelmed by them. If you take charge of your life and come to feel that you are in control again, you can withstand an enormous amount of change and even thrive in the midst of it. On the other hand, if you keep yourself in a helpless position, you'll find that you can hardly cope at all.

Professor Suzanne Kobasa, of the City University of New York, has described certain attitudes of hardiness and a coping style she refers to as "transformational." People who refuse to see themselves as victims of circumstances transform awful experiences into challenges. They believe they can influence events and they approach change as an opportunity for personal growth. By contrast, people who lack hardiness often have learned to think of themselves as helpless. Instead of facing crisis and stress head-on, they get lost in their emotional reactions, withdraw from others, and have little motivation to do anything about their problems.[26]

People who feel powerless to change things, says Dr. Joan Borysenko, are low in hardiness and are "threatened by anything that rocks the boat." Such people are the ones who are the most likely to become ill from stressful events.[27]

The defense mechanism of denial is a prime example of an immature coping style. We all try to wish away our problems and sorrows at times, denying their existence to spare ourselves some pain. If you overuse this coping mechanism, however, your problems are likely only to get worse.

While I was writing this book, I learned some important lessons about denial through a difficult personal crisis of my own. The man with whom I had been in a love relationship for several years died suddenly. His death was shocking and so painful that I tried to deny even to myself the extent of my sorrow. Under contract with the publisher to produce this book by a certain date, I allowed myself a few days of weeping and plunged back into my work.

I worked at my desk for several weeks without telling even most of my closest friends that this man that I loved had died. I was protecting myself. Sometimes, even when we know better, we avoid facing our feelings of hurt and anger. Such feelings can be frightening to anyone.

My neck and back turned into aching knots. I experienced difficulty sleeping, a problem with concentration, and a near shut-down of creativity and productivity. I was often irritable with my dear young daughters and unhappy with myself for having so little patience. Finally, I became aware that I couldn't hide any longer and needed to face the full range of my emotions. I reached out to my friends for comfort and help and for a time saw a professional therapist.

Stress is the result of a failure to master a threatening situation. Difficulties ignored or denied don't go away. Unresolved problems press against us, tighter and tighter, as if we're in a vise. More and more stress occurs until we find a way to grab hold of the lever and decisively turn it the other way to release the pressure.

Confronting our worrisome thoughts and feelings, we come to understand and accept them. Facing our problems, we find solutions and go on with our lives. An event that was disruptive or even devastating is transformed into an experience that leaves us wiser and capable of building something entirely new.

Healing does take a long time. Author Stephen Fineman says that some people who lose their jobs will confront their problems head-on and with high energy; they set about to retrain, actively job search, and network in order to find a new job. Others will quickly reformulate domestic rules, such as adjusting to no longer being the primary breadwinner, and begin to meet their threatened achievement needs through part-time work or hobbies.[28] But I believe that only a pretty unusual person is capable of moving immediately into that kind of high-level coping and problem-solving mode, and there may be a price to pay. When a person makes a so-called recovery too quickly, unresolved hurts and hostilities can follow that person into the next job and interfere with happiness and success.

If you are like most of us, you will need the passage of time to achieve mastery in the aftermath of your crisis or loss. You need the support of others and the special strength that comes from having a confidant to help you develop your own transformational coping style.

Marie Christopher: Strategies for Surviving the Stress of Dealing with Multiple Losses

Sometimes there is so much pain from other crises or sorrows that job loss, at least for a time, seems the least of one's problems. Multiple losses hit especially hard. Psychological insight and thoughtful strategies for survival are needed. If you are trying to cope with other stresses or another major loss in addition to unemployment, Marie Christopher's story may be especially helpful to you.

Marie is a fifty-two-year-old mental health nurse. After fourteen years of experience at a university hospital, during which she obtained an advanced degree, she took a middle-management position at another Baltimore hospital and began on a new career track.

Just over a year on the job, Marie suffered life's greatest loss, the loss of a child. Her twenty-two-year-old son died tragically of suicide. Marie, her husband, and their surviving three sons were devastated. Four months later, her mother-in-law died, a woman whom Marie loved a great deal. Three months after that her nursing position was eliminated.

There had been warning signs at the hospital. Many midmanagement nursing positions had been eliminated because of restructuring. But Marie was too lost in the shock and grief of family sorrows to pay much attention. She just kept on working hard since that was her way of coping and surviving. When the reduction-in-force came to her doorstep, she was the last person still holding one of these midmanagement jobs.

Compared with the devastating loss of her son seven months earlier and the death of her mother-in-law, losing her job seemed a small matter to Marie. She was barely beyond the worst possible pain.

When she attended outplacement services, Marie heard others say that they had insomnia and gastrointestinal symptoms, but she had already had those symptoms while mourning her son. When others asked why the job loss didn't seem to bother her, Marie replied, "Listen, my cup is already full. If I add one more thing, my cup will overflow and I won't be functional."

Often when life hits us brutally with a terrible loss, then another loss, and still another—we close down some of our sensitivities in order to survive. "I was still numb over the loss of my son," Marie remembered.

Suicide is a brutal loss. Almost inevitably there is second-guessing. Loved ones ask, "What could I have done differently? What if I had seen that he was in despair? Were there danger signs? How could he do this to us? Why didn't I . . . ? If only . . . "

Almost immediately after her son's suicide, Marie reached out for help. She contacted me since she had taken several of my college psychology courses. I suggested whom Marie might call for family counseling, and only a week after their tragic loss Marie and her husband came to a lecture I gave at Compassionate Friends, a nationwide support group for bereaved parents. It took courage for them to come to a public lecture and acknowledge their need for help while they were still so vulnerable and anguished.

Three months after losing her job, Marie took a nursing position outside her specialty area of mental health. "Given my emotional state, it probably was not a good time for me to be learning a totally new area," she recalled. After just a few months, Marie and her new boss mutually decided that she should leave. Now that *two* jobs had been lost, Marie's emotional world crashed down around her. "I felt like a failure," she said. "You know when you grieve about something, and then you lose something again, all the previous grief really hits you."

After the second job loss, Marie detailed in a journal her feelings of self-doubt and discouragement. She also wrote, "These are the things I accomplished today. I cleaned the fish tank. I did the laundry. I did this much networking. I sent out this many letters." Life was a matter of back-to-basics.

"I got so depressed it scared me," Marie remembered. After about a week of feeling hopeless, she reminded herself of the wisdom gained from the two bereavement support groups she was regularly attending, Compassionate Friends and Seasons (the latter for people who have a lost a loved one to suicide). "You have to make a choice in life," she thought. "You can choose to be paralyzed or you can choose to live."

Marie used her knowledge as a psychiatric nurse for insight into her own mental state. She told herself to "Shape up!" and when she

did start to feel better, she knew that she didn't have a clinical depression, requiring medication, because if she did then telling herself to shape up wouldn't have helped.

Marie examined what her sadness was mostly about and realized
that the grief over the loss of her job and of her son were just building on each other. She also recognized that if there was something
she needed, she had better ask for it. She reached out to the new
friends she had met in support groups and to several old friends,
especially those who had had crises of their own.

There is a lesson here in preventive medicine. Marie was able to
stay as well as she did because, as a mental health nurse, she knew
what to do—hard as it was—to take care of herself: write in a journal, read books, attend lectures, and network for needed support.
You also can accept the responsibility for taking good care of yourself, even when life is brutally unfair in doling out burdens to bear.

Marie eventually found another job by asking others for assistance. You too can find sufficient strength for bearing your sorrows
and moving beyond the pain in your life by having the courage to
ask for help.

Finding a Good Support Group

If you, like Marie, are dealing with problems in addition to job
loss—a serious illness or disability; a loved one's death; a problem
with alcohol, drugs, or food; or some other difficulty—joining a
support group will help you not to feel overwhelmed by so much
change and pain all at once. You can look in the newspaper for a
list of groups and meeting times, call a local hospital, mental health
agency, or crisis hotline, or ask your clergyperson, counselor, or
physician about support groups that meet in your area.

There are groups for people battling depression, cancer, and
many other illnesses. Support groups exist for bereaved parents,
people who have lost a loved one from homicide or suicide, wid-
ows and widowers, people overcoming addictions, the relatives and
friends of alcoholics and drug addicts, rape and incest victims, and
victims of domestic violence. There are support groups for parents
without partners, adoptive families, single parents, gays and les-
bians, parents of homosexuals, infertile couples, people with eating
disorders, men dealing with impotence, and families of the mentally

ill, including Alzheimer's patients. There are groups for parents struggling with their children's behavior problems, learning disabilities, or illnesses; as well as support groups for people who have had heart attacks or strokes; and many more.

Whatever your situation and regardless of where you live, you can join or start a group where people come together to discuss the kinds of problems that concern you. A support group provides a comfortable setting where people can give and receive encouragement, information, and advice.

Studies have shown that group support offers such healing benefits that regular membership in a support group can add length as well as quality to a person's life. Stanford Medical School researchers recently found that women with breast cancer who met in weekly support groups for a year survived, on the average, almost twice as long as similar women who did not participate in such groups.[29]

Even membership in a support group for a few weeks can have a healing effect. Researchers at the UCLA School of Medicine found that melanoma patients meeting weekly in small groups for six weeks had reduced rates of cancer recurrence and death five to six years later when compared with similar patients not in the groups.[30]

While you are trying to cope with the aftershocks of job loss, it is difficult not to feel that your destiny is out of your control. And as long as you continue to *feel* powerless, you will be. What people in similar circumstances receive when they come together to talk and listen is a sense of *empowerment*.

You'll take a giant step toward helping yourself by getting involved in a support group. Instead of feeling weak and alone, you will begin to feel stronger, braver, and more hopeful.

Dave Elway: Looking at the Stress Left Behind

Although job loss can be harmful to your health, it is sometimes beneficial. Dave Elway is a former timber worker whose wide smile is undiminished by the difficulties he and his family have faced. As with many workers in declining industries, Dave made frequent trips to the unemployment office. Standing in those long unemployment lines waiting to fill out another stack of papers rankled him; Dave saw it as asking for a handout, a degrading experience.

A family man, he enjoyed using some of the layoff periods to build bedroom furniture and creative playthings for his children. Still, the repeated layoffs mostly made him miserable: It was difficult to plan, budget, and make ends meet.

Thirty-eight years old, Dave had spent half of his life working in rural Montana's timber mills. After years of denying even to himself many unsettling feelings, Dave finally began talking to his wife about how much he hated the constant uncertainty the family lived with. When would the next layoff occur? For how long? Would the job loss be permanent this time? It galled him to have worked so hard, to have a higher skill level than most of the men at the mill but still know that at any time his job could be gone.

Dave had many quiet moments of pondering the conditions at his workplace. Daily, year after year, he realized, the mill worker's senses are assaulted by the smell and taste of sawdust. Dust was always floating in the air and almost nobody wore a protective mask. The fine, powdery stuff got in his clothes, hair, nose, mouth, and eyes. A roaring racket from the gigantic buzz saws always penetrated the protective shield of the men's earphones, like fighter planes strafing bunkered soldiers in past wars. At least in the old war zones, the planes zooming low and firing machine guns soon flew away. Here the brutal pounding never ceased.

Dave imagined other places, where it would actually be possible to have a conversation with a co-worker. At the mill, workers could only yell over the noise of the machines, grunting out loud utterances like wrestlers over the roar of the crowd. "Uh, yeah!" one man would scream. "Hey, here!" shouted another. Smoking wasn't allowed but virtually everyone would chew and spit. Sawdust and chaw were everywhere together in messy piles underfoot. "When a person gets to thinking about it," Dave says now, "it was a miserable work environment."

Dave began work twenty years ago at the entry-level job where most mill workers start—on the "green chain," a conveyor belt that carries huge, rough-cut lumber. Cut trees are dense with water, and moving the heavy, water-laden planks was strenuous labor. Beginning at $6 an hour, Dave gradually moved up the mill hierarchy. He became "head planerman," the person who sets up and operates the machine that planes rough-cut lumber into precisely measured dimensions. The money was good, $12 an hour. As with many of the men, and their fathers before them, mill work was the only life Dave had known.

This man is a survivor. Not only had he made it through countless layoffs and firings, but he had managed to advance to a respected position with all of his fingers and toes intact. Still a restlessness grew within him. Like many psychologically healthy individuals nearing midlife, he began to reevaluate his goals. Even if he had wanted to remain in mill work, Dave saw the handwriting on every dusty wall: The Montana timber industry is dying, he realized. When he was laid off for the last time, he saw that it was time to make a new life.

Dave talked things over with his wife and then enrolled in a community college program to train as an EMT, an Emergency Medical Technician. Several layoffs ago he had begun volunteering for a community rescue squad and found the work appealing. Now he was in a race to finish school before the unemployment money ran out. Dave knew that he was taking a risk because there was no guarantee of finding a job once his training was completed. Through his volunteer work in surrounding towns, however, Dave had already begun to network with rescue squad workers and firefighters.

Dave Elway and his family endured some great hardships as they struggled with financial problems and uncertainty while Dave prepared for a new vocation. Eventually, however, Dave experienced an enormously increased feeling of well-being after leaving the timber industry. Now, employed full-time with a fire department, he remembers how physically and mentally strenuous it was to work ten-, fifteen- and sometimes twenty-hour days at the mill. He is also thankful no longer to have that daily exposure to dirty and dangerous work conditions.

There is more family time and job security now, and much less stress, despite the fact that Dave is earning considerably less. While it may take him five years to reach his pay level at the mill, he is now doing work that is satisfying, and the entire Elway family is enjoying life more.

Like Dave Elway, you can benefit from looking carefully at the stresses you have left behind. Your responses to the following questions may show you that your job loss stands to be good for your mental and physical health. Ask yourself:

- In what ways were you dissatisfied with your job?
- What problems, pressures, restrictions, or unhealthy work conditions are you pleased to be without?
- Which miserable or annoying individuals are removed now from your life?
- Were there ways in which your integrity was compromised?
- Did you feel respected as a person by your supervisors and co-workers?
- Did you respect yourself?
- Were you harassed or discriminated against for any reason?
- Were there work-related troubles which you regularly took home with you?
- Were your talents recognized and was your hard work appreciated, or did you frequently feel unfulfilled, frustrated, or undervalued?
- In what ways did you routinely live with too much mental stress or physical exhaustion?
- Was it time for a change?

Without a doubt, job loss can improve your health both mentally and physically. In one survey of 954 workers who were unemployed on average for five months, and in another study of 1,698 men unemployed for a year, approximately 8 percent for each study said that psychological health had improved, almost always because they were free of their job stresses.[31] With respect to physical health, Fagin and Little (who studied unemployed families in England) found that those who had been in ill health because of job stress showed a health improvement after losing their job. Those who had been dissatisfied with their job also showed a health improvement afterward.[32] Similarly, David Jacobson, who studied engineers, scientists, and technical managers, found evidence that those who described their preunemployment work as "stressful" and "dissatisfying" had a positive attitude toward their job loss.[33]

Even if you would return in a minute to the job that you lost—because it was fulfilling, because the work conditions were terrific, or because the money was well worth whatever stress you had to contend with—your job loss can, in the long run, lead to an improvement in the quality of your life. If you decide that it *will* be so, eventually you can make the best of an awful situation.

Many times in my life I have looked at wrenching changes as cata-strophic. I've wondered how I could face certain losses or altered circumstances and remain standing or continue to affirm life's goodness. I didn't want my marriage to end, for example, and mourned bitterly for a long time. And then, over time, the changes I had feared and resisted—often accompanied by intense feelings of loss—opened up new avenues of opportunity, new joys and rewards. Even devastating losses have the potential of offering a new beginning, a more fulfilling life. But you have to decide to make it so.

VI

Danger Signs:
Severe Depression and
Suicidal Thoughts

What is called resignation is confirmed desperation.

—HENRY DAVID THOREAU

Researchers have observed an increased risk of suicide among unemployed people in many countries, including the United States, Canada, Japan, France, Italy, Brazil, Sri Lanka, India, and Great Britain. According to World Health Organization statistics, job loss increases the suicide risk of men more than women.[1]

Stephen Platt, known for extensive studies on suicide attempts and joblessness, says that as much as half of the recent attempted suicide rate in Edinburgh, Scotland, may be "attributable to unemployment."[2]

In my own view, it can be misleading to use the word "attributable" in this context. After carefully reviewing the research, I believe that unemployment has not actually *caused* half of the suicide attempts in Edinburgh, or anywhere else. Virtually no one commits suicide *only* because of joblessness, although in many cases unemployment is seen as the "last straw." It's true that many men and women find unemployment so devastating and depressing that they come to the brink and wonder what remains worth living for. But the evidence shows that self-destructive acts rarely follow job loss unless a cluster of life's problems and a severely depressed mood have become unbearable burdens. The *cause,* then, of the suicide or the attempt is most likely an untreated depression and also a lack of knowledge about how to get help for solving a tangled web of problems.

In a highly respected work called the Lundby Study, Olle Hagnell and Birgitta Rorsman of the University of Lund investigated the role played by stressful life events in completed suicide, concluding "that persons who finally commit suicide have received more than their due share of the hardships of life." A blow to self-esteem, the loss of someone or something precious, an occupational crisis, an illness, or an unwanted move from one's home—all of which can be associated with job loss—were important contributing factors.[3]

But, in perhaps the most important finding of the Lundby Study, the researchers reported that 93 percent of those who committed suicide had some mental illness at the time of their death, often an illness that had suddenly changed for the worse a few days before the suicide. Many of these individuals had been troubled or ill previously, and more than one-third had attempted to kill themselves on at least one earlier occasion.[4] Researcher Keith Hawton also found that many of the suicide attempts and suicides in Edinburgh occurred among those who were "psychologically vulnerable" before losing their jobs, people with preexisting mental health problems such as alcoholism and previous suicide attempts. Workers unemployed for more than a year had the highest rates of attempted suicide.[5]

As an unemployed person your difficulties may seem unsolvable because you are feeling severely depressed, hopeless, and alone. Anyone who has been jobless for a long time tends to grow exhausted at times from trying to cope with many problems.

Prolonged unemployment often leads to role changes in the family and to a related increase in tension, arguments, and sometimes even family violence. You might experience heightened feelings of isolation from others, a loss of self-esteem, and diminished self-confidence. Financial hardships are troubling, too. Understandably, any combination of these problems experienced simultaneously can throw anyone into despair. A provocative event, such as an argument with a spouse, can make you far more likely to think of suicide in the presence of unemployment and the many stresses that come with it than when you are employed.[6]

If you are like many other unemployed workers, you may especially be troubled by a lack of companionship. Missing your former co-workers, perhaps you have become more withdrawn or hesitant to share with friends or family any negative feelings. Unfortunately, the longer the period of unemployment, the greater the tendency to reduce the number of your social contacts. This is self-defeating behavior, since empirical research has shown that "the more time unemployed workers spend with friends, the less depressed and anxious they become."[7]

Maintaining strong friendships is important, explain authors Carrie Leana and Daniel Feldman, not only because good friends help to alleviate psychological distress. Close contact with others also provides encouragement and some healthy social pressure to get a new job.[8]

"One way of looking at suicidal behavior," writes Dr. Robert Yufit, a professor at Northeastern University Medical School and recently the president of the American Association of Suicidology, "is to consider the individual's desire to disconnect everything. Often one wants to be disconnected from the pain being experienced, the pain of loss, failure, or depression." What good relationships can provide, Yufit continues, is help in "coping with stress, in reducing feelings of loneliness, and, perhaps [in providing] the most important continuous relationship of all, the sense of belonging to oneself" or self-acceptance.[9] In times of crisis, when feeling depressed and discouraged, we all need friends to help us accept our humanness.

Unemployment combined with depression can be life threatening unless steps are taken to prevent depression from becoming overwhelming and unless one's self-esteem can somehow remain intact or be restored. Under the dark cloud of severe depression, an individual's judgment is impaired and life's difficulties seem impossibly complex and hopelessly unmanageable. Yet when there is good support from loved ones and medical treatment for the depression, most people choose to live.

UNDERSTANDING DEPRESSION

The word *depression* means different things to different people. It's a complex condition, and even in the medical and counseling fields, its meaning has been evolving. This section will explain the difference between normal responses to life events and the serious illness of clinical depression.

Depression can simply be part of an expected grief reaction to losing someone or something precious. Sadness, tearfulness, longing, regret, remembering, and a deep feeling of disappointment in life can all be a natural and healing response. Not uncommonly a grieving person has trouble sleeping for a time, has difficulty concentrating, and is preoccupied with thoughts about the loss.

Bereavement lasts weeks, months, and often a year or more, with progressions and regressions, but gradually the grieving person begins to feel better. Inspirational experiences, talking out one's feelings, and acts of human kindness help to lift the spirits. Whether grieving the loss of a job or some other loss, usually the individual responds with heartfelt appreciation when others do something helpful or show compassion. A grieving person often temporarily experiences a diminished level of energy and less interest in activities normally pleasurable. Although there may be an impairment in day-to-day functioning, one's usual daily activities soon resume. An individual may get very upset at times and feel overwhelmed by various problems, but as solutions are found to these specific problems, the person's mood shows improvement. In time, the mourner notices a gradual return of the ability to cherish and enjoy life. Although the pain from certain losses (such as a loved one's death) never entirely goes away, over time healing occurs and one is sustained by present relationships and sweet memories.

By contrast, when a person is severely depressed—with the type of depression that is an illness rather than an uncomplicated grief reaction—one's mental state may be characterized by apathy, listlessness, emptiness, and despair. Feelings of hopelessness, worthlessness, or excessive or inappropriate guilt often are present and nothing much seems to help the person feel better. A feeling of "something is wrong with me, wrong with my body, my being" often characterizes how he or she feels. The severely depressed person is absorbed in troubled thoughts, is apt to be irritable or socially withdrawn, and is unaffected by the kindnesses of others. There is little or no sense of "things gradually getting better," mostly a feeling of "not caring anymore," or of darkness, alienation, or deadness.

For most of the day, nearly every day, for at least two consecutive weeks, a person suffering the illness known as Major Depression has a depressed mood or a loss of interest or pleasure in nearly all activities. He or she has at least four persistent, additional symptoms drawn from a list that includes changes in appetite or weight; a sleep disturbance; decreased energy; feelings of worthlessness or guilt; difficulty thinking, concentrating, or making decisions; or recurrent thoughts of death or suicidal thoughts, plans, or attempts. Such symptoms persist and cause significant distress or impairment in functioning. Even the smallest tasks can seem to require substantial effort.[10]

If you have ever experienced a prolonged period of debilitating depression prior to your job loss, had a problem with alcohol dependence, or previously attempted suicide—you are more vulnerable now than most unemployed people and you need to get help. If before becoming unemployed you were already grieving other losses, struggling with marriage, family, or financial problems, and suffering from low self-esteem, you also probably need professional help, just because there is too much stress for you to try to handle it all alone and all at once.

A foreign affairs officer who was injured on assignment and forced into temporary retirement in her thirties told me that she suffered with depression for several months. Although her spirits were much improved now, she recalled having had sleep problems, anxiety attacks, fatigue, and suicidal thoughts. She was helped by escape reading, church attendance, and periods of positive introspection. Had the woman's depressed mood not improved, she probably would have needed professional help, since her depression was severe enough to make her wonder whether life was still worth living.

A man who had lost his job as a "Class A" welder said that he had lost weight, his sleep was disturbed, and he was feeling irritable and anxious. He was also smoking marijuana regularly, drinking more alcohol, getting into arguments with loved ones, having thoughts of wanting to hurt someone, and thinking of suicide. All of these symptoms are commonly associated with severe depression, especially when clustered together. Not surprisingly, the man's children had recently begun to have behavioral and academic problems in school. Professional help was urgently needed. Such severe depression causes a great deal of unhappiness unnecessarily because most people can be helped when properly treated with prescribed antidepressant medication, professional counseling, or preferably both.

A woman who lost a factory job seven years ago and is now working as a waitress told me that she often considers separation and divorce, has trouble sleeping, feels increasingly isolated from family and friends, has lost pleasure in the activities that once made her happy, and often thinks about suicide.

If you are experiencing similar physical or emotional symptoms, or you are worried about a loved one who is, get medical advice. Your family doctor can be a source of guidance. He or she may prescribe an antidepressant medication and would need to monitor its use. You can be referred to a psychiatrist if more expertise in treating depression is needed in your case.

Far and away, the number one reason that people commit suicide is that they suffer from a biologically based, severe depression. Dr. J. Raymond DePaulo, a noted researcher at the Johns Hopkins Hospital, emphasizes that in the famous Lundby Study no suicides were found among men suffering from a mild form of depression, whereas the most severely depressed men showed a startlingly high suicide rate.[11]

Untreated depression can be almost as deadly as "Russian roulette." "As many as 15 percent of severely depressed people take their own lives," write Drs. DePaulo and Ablow in *How to Cope with Depression*. This is a tragedy, since 80 percent of those with depression or mania go into complete remission once they are diagnosed and completely treated.[12]

Especially if you have a plan in mind for how you would kill yourself, please confide in someone you trust and ask that person to help you find good professional assistance. Explain that you need help urgently. Despairing people with a suicide plan in mind often attempt suicide on an impulse. Get help while you are still strong enough to do so.

An unemployed project manager for an engineering firm, an unemployed plumber, a former salesman, a laboratory technician, and an out-of-work male nursing assistant were among many men who answered an anonymous questionnaire and reported a decreased interest in lovemaking, a change in appetite and sleep patterns, depression, irritability, fatigue, negative introspection, less patience with loved ones, and greatly increased television watching—all symptoms that can be associated with depression.

It is hard enough, in today's tough job market, to find employment when you are feeling well, let alone when you are depressed. If your depression is severe enough that it affects your ability to plan for the future, make decisions, and search for a new job—get help. A well-trained professional counselor can help you evaluate your situation, talk out your problems, and decide whether a medical consultation is needed. Don't assume that professional help is too expensive. Many local mental health and pastoral counseling centers have sliding fee scales.

William Dressler, who studied the relationship between unemployment and mental health in a black community in the South, found high rates of depression among African Americans who lost their jobs. In this traditional black community, unemployment was seen as a major problem because of the belief that "work, at any kind of job, is essential for a decent life." The sense of loss felt because of the significance of work was said by Dressler to lead to depression and be clustered with other difficult life events such as marital separation, residence changes, and changes in habits and social roles.[13]

It is true of virtually all groups living in various regions of the United States and in many other parts of the world that job loss is a major stressor almost always accompanied by other stressors, all leading to some form of depression. Too much change and stress all at once can overwhelm even the strongest, most psychologically healthy person—especially if the person is not reaching out for help. It also stands to reason that someone already prone to depression would find the loss simply devastating. If your depression seems unshakable, you need to get help.

Friends and Family Members: Here's How to Recognize the Danger Signs

If you have a loved one who is severely depressed, you need to know that hopelessness is the primary connection between unemployment and attempting suicide.[14] It is a connection that can and must be broken.

Dr. Robert Yufit has written that the typical suicidal person is highly involved in thinking about the past, feels very negative about the present, and is minimally involved in the future. This is in contrast to the nonsuicidal person, who is highly engaged in the present, cares a great deal about the future, and doesn't live in the past.[15]

A person who is not a suicide risk is free enough from personal despair to feel deeply attached to loved ones and to want to stay alive for them. While life may be very painful at the present, it is clear to the nonsuicidal person that there is much to live for. He or she has the capacity to hope.

Middle-aged men in the lower social classes with families to support tend to suffer greatly (both financially and psychologically) as a result of becoming unemployed, and they have a high rate of suicide.[16] But suicide in general is more common among white-collar workers, including people with college degrees, and particularly among those with graduate degrees.

Women *attempt* suicide three to four times more frequently than men, but men *commit* suicide three to four times more frequently than women.[17] Because those who die in suicide attempts tend to use more lethal methods, any firearm in the household of a discouraged and depressed individual needs to be removed. Potentially lethal illegal drugs (such as heroin and cocaine) and prescription drugs (including most antidepressants and sleep medications) also pose a grave danger in the hands of a suicidal person. In addition to the risk of drug overdose, cocaine is a particularly deadly drug in that an already depressed person who gets high plunges into an even worse depression coming down from the drug.

Especially at risk of severe depression and suicide are people with a personal or family history of depression, those who have had a close relative attempt or commit suicide, those who have an alcohol or drug dependency or have a close relative with a substance abuse problem, people suffering multiple losses or undergoing multiple surgeries, people who have attempted suicide in the past, and men over fifty suffering chronic, debilitating illnesses. Many people who kill themselves talk about suicide beforehand, give away prized possessions, draw up or revise a will, or behave as if they are going away on a long trip.

How to Get Help

Studies reveal that the most effective treatment for severe depression is a combination of medication and supportive counseling. Medication is needed because severe clinical depression alters brain chemistry. Supportive counseling usually is needed, too, because depression is difficult to cope with unless one has the understanding and assistance of someone knowledgeable about depression and qualified to help find solutions to everyday problems.

A psychologist, psychiatrist, certified mental health counselor, licensed social worker, or qualified pastoral counselor can provide supportive counseling. Your best bet is often a personal reference from someone who knows the professional and has benefited from his or her compassion and ability. It's also a good idea to ask a professional whom you respect for help in finding the right person for you. When you ask physicians and other professionals *where they would send their own family members* for help with depression or any other problem, you get a different answer than if you simply ask for a nonspecific referral.

You can also call the suicide or crisis hotline in your phone book. You may find these numbers listed under your local hospital or mental health agency. Turn to Appendix D in the back of this book and read the page entitled "For Help with Severe Depression." Also listed in Appendix D is a suicide referral agency and the number to call to ask for your local suicide hotline.

I have known many people over the years in such a state of despair that they wished to die, people who got professional help and are deeply thankful today to be alive. Just as they did, you can relieve your unrelenting depression, anxiety, and feelings of hopelessness by taking medication prescribed by a physician and/or by talking with a good therapist.

Make a commitment to someone you respect not to attempt any action destructive to yourself or others without first calling for help. Some of the finest people in the world have suffered from severe depression, received needed treatment, and gone on to live extremely rewarding and productive lives. So can you.

VII

Family Problems: Finding Solutions

It is my experience, and I suspect yours as well that family relationships provide our greatest heartache. But they also provide our greatest joys.

—DAVID G. MYERS

"I had these fits of absolute blackness," said an unemployed design engineer. "As far as I was concerned I was a complete failure, with a Ph.D. and a bachelor of science." He was "a qualified architect and land surveyor, and not getting anywhere." His wife said that he started getting resentful, taking it out on her and the children. His daughters complained that if they turned on the radio, he'd start shouting at them. The girls had to make sure they didn't do anything wrong and used to stay in their bedrooms not to get in his way.[1]

Unless you're single without dependents and live alone, job loss is sure to have a powerful impact on your family. Psychological distress is contagious, often moving right through a family like a disease. This phenomenon has been borne out by study after study. For example, it was found that if the husband was still unemployed after four months, the wife started showing substantial psychological strain.[2]

Unemployed women and wives of unemployed men are likely to show high levels of depression. However, in one British study, husbands of unemployed women did not seem to have a similar decrease in psychological well-being.[3]

Unfortunately, most of the enormous body of research regarding unemployment and families over the last forty years has focused exclusively on out-of-work men; we don't have sufficient studies to teach us how husbands and children respond when a wife or mother loses her job. Years of counseling experience and the numerous interviews we have conducted with unemployed women, however, lead me to believe that the entire family is always affected when any family member is feeling distressed. And job loss upsets virtually everyone who wants or needs to work for financial or emotional reasons.

While much of this chapter is based on studies that pertain to unemployed men and their families, the information is beneficial to unemployed women and their families as well. I hope you'll ask your spouse and young adult children to read this book (or at least this chapter) so all of you can better understand the problems you face.

How stressful is it to be married to a man suffering the ordeal of long-term unemployment? Could it possibly be as stressful as living near a nuclear power plant when a nuclear accident occurs? One astonishing study shows that it could be. Because of happenstance, it was possible to compare the long-term mental health consequences of the Three Mile Island (T. M. I.) nuclear accident in 1979 and widespread unemployment due to layoff in another part of Pennsylvania. Wives whose husbands suffered long-term unemployment showed symptoms of psychological disturbance remarkably similar to those seen in women who lived near the T. M. I. nuclear reactor during the period of intermittent radiation leaks, ongoing problems with the cleanup operations, and several years of public controversy. Women who were already distressed over other personal difficulties showed the most symptoms. Also women who had been treated in the past for severe depression or an anxiety disorder were more likely to become depressed or anxious during the study period than women who were not previously ill.[4]

Among a group of 465 wives of blue- and white-collar primary breadwinners, the husband's level of distress was a better predictor of his wife's symptoms than was his employment status. In other words, if the husband was highly upset, eventually the wife was likely to show a similar level of distress. On the other hand, unemployed husbands who were able to cope well with job loss had a calming effect on their wives and children.[5]

How is your situation affecting your children? Some children whose fathers lost their jobs have had eating disturbances, minor gastrointestinal complaints, sleep problems, accident proneness, and behavioral disorders.[6] In one study, parental unemployment doubled the risk of young children being admitted into a hospital, and in another, adolescents and younger children of unemployed parents were twice as likely to be admitted to a pediatric emergency room for a suicide attempt than were children with employed parents.[7]

It is important to emphasize, however, that many children—perhaps yours included—are relatively unaffected by their parents' unemployment. Children differ in their resilience in the face of family stress, and sometimes the child's personality and temperament protect him or her from psychological injury. Besides, not all changes are for the worse: Your children might be benefiting from your unemployment, such as in spending more time with you. It is the quality of family relationships that determines who seems scathed or unscathed by unemployment. The best protection against any kind of family stress, including a parent out of work, is family cohesion and support.[8]

Perhaps your marriage is suffering. A man whose wife had lost her job in a Canadian plant closing said that the consequence was a breakdown in their marriage. "She is still not comprehending why SKF [the factory] closed, as her whole life revolved around her job, to the detriment of our marriage," the husband said. The couple separated and the husband moved out of the house.[9] Some women reading this book might similarly say that their husband's life was so wrapped up in work that after he lost his job, their deteriorating relationship broke down even further.

Said one worker, "I was really shaken when my first job [offer] went sour . . . because I thought the job would be easy to get. . . . I think the family started disintegrating then." The man described his increased drinking and resultant vicious tempers. "I was easily angry and upset and I used to snap at the children all the time. I started having these deep depressions, and nobody could help me."[10] While this particular case sounds severe enough to warrant medical treatment, often entire families ride an emotional roller coaster when applied-for jobs fail to come through, writes anthropologist Katherine Newman. The discouraged job seeker dreads having to face a roomful of disappointed faces.[11]

If you once performed an important role but no longer make the same contribution, the role of your spouse and older children might have changed accordingly. "My wife is self-employed, works very hard for her money," said a former steelworker. "We make ends meet, but I feel I'm not pulling my share of the load. I apply for all types of jobs for which I feel I may be qualified [but] nothing seems to work out. It hurts inside not to do my share."[12]

It's probably true that long-standing notions about gender roles have caused men to have a greater ego involvement in work than most women. If you are a man, you may define your worth narrowly in terms of competency at work and ability as a breadwinner rather than in terms of your relationships with others. Women, although they take competency at work very seriously, tend to define themselves more broadly, according to a wider variety of roles and relationships. Work is definitely important—employed women suffer less depression than both unemployed women and homemakers—but women are sustained as well by meaningful relationships at work and at home. The nurturing roles of mother, wife or lover, daughter, sister, friend, and community member fulfill us.

A forty-six-year-old man named Jack Blum reflects while standing in an unemployment line: "I'm at the bottom and nobody likes it at the bottom. But okay, somebody's got to be at the bottom. Poor people, all walks of life, ethnic types, black, white: You don't make money, down to the bottom! Here's the real melting pot of this country."[13] Such strong feelings of disillusionment, anger, and depression are almost inevitable. Yet to survive you must rise above your feelings.

One psychologist found that men who were out of work a year or more began to blame themselves for their loss. In the earlier months the men had shown anger at their former bosses or the government, but now the anger that was once a life force made them weary. "In its place was born an intensity of shame."[14] A man's shame might emerge as anger directed at his children. In such cases children learn early on not to talk about the situation and never to question their fathers about it.

How unemployment affects your family depends considerably on what stage of the life cycle each family member is in and how you and your partner envision your roles as parents. For example, consider the Jamesons, a family with three preschool children. During the father's five months of unemployment, his wife was happy to have him at home to help her at this stressful time in her life as a mother. His unemployment had the effect of a parental leave of absence for a child-care emergency.[15] He slipped comfortably into various caretaking roles, and she was so glad to have his help that a drastically reduced income was not seen to be a major problem. In such a setting, the self-esteem of both husband and wife could be enhanced by their ability to make the best of a period of unemployment.

On the other hand, when a husband is out of work and has the time to help but is unwilling to do so, marital conflicts arise. This fact undoubtedly helps to explain why couples in an egalitarian relationship fare better in coping with the primary breadwinner's unemployment. When roles are not too narrowly delineated or sexually stereotyped, they can comfortably be exchanged, with the usual breadwinner becoming the caretaker and vice versa. If you and your spouse can share the roles of parent and provider with mutual respect, everyone in the family will benefit from your flexibility, especially your children.

In one study of blue-collar families, unemployed husbands who were willing to change from a traditional to a more egalitarian role had higher self-esteem, since in times of joblessness the power of the traditional husband is diminished. This study found that couples in a traditional marriage suffer much more disruption of family harmony than those who believe in equal human relationships, since "traditional husbands may perceive themselves as losing bargaining power and status in the family as they lose their breadwinner role."[16]

In a marriage with flexibility and equality, the wife entering paid employment is free to grow in independence and pride, and the family can enjoy her accomplishments without disparaging the unemployed man of the house. Over time, job loss can strengthen your family as you face new challenges. Each member can become more confident and proud of his or her contribution.

THE JACKSONS: A BREAKDOWN IN COMMUNICATION

Kristin Jackson was a twenty-year-old college student living at home and working part-time as a cashier at a five-star restaurant in Dallas.

Her dad had an $85,000-a-year job as the sales manager of a large office equipment company. Then they both lost their jobs. Kristin was demoted to waitress. Mr. Jackson was offered, in his words, "a lowly sales job while some hot shot young kid took over the managerial position at half the pay." He walked away, deciding that he had had enough not only of that company but of business management altogether.

"Our family went from feeling very secure to feeling absolutely insecure," Kristin told Rick Lamplugh. The Jacksons immediately lost the perk of always having a late-model company car. They were a one-car family now—with a college girl and a teenage son eager to have the car for social events, twin third-graders who always seemed to need a ride somewhere, a mother who needed to move from part-time to full-time work, and a dad who had to go on job interviews. Mr. Jackson was home most the time, drinking beer—at least two cases a week—eating snacks, and watching sports on television. He and Mrs. Jackson fought about the abundance of empty beer cans in the trash. The four children, who got little of his time when he was working, were resentful that they were still not getting quality time with him. In fact, their instantaneous family togetherness got on everybody's nerves. Furthermore, Mr. Jackson had never been the children's disciplinarian, and when he tried to interact with them now, he did so without much skill. "Our whole world was thrown completely out of whack in a very short period of time," Kristin remembered.

Kristin and her seventeen-year-old brother secretly thought their father should have taken the sales position until he found something else. Mr. Jackson didn't know how to confide in these older children or make them understand how humiliating it would have been to become a salesman under someone so young and inexperienced, a man he had supervised. Had they been helped to understand their father's perspective, perhaps they could have supported him and respected his decision not to compromise his integrity.

Mrs. Jackson became the breadwinner while continuing to be in charge of most family decisions. She gave up her part-time job and admirably took two other jobs, working seven days a week. Regrettably, however, Kristin's mother set a negative example in the treatment of her husband. She frequently complained about "not being appreciated" and "working so hard while your father is piddling around," not realizing that Mr. Jackson was working through a grief reaction to his feeling of betrayal by the boss who fired him after twenty years. He was trying to reevaluate his life and make a major career change, which included taking commercial real estate courses and studying at home. Mrs. Jackson focused on his excessive drinking and also attributed the strained family relationships to that and to his idleness. In front of the children she pushed him, saying, "I don't care what you do, just find a job."

Adding to the problem, the family maintained their old lifestyle, supporting it through Mrs. Jackson's income plus a home equity loan. There were many arguments between the couple, between the parents and their children, and among the siblings. Kristin felt that her mother was "a control freak," coming down hard on her children for not doing more around the house, and pushing her husband to take just any job right away. "My father started to regress and become one of the children," observed Kristin astutely. "He didn't stand up for himself. He wouldn't make decisions and he gave all the control to my mother. I really hated that."

When Kristin and her brother asked their dad why he no longer wanted to work in business management, he said he was "sick of wheeling and dealing" and hated the politics of it all. These were not sit-down, heart-to-heart discussions, however, but more a matter of passing comments. Their dad would say that there were more reasons than they could understand and left it at that. "I didn't understand why he would say that to me," Kristin told us. "I'm a pretty intelligent person and I felt like he didn't want to share with me what he was feeling."

Meanwhile, the family was breaking down. The younger girls had trouble at school, developed sleep problems, and had crying spells. Kristin's brother started running with a crowd of boys in high school who were a bad influence and his grades fell. And Kristin, fed up with family tension and conflict, left home, moved in with some friends, and considered quitting college. She became the "black sheep" in her parents' eyes, because she was seen as bailing out when the family most needed her.

Mrs. Jackson became a one-person lobby for family counseling, and the others finally agreed. Some marriage counseling, family therapy, and a few individual sessions with a qualified, affordable social worker went a long way to restore family cohesion. The Jackson family began to appreciate the strength and courage of their husband and father in moving toward a new career despite an initial lack of support at home. The children began to cut him some slack. When he finally got started in a new career and began to earn money, things improved even more. Mrs. Jackson quit one of her jobs, and the couple and family arguments decreased. How different things could have been had the family been able to work as a team and the parents been able to function as equals much earlier. But most people do the best they can at the time. It is often the case that personal crisis moves people to change in positive ways.

At a time of family crisis it is very important to strengthen the lines of communication. If you are the spouse of an unemployed parent, it is vital not to diminish your partner in the eyes of the children. It is important to include the children in at least some discussions about the job loss so they can understand why certain decisions are being made and can be given the opportunity to be supportive. Older children need more information than younger children, but all children need to see that conflicts can be resolved and that the family is still their haven. In addition, couples who obtain counseling are doing a great service to themselves by promoting the healing process of the entire family.

Another issue in the Jackson family was maintaining their lifestyle. Decisions about whether and how to maintain previous standards need to be made by both spouses as equal partners and usually should include children old enough to contribute through chores or outside jobs. Who works how much and when, division of household responsibilities, and career and school plans should all be dealt with in family discussions. When couples respectfully communicate with each other and their children in this way, tensions diminish and feelings of intimacy and mutual support increase. Job loss can be a time of strengthening family ties and demonstrating to children how to live through personal crisis and yet stay close as loved ones.

HELPING CHILDREN COPE WITH DOWNWARD MOBILITY

Downward mobility is more widespread than most people think. In the United States, low-wage jobs are proliferating and large numbers of well-paid ones are disappearing, so both blue-collar and white-collar workers are being affected.

Many parents forced to downsize try to stay in the family house so that their children can have as little disruption as possible. This strategy can backfire, especially with teenagers. Even though staying in the same neighborhood enables teens to keep their old friends, it also places them in a lifestyle that their parents cannot afford. Children may pressure their parents for money or clothes so they can be like their friends, and parents may feel distressed that they cannot live the way they used to and that their children can't seem to understand that fact.[17]

I nevertheless believe that remaining in the same neighborhood, if possible, is probably best. Unless you can find a less expensive house in a similar type of neighborhood, too many changes may be thrust upon the family by moving. When numerous changes are occurring, the stability of the familiar will go a long way to help all of you cope with stress.

Many people sell their houses in order to cash in on the equity, get a lower mortgage, and make a fresh start in a lower socioeconomic neighborhood, a place where they are not known. If you are considering this, take into account that the great differences between the new neighborhood and the one you left can leave you all feeling isolated and a bit disoriented. Children and teenagers in particular can find it difficult to make the transition and to adjust to and be accepted by different kinds of people in a different environment.[18]

It is important for parents to provide a sense of permanence and security and to help the entire family adapt to whatever downward mobility occurs. Even if you must make certain lifestyle changes, you are not powerless over your economic situation. We know that the children of downwardly mobile families often worry about money and security as adults. Do your children a lifelong favor and be careful not to transmit to them an attitude of negativity, cynicism, and powerlessness.

One of the downsides of living in a materialistic culture is that many of us connect our sense of worth to acquisitions, status, and accomplishments. More wisely we would define ourselves by our intrinsic worth, as intelligent creatures of the Universe and children of God. Consider whether your family might benefit from a reevaluation of basic values. If you believe there is a higher meaning to life than money, communicating this perspective to your children—by your actions and words—can help them gain a more positive outlook and grow in self-esteem.

Years ago in graduate school, I read an interesting article about mobile families coping with change—parents and children uprooted from the familiar world of home, school, neighborhood, family, and friends. In various families, how the children adjusted to piling into a car in front of a U-Haul trailer and moving to a new state was almost entirely dependent on how their parents coped. If the parents were happy to seek out new opportunities and had a positive attitude about the move, the parents' attitude was contagious and the children made the transition to new schools and friendships with relative ease. On the other hand, if the move was tumultuous for the parents, it was also difficult for the children.

In the late 1950s, our family farm fell on hard times and my father had to leave farming and find work elsewhere. Because he took government jobs in New Mexico, we moved often and lived in four different towns in three years. Although I had to leave my friends—including my first boyfriend—and start all over at a new school every year, I still remember those years as happy times. For the first time in my life my mother and father were free of the burden of heavy farm work and the daily responsibility of taking care of livestock with no days off and no vacations, so the life we led in an urban setting was relatively easygoing. We left behind a spacious, modern ranch house to live modestly in a series of small, one-bedroom apartments and we didn't have much money to spare. But my parents had an upbeat attitude toward change: They found the new environments stimulating and transmitted a positive attitude to me. Because my parents were happy, so was I. To this day I remember fondly those New Mexico years, which financially speaking were austere.

MARITAL PROBLEMS

More than half of the men I have surveyed anonymously in my job loss seminars report a "decreased interest in lovemaking" since becoming unemployed. Women who had lost their jobs were not as likely to say they were less interested in making love. A majority of both sexes acknowledged "more arguments with spouse or love partner," "less patience with family members or friends in general," and "increased feelings of isolation from family or friends." One in three said there were "more arguments with children in the family" and that there was "more yelling at loved ones. One in five said they had "increased thoughts about separation or divorce." Noteworthy, however, is the fact that one in three reported "increased 'quality time' with spouse, children or other family members." While my surveys were not scientifically controlled, the reported marital problems are consistent with those repeatedly described to Rick Lamplugh and me in dozens of interviews and have been established in scores of tightly controlled studies.

Two researchers studied 111 couples during the 1929–1933 Depression years and followed them into the 1940s. For many of the middle- and working-class couples, economic constraints produced a significant decline in the quality of their marital relationship. Men who lacked adaptive skills became more difficult to live with, more tense, irritable, and explosive, said the researchers. But not all the couples experienced such conflict. The researchers found that couples who had a strong marital bond before having to struggle with hard times showed a remarkable personal and marital adaptation. Men and women who were emotionally stable prior to the Great Depression tended to remain so.[19]

While the overwhelming majority of families stay intact, unemployment can destroy relationships. The *British Medical Journal* points to evidence "that family life is shaken by unemployment—often unto disintegration": Divorce, domestic violence, evidence of failure of growth in children, and other significant family problems occur.[20] Various studies have reported a deterioration in the marriage relationship, an increase in arguments, and one of the partners either leaving or having considered doing so. According to data collected in Britain in 1979, divorce among the unemployed was double that of the national average. In cases of wife-battering studied in Australia and Britain, almost half of the men involved were unemployed.[21] In the United States spouse abuse is the number one cause of injury to women, and 4 million women are victims of domestic violence every year.[22]

As the size of the U.S. military shrinks, family violence is also significantly increasing on America's military bases. This rise in spousal and child abuse, according to an Army study, tends to escalate at bases scheduled for closure. According to Gail McGinn, a personnel official at the Pentagon, "Everybody is wondering about what their own careers and their own finances will be"; she believes that financial issues are major contributors to family tension and violence. It would be inaccurate, however, to assume that the threat of job loss or financial worries *cause* domestic violence in the military or elsewhere; many other factors come into play. The military population, according to *Time* magazine, is younger and more violence prone than civilian society: "Alcohol abuse is relatively high, pay tends to be poor and the military attracts men who have authoritarian tendencies."[23]

Most sizable cities have at least one Sexual Assault and Domestic Violence center, a domestic violence hotline, and separate support groups for both the abused and the abusers. Call your local Mental Health Department, a hospital in your area, or check the yellow pages of your telephone directory. If you are a victim of such violence, be sure to seek medical treatment. If you are an abuser, saying you're sorry is meaningless unless you also have the courage to get professional help and stop this criminal behavior.

When people lose their jobs, suddenly their lives move into a holding pattern, a period of anxiety, frustration, and uncertainty. This time of "living in limbo" has a way of disrupting marriages. For many couples, "limbo" can be a time when previous flaws in a couple's communication patterns are exaggerated and new or dormant ones are brought to light.[24]

If you were emotionally stretched prior to your job loss, you are apt to become even more distressed now. If your marriage was already in conflict or other family relationships already strained, there will probably be even more tension and conflict now. When people are hurting and their relationships aren't working, there is an understandable tendency to feel that a situation is hopeless or that one's options are extremely limited. Try to resist that inclination of resigning yourself to a bad situation.

THE MISTREATMENT OF CHILDREN: WHAT CAUSES IT AND HOW TO AVOID IT

Experts have agreed for many years that a relationship exists between unemployment and child abuse.[25] Two 1983 studies found that unemployed fathers and stepfathers were from three to six times more likely to abuse their children than employed fathers and stepfathers.[26]

Researchers who tracked the number of child abuse cases over a twenty-year period—Professor Richard Krugman and his associates at the University of Colorado School of Medicine—found that unemployment was present in 49 percent of the families where there was physical abuse. Damage to children included fractures, head injuries, subdural hematomas, burns and bruises, and neglect. Key contributing factors appear to be psychological stress, an increased number of hours spent with a child, inability to obtain child care, alcoholism, and substance abuse.[27]

Unemployment, of course, does not *cause* child abuse. Not all abusers are unemployed, and the vast majority of people who are out of work do not abuse their children. Yet if we look carefully at the abuse that does occur and understand why it occurs, we can get a better picture of specific family stressors. It is important to understand the potentially devastating consequences of not finding healthy ways to alleviate the stress of unemployment, and it is important to search intelligently for solutions to family problems.

Punitiveness or excessive punishment comes in many forms. Mental abuse is even more common than physical abuse. Name-calling, threats, accusations and insinuations, belittlement, shaming, withdrawal of parental love, and meanness of any kind—all are examples of mental abuse. Also, whenever a child's punishment for various infractions is unfair or out of proportion to the seriousness of the behavior, it can be said that the parent is abusing his or her authority. Furthermore, any troublesome behavior on the part of a youngster almost always gets worse rather than improving when a child is handled with undue severity. Help is needed so a more reasonable, compassionate, and effective discipline can be maintained in the family, to everyone's benefit.

Unemployment tends to intensify the parent-child relationship. If a parent has had a poor, coercive relationship with a child before the job loss, that relationship probably will deteriorate further.[28]

Children often respond to anxiety in the family by acting out their troubled feelings. Tearfulness, sleep disturbances, withdrawal, or moodiness; more arguments with siblings and parents; truancy, poor grades, or other school difficulties; increased conflicts with playmates or classmates; unexplainable illness or accident proneness; bedwetting that resumes after a child has outgrown it; and getting into trouble with the law often signal a distressed child. If the child or teen is also having to cope with mental or physical abuse, the youngster's problems will almost always go from bad to worse until someone intervenes.

Child abuse can occur from infancy through the teenage years. Another regrettable reality is that parents who are physically or mentally abusive when their children are young tend to continue the abuse through hurtful words when the children are adults.

Parents who lack a support network have an increased risk of mistreating their children. So do those who did not receive enough nurturing when they were young. In such cases, parents may be providing too little nurturance to their children while expecting far too much care from them, perhaps because of trying to fill their own long-standing emptiness. Some people don't know how to be good parents because they didn't have good parents as role models. Remaining emotionally incomplete and needful, they may need professional counseling to become capable of providing proper child care.

Parents may be at risk of child abuse for a variety of reasons. The most common predisposing factor is mental or physical abuse by one's own parent(s), often closely intertwined with alcohol or other substance abuse. Researchers Blair Justice and David Duncan reported four types of "perilously stressful situations for [those] susceptible to child abuse: (1) unemployed fathers caring for children at home; (2) working mothers with job and domestic obligation overloads; (3) husbands, especially professionals, working so long and hard that they neglect their wives [and contribute to an unhealthy situation between the wife and children]; and (4) traumatic experiences on the job resulting in undischarged tension."[29]

Particularly in families where there is existing tension or a parent who has been violent in the past, material deprivation and loss of status may cause frustration and anger, and these feelings may be displaced onto the children.[30]

Study after study indicate that economic stress is the obvious culprit. Financial stress can accentuate a husband's irritability, moodiness, and tendency to parent his children in an arbitrary way.[31]

An excessive number of unsettling changes over a period of time can also predispose parents to start abusing their children. Such parents can become worn down by the repeated necessity to adapt to new circumstances.[32] Job loss requires a succession of wearying coping responses. Filing for unemployment or welfare, undertaking job search or retraining, losing former co-workers, considering possible relocation, and adjusting to a decline in standard of living—all require effort and emotional energy. A parent who is dealing with all that is more apt to be distracted and impatient, unfortunately while spending more time at home and having more contact with the children.[33]

Some fathers especially, unaccustomed to caring for children in a full-time child-rearing role, may struggle with the role transition and begin to mistreat their children. The normal difficulties in managing a child may provoke more abuse from these substitute caregivers than from the child's regular, more experienced caregivers.[34] Such parents may need to protect the children God has given them by placing them, at least temporarily, in someone else's good care.

It is essential that families get help to find solutions for financial problems (see chapter 4), since reducing financial stress often improves the emotional climate between parents and children. But in any event, just because there is a great burden of worry over money or other problems, don't let yourself justify or rationalize the mental or physical abuse of your children.

As should be apparent now, there is increasing agreement among professionals that the mistreatment of children results, in part, from stress.[35] Therefore, if you are hitting your children or striking out at them with hurtful words, what you need is a comprehensive plan for managing and reducing your stress. Just as the person who drives a car is morally responsible for staying sober so as not to inflict injury on innocent victims, a highly stressed person has an obligation to take steps to maintain emotional stability.

If you use alcohol to excess or use controlled substances, as many unemployed people do, it is very important to understand that it is dangerous to use such drugs especially when you are depressed, anxious, or angry and when there is family stress. Alcohol is a depressant. It will worsen your moods: Family conflicts and arguments will heat up, self-doubt and defensiveness will intensify, and most of your problems will get worse. When alcohol or other drugs loosen inhibitions, heighten paranoia, impair judgment, and diminish self-control, all forms of family violence are far more likely to occur, including ridicule and name-calling, child-beating, spouse-beating, and incest. Don't let alcohol or other drugs ruin your life and injure or destroy a loved one's life. If you can't control your alcohol intake once you start drinking or are tempted to use other drugs, make a decision now to stay entirely substance free, for your own sake as well as for your family.

Reach out for the help you need from trusted friends, relatives, a family counselor, or Alcoholics Anonymous. If expressing your sorrows and frustrations by lashing out at family members has been your pattern, decide to get help before further damage is done. Find the courage not to consider yourself self-sufficient (as none of us are) or somehow above all that psychological counseling business.

Basically, I believe that the truth makes people free. People who attend Parents Anonymous (a support group for parents who physically or mentally abuse their children) have made a decision to live truthfully. Getting individual or family counseling is another way of living the truth. You are saying, "This job loss really did happen. I really do have all these family problems and troublesome feelings to deal with. I know my life has changed. I have to become a stronger person than I was." Living in truth means having the mental health to face all that, get help, and move on with your life.

INOCULATING YOUR FAMILY

We know that education helps inoculate families against the worst aspects of unemployment, as researcher Loring Jones has stated.[36] You can reduce your anxiety and avoid many pitfalls by making use of the resources that are available to you. In addition to my book, ask your spouse to read *Surviving Your Partner's Job Loss* by Jukes and Rosenberg. Both parents and grandparents will find helpful *How to Talk So Kids Will Listen and Listen So Kids Will Talk* by Faber and Mazlish, which is also on audiocassette. These and other readings listed near the back of this book, in the "For Further Reading" section, can go a long way to alleviate stress and improve family relationships.

Family counseling, too, can help your family learn conflict resolution skills and improve communication. It can help all of you cope with the economic and emotional changes your family has been forced to contend with, so you can avoid taking out your frustrations on each other.

Older children are likely to react with anger and withdrawal unless you explain the reasons for the job loss. Younger children, on the other hand, because of their self-focused view of the world, tend to blame themselves for the changes they see in the home. You need to take every opportunity to talk openly about the circumstances of the job loss with your middle school and teenage children, as well as with those aged three to ten.[37] Psychologist Paul Lerner advises that you explain to your children what changes to expect, what they should say publicly about the lost job, and how they can help.[38]

It is important to provide repeated reassurance and specific information in words that your children can understand. You can say, for instance, "It isn't anybody's fault, but here's what's happening at the workplace and here's why I lost (or your father/mother lost) this job." Explain that the plant closed or moved out of the country, the company or the boss decided to fire a lot of people to make more money, the business couldn't survive any longer, the government didn't provide enough money to pay people's salaries, the boss was a terrible person to work for and didn't treat people fairly, or whatever. You might add, "These changes in our family are hard for all of us because we don't have as much money now and everybody is upset because things aren't the way they used to be."

If the job loss was somehow your fault, tell your children there were some problems at work and that mistakes were made. Say only as much about these events as you can comfortably say, appropriate to the children's ages. Emphasize that we all make mistakes and that the important thing is to learn from them and grow stronger. Be sure to say, "But I want you to know that in our family we don't blame each other when things go wrong, we just try to fix the problems."

Apologies followed by changed behavior go a long way to improve relationships between all family members. It's also important to be specific when apologizing or asking others to change in some way. "I'm sorry I've been cranky from worrying about money and worrying about finding another job," you might say. "I'll try to be nicer and not to yell at you; I'll try to take more walks to let off steam. But I need more help with jobs around the house and I need your encouragement, too." Children as well as adults respond better to direct requests than to generalities. Tell your child or teen: "Sometimes I need you to be quieter, not to fight with your sister so much or ask for money so often." *Don't* say: "You never appreciate anything I do. All you ever do is fight with your sister and ask for money!"

From time to time, family conferences are helpful. You can set the stage by explaining that everyone needs a chance to express the worries, hurts, or angry feelings they've been bothered by lately, and they can do so without blaming someone else. Lead the way in describing specifics so you will encourage others to do the same. Various people might say, for example: "I wanted to go to the movies and get that new dress but I couldn't because we didn't have the money and I felt bad about it." Or "I know daddy has been upset but it scares me sometimes when he talks to mama or me in that angry way." Or "Sometimes I need more hugs and loving words said to me because I get discouraged and worry a lot, even if I am a grownup."

After both children and adults have had a chance to express their concerns and feelings without being cut off or criticized, often it is helpful to shift the focus toward action and problem resolution. You or your partner might say: "I'm sorry that we haven't been very happy in our family lately. Let's all think out loud and tell about one thing we can do to help the others feel better. If we all work together and give each other some extra love and help, we can be happy again as a family, even with the lost job."

FURTHER IMPROVING COMMUNICATION AMONG FAMILY MEMBERS

All human beings have a need to be heard. The famous psychologist Dr. Carl Rogers, addressing a group of us who were his students on the subject of emotional healing, once said, "There is one thing we all want more than to be loved, and that is to be understood." A certain quality of communication with another person is necessary for individual psychic repair. You can heal yourself and mend your relationships if you put yourself in the company of empathic and understanding people.

But others need to be heard, too. The less careful you are to listen to those closest to you, the more they will fail to recognize your own need to be understood. When another person doesn't understand exactly what we mean, we feel misunderstood or neglected and tend to blame the listener. Yet the reason communication often fails is that we are too intent on protecting ourselves, controlling others, and proving we are right.[39]

Schools, colleges, and churches and synagogues often sponsor lectures or workshops to improve communication skills. Avail yourself of the kinds of learning that can help you to become more open and less defensive, and you'll also become a lot happier in your relationships.

We all have a tendency to resist criticism because it makes us feel uncomfortable, especially when it comes from someone we care about. Most people haven't learned how to give criticism without attacking or belittling, and that is another reason why we avoid it. Yet it's very important not to close yourself off from honest feedback from others. Criticism can be the first step in solving minor problems and keeping them from becoming major ones.

Remember, though, that any criticism needs to focus on *problems and solutions* rather than on *personalities and blame.* In dealing with both children and adults, it is extremely important to avoid attacking someone's character or questioning anyone's integrity and motives. As Dr. Haim Ginott has shown in his books, you can describe events without assigning blame and can explain your own feelings of discomfort, anger, disappointment, or hurt without criticizing the other person directly. For example, a parent might say to a youngster: "I am upset that your dirty dishes are still lying all over the place in the television room. I want you to pick them up now and take them to the sink." (*Not* "I can't believe you're so lazy and never listen; I'm sick of the way you are . . . ") A spouse might say: "I'm really worried about how much we owe on our credit cards. Let's try to figure out a strategy for paying these off and not using the cards in the meantime. Can we work out a solution that feels comfortable to both of us?" (*Not* "You never think about anybody but yourself. You just spend, spend, spend . . . and your mother was the same way!") Such character attacks never solve problems and only bruise and alienate family members. But if you hold a family conference and discuss ways to improve communication, you can all agree on some guidelines for handling problems.

When my daughter Ashley was seven years old, I violated a family rule on the expression of anger. I was irritated at her for misbehaving at a church function and I hissed in her ear, "Stop acting like a brat!" She immediately felt hurt and angry but it took her only about ten minutes to set me straight: Ashley crawled on my lap in this public setting and quietly but firmly declared, "You hurt my feelings and I'm not a brat! In our family we don't call names, including you!" I was proud of my second-grader for speaking so clearly and for holding me to my own rules. As a child I would never have been allowed to address my father like that. And you might note that Ashley spoke up for herself in a way that followed the rules: She said what the problem was and how she felt about what happened, but she didn't attack me or retaliate. Remembering how some of the adults I grew up with never acknowledged error, no matter how awfully they behaved, I told my daughter, "You're right. I shouldn't have said that. I was angry with you because of how you were acting and I want you to behave. But you aren't a brat."

Try to remember that your children have to struggle with feelings of loss and disruption in their lives just as you do. All children need help to understand how a parent's job loss will affect their lives. Will the family still take their usual vacation? How much fighting will there be with siblings who have to share bedrooms because an addition to the house must be postponed? Will expensive orthodontics have to be delayed? Will college students have to transfer to a cheaper school or even drop out? Will the children have to lower their personal aspirations?[40] Will it be necessary to move to a new region or a less expensive house?

"Children are like scientists . . . testing hypotheses all the time to see what the world is like," psychologist Lee Salk believed. "But if their world is chaotic—if the rules and [their] parents' reactions keep changing—their ability to predict the consequences of their own behavior is diminished and their capacity for coping with freedom and choice is compromised."[41]

Your children can support you in times of trouble but first they need your love and protection. They need rules that are fair and predictable. They need you to take care of yourself so that you have the energy and patience to care for them, share activities as a family, and simply enjoy each other.

Spouses can be helpful in a variety of ways, say authors Jill Jukes and Ruthan Rosenberg in *Surviving Your Partner's Job Loss*. Spouses can serve as a sounding board; offer hugs and smiles; remind the partner of his or her talents, accomplishments, and strengths; frequently remind the spouse that the present stressful situation is only temporary; help with job search tasks in whatever ways both partners are comfortable with; and provide understanding and optimistic encouragement but without making the job-seeking person feel pressured. Often the out-of-work partner is extremely sensitive to any possibility that the spouse is asking for an accounting of how the day has been spent.[42] Since there are good days and bad days, productive and doldrum days, the supportive spouse should either wait to be told about the day or say something general and nonprobing like, "How was your day? Did anything happen today that you want to talk about?"

People who are out of work tend to wear casual clothes and pursue weekendlike activities. Their spouses need to resist making suggestions that they, for example, redo the basement. To lessen the likelihood of your spouse coming up with such projects, it's a good idea to dress every morning, shave or put on makeup, and follow a daily routine. Jukes and Rosenberg describe one woman as being dismayed because her husband bought a cozy-looking athletic warm-up suit and seemed to be getting ready to spend the winter hibernating in his basement office. By contrast, another woman took heart in the fact that her husband made himself look ready for an interview nearly every day. Also, if you dress the part of someone who may get hired today (instead of someone who looks unemployed), you will improve your own morale and your image to anyone you may run into.[43]

Be sure to show appreciation to a family member whose words or actions are helpful. Make your feedback specific, such as, "Thanks for reminding me of my strengths—sometimes I kind of forget them these days," or "I really appreciate it that you're cutting back on spending and not complaining about it." In addition, without attacking the person, you can give feedback on words or actions that are not helpful: "Nothing personal, but I'd rather you not keep asking how my job search is going because often I'm already feeling discouraged," or "When you say you wish we had the money to buy such and such, I wish the same thing and feel sad about it." Even the people who know and love us best aren't mind readers: They need to be told how we feel and think about things.

Family ties are important, of course, but people who have been accustomed to having a wider network of relationships need to remain in contact with former associates and friends or develop some new friendships. While you probably do need your closest loved ones close by, beware of clinging to them so tightly that they grow weary. I like the analogy of a friend of mine, the Reverend Lewis Morgan. If you scoop up a handful of sand at the beach and make a fist to try to contain it, your tight grip will cause the sand to slip through, Lewis explained. On the other hand, the sand that you hold onto more loosely will remain yours. People are like that in relationships.

Especially with long-term unemployment, core network supporters may get "burned out" in response to repeatedly being called upon for help.[44] Excessive dependency can become a problem on both sides of the equation: Those who are giving constant assistance eventually resent a lopsided relationship in which they are doing most of the giving, while the unemployed person, who hates always to be asking for help, also feels resentful.

"Dependency breeds hostility," said psychiatrist Haim Ginott. Clearly Dr. Ginott understood family conflict. "Reduce dependency and you'll reduce the hostility," he advised.[45] I'm not saying that you shouldn't look for support from close relatives and friends. Such connections with loved ones are what life is all about. But when support over time is not exchanged in relatively mutual ways, it may be difficult for you, as it is for most of us, to keep receiving and still maintain your self-esteem. More positive self-regard and less conflict exist in relationships where there is *interdependency* and where people more or less take turns.

Unemployment brings out the strengths and weaknesses in families.[46] If your family or marital difficulties are such that it's still hard to see the forest for the trees, then be strong and get some professional help without delay. Your perspective can be put right again. When people unburden themselves to a certified marriage or family counselor, certified pastoral counselor, or social worker—over time, there is often a renewed ability to see what is healthy and positive in relationships that have been in conflict. Anger, disappointment, and hurt cloud a person's perspective and block feelings of warmth and love. Once the troublesome emotions are expressed in a therapeutic setting and understood, so often feelings of love and appreciation are released.

Many find that it's still possible for couples to live with thankful hearts while earning less money and living more modestly. It's possible as well for a family to grow closer by working together, sharing burdens and responsibilities, and valuing the contributions and special qualities of each family member.

Celebrate what is good in your life. Look at the people who have supported your family in various ways and remember to thank them. Praise your children for the sacrifices they have made or for pitching in as needed. Show appreciation to your spouse or lover, your neighbors, and friends. Recognize the blessings you continue to have.

VIII

Surviving in a Changed and Changing Workplace

More changes are coming.
Those who can be nimble
will survive.

—James Carville

Most likely your situation is due to circumstances beyond your control. However, although you can't change what has already happened, you *can* get some significant control over what will happen in the future. Understanding the changed and changing workplace is essential to survival, will put you ahead of the competition in your job search, and ultimately will empower you.

DRAMATIC CHANGE

"The buoys that have marked the channels of our lives have all been swept away," wrote Barbara Tuchman in *The Guns of August.*[1] Tuchman was referring to the profound worldwide changes associated with the First World War, but her words well describe the dramatic changes of our times, too. Transformations at the workplace and rapidly changing social and economic trends are producing turbulence in the United States, Canada, Japan, Great Britain, and many countries on the European continent. Millions of people, adrift in unmarked seas, are searching for familiar buoys. But the old markers are being replaced by new ones.

After World War II, writes an editor at the *Washington Post,* the wealthy countries entered into a social bargain that is now in the process of becoming unraveled. Over time, that bargain involved an increase in living standards for average workers, many social benefits, and a large and powerful private sector. Increasingly affluent blue- and white-collar workers fueled economic growth.[2]

However, although the average American's wages increased continuously after 1947, wages stopped rising in 1973. And today, the average wage of a U.S. worker is still no higher than it was in 1973, adjusted for inflation.[3] This means that baby boomers (born between 1946 and 1964) are entering middle age with the feeling that they are not getting ahead. There have been too many baby boomers who want the best in jobs and housing, but not enough of the best to go around. Thus, according to one observer, "The endless economic expansion that was supposed to be an American birthright was yanked away just as the biggest generation in American history reached for it."[4]

Explains Professor Katherine Newman of Columbia University, "The problem is not simply that people are being laid off from jobs in large numbers. It is that the jobs themselves are evaporating. The industries in which these jobs were once found have packed up and left, and they are not being replaced by equivalent jobs."[5] The result is downward mobility. It is important for you to become or remain aware of this sobering information so you can equip yourself to work toward survival and even triumph.

Deindustrialization has taken jobs away not only in America's older or "sunset" industries but also in the "sunrise" sectors (for example, microelectronics), where assembly jobs are being exported to Asia. And, continues Newman, since satellite technology has made international data transmission comparatively inexpensive, many data entry, airline reservation, and other clerical jobs have moved to the Caribbean, Ireland, and China, where wages are one-fourth to one-fifteenth of those earned by Americans. Computer programmers are developing software in India for the U.S. market.[6]

Management jobs have been permanently lost because of corporate mergers, acquisitions, hostile takeovers, and "lean and mean" business maneuvers designed to trim costs.[7] A recent survey of 8,000 members of the American Management Association reported that 47 percent reduced their staffs (by an average of 10.4 percent) in 1993. It is a trend that is continuing. Even companies that are consistently profitable and those that have already downsized several times continue to shrink.[8]

Giant corporations such as IBM, General Motors, United Airlines, and Eastman Kodak are still cutting their payrolls. And small start-up firms, which created 20 million jobs in the 1980s, are having trouble borrowing the capital they need to grow, writes John Greenwald in *Time* magazine. Workers are being let go even in industries such as health care, as many drug firms and hospitals are consolidating and closing facilities. American industries and institutions from education, insurance, banking, and telecommunications to information processing, manufacturing, real estate, and construction have seen personnel reductions and cost cutting.[9] The net result of these changes is that even in a nonrecessionary period, such as April of 1995, the number of unemployed persons in the United States increased by 428,000, making a total of 7.7 million unemployed.[10] In addition, union members from steelworkers to airline pilots have been forced to accept benefit reductions, restructured contracts, and other "givebacks." Downsizing has become a way of life.[11]

One unfortunate aspect of corporate restructuring is the fact that many women and minorities are being laid off just as they were making inroads into middle management, says management guru Tom Peters.[12] On the other hand, the gender discrimination that has resulted in higher pay for men for so many years is now working against middle-aged men as cost-cutting companies are deciding whose jobs to eliminate. James Medoff, a Harvard University economics professor, reported recently that men ages thirty-five to fifty-four are twice as likely to lose their jobs as they were in 1981.[13]

To an out-of-work person it can be pretty depressing to think about plant closures, jobs moved abroad, corporate downsizing, and the new era of global competition. It can also get depressing to realize that businesses, government, and other social institutions are changing how they do business—outsourcing, contracting, networking, and temping many blue- and white-collar jobs—so regular full-time, permanent jobs are harder to find. A person can feel both depressed and alarmed over the fact that many workers who would succeed today must learn to use the latest technologies or develop timely skills which may be very different from the skills needed in the last job.

Yet by facing these new realities with honesty and courage, you can find or create a rewarding new place for yourself and earn a living at the same time. You can become a productive member of a company or institution's core permanent workforce or become a successful entrepreneur, independent contractor, consultant, or temporary employee.

There are numerous, varied, and rich opportunities to explore once a person accepts that the rules have changed for most of the workplace games being played. Those who are willing to learn some new plays and adapt to the new rules can become outstanding players with a place of security on one team or another. It's also possible to become a team manager or the owner. You can forge a new working life for yourself.

Job security today is no longer a result of enduring relationships with employers but is based on the skills that workers acquire. Like workers in most major industrialized nations, North American workers must face the reality that trying to stay with one employer or succeed by having one set of skills is not enough. A recent *Wall Street Journal* article quotes a White House economic advisor as saying that "The 'new definition of job security' is one in which workers are 'equipped to handle the next job.'" In fact, government officials are trying to shift from the phrase "job security" to "employment security."[14]

But employment security, says Lawrence Katz, the U.S. Labor Department's chief economist, must now be defined as "having skills that are portable and benefits that are portable." Since many Americans will change jobs seven or eight times in a lifetime, the old ways of thinking about security no longer apply.[15] Another old rule of thumb that no longer applies is the notion that jobs are lost when a nation suffers a recession or other economic downturn and that satisfactory reemployment accompanies economic recovery. In January 1994, major U.S. corporations announced 108,000 layoffs, a level of layoffs topping even the worst of the 1990 recession.[16] And workers laid off at the giant corporations often find that their new jobs elsewhere offer less pay.[17] Although it is true that millions of new jobs are being created in Western societies, including many good jobs for managers and professionals, there is still a need for more well-paying jobs.[18]

Sandy Koicuba, for example, a materials specialist at Caterpillar's manufacturing plant in York, Pennsylvania, was one of nearly 10,000 employees laid off by that company from 1988 to 1993. After the company got its costs down and productivity up and began to re-hire, the forty-four-year-old woman was recalled to pack materials in a company warehouse. Her wage is $9.10 an hour, versus $17 an hour in her old job—and her fringe benefits have been virtually eliminated. "I work sixty hours a week, and I still can't make it," Sandy explains.[19]

Sheldon Joseph, fifty-six, formerly a Chicago advertising execu-tive, began temping for $10 an hour in a community job-training program after he was laid off in 1989. Recalling the mutual loyalty between employers and employees that once defined the corporate environment, Joseph says, "I feel like Rip van Winkle. You wake up and the world is all changed. The message from industry is, 'We don't want your loyalty. We want your work.'"[20]

Sandy Koicuba's and Sheldon Joseph's stories are all too com-mon. Rick Lamplugh and I heard such tales, but we also heard the stories of many people who coped well with job loss and survived, including men and women who have triumphed by creating a life for themselves that is more satisfying than the life they had before. Many have reordered their priorities, taking steps to live more bal-anced lives. Many others have recognized and seized new work-place options and opportunities, sought more education, and developed new skills. These individuals—I call them "triumphant survivors"—have done their share of suffering yet have grown to see adversity as a challenge.

The various stories in this book of people who have begun to re-build their lives and create a positive future may at first glance ap-pear quite different from yours, but there are many universal lessons here despite the uniqueness of each person's situation.

ANAMI RIDGE: CREATING A PATH TO A HAPPIER LIFE THROUGH PART-TIME WORK

Confronting the new economic realities of global competition, em-ployers throughout the industrial world increasingly are relying on part-time workers. According to the *Washington Post*, one out of every seven workers in the industrialized world is now a part-time employee, including 25 percent of the working women.[21]

It is estimated that 60 percent of the new jobs created during a recent six-month period were part-time and at least half of them were taken by people wanting full-time work. The Bureau of Labor Statistics has reported that as many as 6.2 million Americans want full-time jobs but have accepted part-time work because that is all they can find.[22]

Anami Ridge, a disability management professional, reached a career crossroads when her company downsized. Her job was to help disabled workers find new occupations after being injured on the job. Daily she tried to help frustrated workers—often with a high school education or less—face the reality that they wouldn't be making $10 to $15 an hour anymore as construction workers, warehouse laborers, truck drivers, machinists, or loggers. Even with job retraining, $6 to $8 an hour was the best these workers could expect. Suddenly Anami, a single parent, had to wonder how she could support a family with significantly less income: Her company offered to keep her on part-time in lieu of letting her go entirely. It was a keenly stressful job, one that placed Anami in a four-way cross-fire: hostile injured workers sometimes saying she wasn't doing enough to help them; their lawyers, who had heard only one side of the story; the insurance companies, who wanted the workers reemployed quickly because they were paying the consulting firm's fee; and the state disability agency, which was constantly breathing down her neck.

Anami had to decide whether she wanted to change careers. Did she think she could learn to live on a sharply decreased income and have the trade-off of more time with her young son? If she stayed on in the job and worked part-time, could she alter their family lifestyle so the part-time pay would be sufficient? If the company called her back for full-time work some months later, would she still choose to cope with her stressful job only on a part-time basis?

Anami and her son live an hour from the mountains, an hour and a half from the beach, and down the road from a lovely park and stream. As a loving mother, she had wondered for a long time how she could find more time to be with her son and enjoy the outings they both cherish. She had thought long and hard about the quality of family life she yearned to have.

The questions Anami posed for herself are ones she had presented over the years to scores of blue-collar workers: What new ways of thinking were now required so she could accommodate the new workplace circumstances and still pay attention to her own values and yearnings? What strategies were needed for coping and economic survival? "I don't think it's mentally or spiritually healthy," Anami told us, "for people to spend their lives chasing money." Her own crisis of being forced to make ends meet on a part-time income increased her feelings of empathy toward her disabled clients. Just like them, Anami Ridge needed to reevaluate her life.

Although there were definite challenges in getting accustomed to a significantly reduced family income, Anami decided not to look for another full-time job. When she thought it over, the part-time position seemed to be a good one; it paid well and required skills she has and enjoys using. She also can "call her own shots," as Anami puts it; she is in control of her own schedule and approach to working with people.

With more time for "living a balanced life," Anami told us that in addition to spending more time with her son, she is enjoying doing volunteer work at a wildlife rehabilitation center. She finds it rewarding to take care of injured wild animals just as she has found it satisfying to help injured workers at the rehabilitation center. Further, paid employment is more satisfying now: She copes better with a stressful job because she has more family time and the opportunity to pursue her interests outside of work.

Anami didn't change jobs but feels as if she did. She knows she was "burning out" at work before the company downsized and is mentally free of those burdens now. She no longer wants to go back full-time, even though the work load has picked up and full-time work is available. She is *choosing* the life that she is now living.

Like Anami Ridge, you can seize the opportunity to make something that is positive and good for you emerge from the changing workplace. Financial difficulties and other lifestyle changes that may seem devastating at first can become problems with solutions and doorways to a happier life.

"Above the poverty level, the relationship between income and happiness is remarkably small," wrote social commentator Jonathan Freedman.[23] In fact, when asked, "What is necessary for happiness?" or "What is it that makes your life meaningful?" psychologist David Myers has found that most people say "satisfying close relationships with family, friends or romantic partners" comes first.

"Happiness," says Myers, usually "hits close to home."[24]

You may decide that it's a matter of personal survival to alter your goals and redefine personal success. As consultant Judith Bardwick of La Jolla, California, says, many people facing unavoidable change "look to sectors of their lives where they have more control, like creating a wonderful family or contributing to the community." Instead of changing your life, you can change how you experience your life.[25]

GRANT LAIBLIN: STARTING A BUSINESS

Although Grant Laiblin's job did not go overseas or dissolve in corporate restructuring, his story describes survival in the face of occupational disruption. His story is one of a man who made certain life-improving decisions and whose actions enabled him to turn an awful situation into something positive.

Grant was a tall and muscular construction worker whose life was permanently changed when a large pipe fell across his neck at work. After multiple surgeries, his physician finally said that Grant could never go back to a job involving strenuous labor with heavy tools, which is what he had done for most of his adult working life. Grant wondered what was in store for "this banged up, old construction stiff." Like a lot of unemployed workers—especially those who are ill or injured—Grant felt *old*. He was thirty-eight.

For more than a year he was in considerable pain, both physically and mentally. As Grant lay at home recuperating from each surgery, he worried about what his family would do when the insurance money stopped coming. He suffered depression and anxiety attacks, which his doctor treated with medication. At first, his pride was hurt and his marital relationship strained when he stayed home with the three children and his wife went out to work, something he felt she resented.

Grant both challenged and surprised himself with what came next. He had the wisdom to know that he needed professional guidance and opened his mind and heart to benefit from sessions with a vocational rehabilitation counselor. He began to grow and gradually he envisioned making something positive emerge from his troubles.

His counselor helped him realize that what he really wanted to do was go into business for himself, as his brother had done. Articulating and then pursuing that goal were bold steps for Grant, who had not finished high school. He said he was "scared to death" about having to handle tasks such as paying taxes and doing a payroll. Nevertheless, since he was eligible for some limited retraining through the Workers' Compensation system because of his work-related injury, he decided to use those benefits for learning what he needed to know.

At his local community college in Oregon, Grant signed up for a series of valuable courses in business basics such as computers, accounting, and marketing. Grant is intelligent, capable, and willing to work hard, and so, to his surprise, he did very well in his classes. Here was a guy who had operated a jackhammer for a living and never thought of himself as smart, who came home with straight A's. His wife proudly posted his grades on the refrigerator door, along with their children's school work, and his sons literally patted him on the back. It meant a lot to Grant to see what he was capable of and to have his family's support.

Grant talked with his brother, who owned a hose and fitting business in Seattle, selling parts needed to repair trucks and heavy equipment. They saw a potential for a similar business in Grant's hometown of Philomath, Oregon, and Grant did some market research to establish that that was the case. His brother was willing to provide some of the start-up cash if Grant would invest the time that was needed to learn the business.

For several months, Grant commuted five hours every Monday morning to his brother's store. There he worked Monday through Friday, week after week, learning the trade. Every weekend he drove the long distance home and was back at the store again on Monday. Grant knew that success might not come easily or right away. He had learned in one of his business classes that 75 percent to 80 percent of new businesses fail within the first year. He wanted to be well prepared for success.

When he finally opened his own business, Grant had the product and business knowledge, plus about $10,000 in financial backing to make a realistic attempt at starting a business. He worked long hours and did everything he could to stretch those dollars. His wife took care of the paperwork and also worked another job. Their fourteen-year-old son swept the floors and stocked the shelves.

For years before going into business for himself, Grant had stayed in a job he disliked, working for someone he disliked. Grant realizes now that he has moved beyond those doubts about himself.

The Laiblin family's hard work and sacrifice have paid off. "We were in the black within ten months," Grant says proudly. "It really is a business that was needed in our area." In 1992, Willamette Hose and Fitting, Inc., moved from a building with 1,000 square feet to a place with 12,000 square feet, and they have since purchased the property. The company has five employees, including (as general manager) the now grown-up son who used to sweep the floors.

When Rick Lamplugh first told me Grant's story, I remember thinking about the men I've seen operating jackhammers at various road and construction sites. On my way to work, I have often sat in my car at a stoplight and more-or-less stared at the dusty, sweaty face of a jackhammer man and watched the violent trembling of his strong arms and shoulders. Growing up as the daughter and granddaughter of farmers, I learned to admire people who work hard for a living and get dirty, so when a man does the hard labor of road repair, standing knee-deep in a hole no more than ten feet from the traffic, sometimes I am mesmerized. But now I know that I'll never be able to hear the awful noise of a machine penetrating concrete, and watch a stranger harness the power of a jackhammer, without thinking about such a person in a new way. In the future, I'll sit in traffic and say to myself, "There's a guy who may decide to have his own business someday."

You also may decide to make a major occupational change. If you have doubts, as most people do, you can follow Grant's example. Although he was a high school dropout and never thought of himself as very smart, he struggled, reached out for a professional's help, was willing to work hard and make sacrifices to learn what he needed to know, was a gracious receiver when various family members gave their support, and created for himself a new way to make a living. Today's world of work is like that: You have to make yourself nimble to survive.

THE FAST-THINKING MANAGER

Life is a series of transitions for most people, but it is children who most consistently show an amazing ability to adapt and to cope with change. Psychologist Al Siebert says that one of the keys to doing well in life is to strive toward becoming almost childlike in flexibility.[26] He gives the example of a middle manager who was working for Tektronix in Portland, Oregon, where the computer products firm has been constantly going through good times and bad. When he learned he was to be laid off, the fast-thinking manager said to himself, "I'm in an awful situation but really Tektronics needs me in an extreme way. I'm the only one who knows the particular product I've been handling and the process that produces it." So he approached the personnel officer, with the knowledge that consultants are a rapidly growing part of the workforce, and announced, "You need me. Why not hire me on as a consultant?" The company did.

Later, after things got better at Tektronix, the company's local executive decided that they couldn't afford so many consultants, and so they had to hire the manager in order to keep him on. Thus, twice the manager changed jobs, by changing the way he was paid, but he never left his desk. Today's workplace embraces people willing and able to adapt to change in such ways.

"Just-in-Time" Employees: The Challenge of Seizing Something Good from the Changing Workplace

The idea of acquiring needed materials "just-in-time" to assemble them in the manufacturing of goods originated in Japan. It is a concept the Japanese have perfected and American firms are learning to implement. Not bearing the cost of warehousing and insuring extra inventories saves a lot of money. Similarly, employers find it profitable to hire only when employees are needed; they save the huge expense of payroll taxes, wages and salaries, Workers' Compensation, and various costly benefits.

In the United States there are 35 million contingent workers, men and women who are temporary full-time employees, contract employees, consultants, and others who are not part of the core employee base of any company. This *is* the new workforce. In 1988, about one out of four Americans in the civilian workforce was a contingent worker. Already by 1993, one in three Americans held such a job, including part-time workers. And by 2000, contingent workers are expected to be at least half of the labor force. Manpower Inc., a company that places temporary workers in various businesses, now has 560,000 U.S. employees and has overtaken General Motors as the nation's largest employer. In fact, Manpower Inc. has nearly twice as many employees as GM.[27]

Since jobs that are neither full-time nor permanent account for a significant percentage of the available jobs, it is important to recognize certain potential *advantages* to working in this manner. For one thing, you have more flexibility as you handle the conflicting demands of work and family. You can choose a more balanced life with more time for loved ones, recreation, and other pursuits and activities that make you feel useful in your community.

Part-time or temporary work also can be an opportunity to try out a variety of new employment situations—to help you discover different occupations that interest you or to confirm which fields you'll want to avoid. You can develop new friendships while learning valuable skills or uncover hidden abilities which you can eventually take elsewhere.

Numerous authorities report that companies today are happy to replace many current employees with consultants and temporary help, and this may be your most realistic way of getting entrance into such a company. While IBM, for example, set out to lay off 25,000 employees in 1993, it nonetheless has maintained contracts with 300 outside firms to accomplish such tasks as running the computer giant's payrolls and designing software programs.

In many corporations, few jobs are too large or too small to be handled by temps, freelancers, part-timers, leased employees, independent contractors, or consultants—employed as secretaries, security guards, engineers, X-ray technicians, doctors, lawyers, chemists, assembly line workers, bank officers, sales clerks, or computer scientists.[28] Another reason large companies such as AT&T hire new personnel as temps is to ensure that they are the people the company wants for the long run. Later some of these workers will be added to the AT&T payroll. There are opportunities for those who would seize and make the most of them.

Employers, according to Rick Lamplugh, look at their organization and ask: "Who are our essential employees?" These "core workers," those who have demonstrated the importance of their contributions, get the permanent full-time jobs. Those who hold jobs essential only at certain times become part of the contingency workforce; they work when needed. If becoming a company or institution's core worker is your goal, you can better equip yourself by considering temporary work as a means of gaining new marketable skills while earning money. According to a survey quoted recently by *Nation's Business,* two out of three people who work as temporaries gain new skills.[29]

If you decide to make independent contracting or other part-time or temporary employment work for you on a continuing basis, you may need to consider in advance how to take good care of yourself in regard to various issues. According to a recent study by the International Labor Organization, part-timers often are excluded from benefits such as sick pay, overtime, and unemployment insurance, and especially women are usually paid lower wages than full-timers. Generally, part-time workers in the United States also do not benefit from the Family and Medical Leave Act, which allows for an unpaid leave of absence to care for a new child or other family member. And, being outside the traditional system of worker-management relationships, contingent workers can be more vulnerable to age, race, sex, disability, and other forms of discrimination, sexual harassment, and other problems. If any difficulties should arise, it's always a good idea to have a plan in place for where you can turn for help and advice. Think ahead, for example, about who you could ask for assistance if you have a medical or family emergency or if you feel something isn't right about how you've been treated. (See also Appendix A for whom to call in situations of discrimination or sexual harassment.)

Many professionals are finding that they prefer the life that the changing workplace can provide. For example, forty-two-year-old Los Angeles attorney John Andrews told writer Janice Castro of *Time* that he remembers working seven weeks without a day off as a young lawyer. Since there's no longer any security and partnerships fold up overnight, Andrews avoids the "ultimate rat-race job" of being a lawyer by temping at various law firms and makes enough to support the lifestyle he prefers. "I like to travel," Andrews says. "My car is paid for. I don't own a house. I'm not into mowing grass."[30]

Temping is also convenient for Veronica Bryant because she has a six-year-old daughter. The forty-eight-year-old secretary lost her job when her employer went out of business. "I prefer long-term assignments," she says, "rather than one day here, one day there. It's not very difficult. I more or less fit in. I pick up my check and I leave. I don't even know if they know me."[31]

In such circumstances, it becomes very important to have a strong social support network, family and friends you spend time with regularly, since in most cases you are no longer able to enjoy ongoing relationships with co-workers. Church or synagogue connections, membership in social or health clubs, athletic or musical groups, or community volunteer programs can provide the meaningful human contact that the workplace once offered. On the other hand, you may meet some people while temping whom you decide to continue to see socially. Relationships in a changing workplace simply require more intentionality and a conscious effort to maintain them.

How you decide to think about your situation will shape, in large measure, how happy or unhappy you will become in a job that is not what you thought you wanted. Whether you decide to work part-time or in a full-time temporary job, become an entrepreneur or a consultant, or accept any job while seeking eventual employment as a "core" employee—if you choose to see yourself as a second-class citizen in an inferior job situation, then that is how you will feel. Instead, you can view yourself as a first-class human being making the most of a temporary or permanent workable alternative to the type of employment you may have enjoyed before.

KELLEE HARRIS: THE IMPORTANCE OF CREATING JOB SECURITY FOR YOURSELF

Kellee Harris had a stunning wake-up call to the reality of the rapidly changing workplace. A woman with an M.B.A. and fifteen years of marketing and management experience with top national firms, she had managed product lines generating tens of millions in gross dollar sales. After a stable work history, Kellee was laid off from three midmanagement jobs in twelve years.

A marketing manager with a competitive track record, a quick mind, high energy, and a positive attitude—and the only person left in her department at the last job—she had believed her position to be secure. But no position is safe anymore, Kellee finally realized: The only security that exists is what you create for yourself.

After the first layoff, Kellee had easily found a new position through networking. After the second layoff, the search was longer. A want ad led to Kellee's second new job. Then following the *third* layoff, Kellee's networking contacts said they had no idea where another marketing job might be available; what's more, many of her contacts suddenly were frightened of losing their own jobs to downsizing and outsourcing.

Kellee realized that even though companies were cutting jobs in the area of her expertise, there was still marketing work to be done. She saw that many businesses were striving to stay lean and profitable by outsourcing—getting their work done through vendors, consultants, and temporary employees. After getting some good advice from people she respected—self-employed and other experienced professionals—Kellee was determined to go out on her own. She decided she would find companies with marketing needs and contract with them to provide a specific service over a certain time period.

Kellee told Rick Lamplugh that, from a company's point of view, outsourcing made sense because it's a short-term arrangement with no commitment. She laughed then at the idea of no commitment, adding, "That's how companies are treating their employees anyway!"

With her husband's understanding and support, Kellee tapped every possible savings resource they had, including using large credit lines on several of her credit cards to buy a computer, printer, and fax machine. For some individuals it would be foolhardy to walk out on a financial limb as far as Kellee went to get her business going, but her husband had a job and Kellee had confidence in her abilities. After all, although she had lost three jobs, she had also been able to *find* three jobs—so she obviously had skills that were in demand. Kellee also knew she was willing to work hard to succeed and that she would seek whatever advice was necessary and learn whatever she still needed to know to make contract marketing successful.

Nonetheless, there were sleepless nights. Starting her own business, MarketSpark, carried a burden of responsibility along with the challenge and excitement. Kellee lost weight, had migraine headaches and a miscarriage, and was often worried, irritable, and mentally preoccupied at home. Family relationships were strained at times, as Kellee's husband and their two young daughters inevitably absorbed some of her stress. Finally Kellee's husband urged her to develop a plan to take better care of herself. She started to use an alarm clock to remind herself to take breaks, she dropped off and picked up her little girls at preschool, and she spent more time with family members at home. Living a more balanced life reduced Kellee's stress considerably, adding to her energy level and optimism.

After six months of hard effort, Kellee had one good client and "a real dry summer," but she was determined not to give up until she had tapped every single resource. With a strong sense of commitment to achieving her goal, Kellee carefully planned strategies for capturing business. She wrote an article on contract management for a widely read business journal, found several mentors, got helpful advice from the Small Business Administration (SBA), and also received free advice from retired business executives through the SBA's Service Corps of Retired Executives (SCORE).

"You don't have to jump into entrepreneurship without an informational life raft," says Meg Whittemore in *Nation's Business.* There are numerous good government and professional agencies where you can get advice to help you get going. In forty-two states, local centers of the SBA offer training and counseling to owners of new and established businesses, and 13,000 SCORE volunteers offer free assistance and advice.[32] (For more information about the SBA and SCORE plus a list of phone numbers, refer to Appendix E at the back of this book.)

Clearly, as Kellee Harris demonstrates, success in life isn't as much a matter of luck as it is persistence, resourcefulness, and effort. After several years of struggle, Kellee developed a successful marketing consulting business, specializing in sports and fitness marketing. Now she is busy operating a two-person business. She contracts with companies to develop marketing plans for their products and services, attends sports trade shows to source new business and support existing clients, rents displays, and coordinates the marketing activities of the company's permanent full-time staff—just as a permanently employed marketing manager would do but on a temporary, project-oriented basis. When the contracted work ends, she moves on to market manage another company's new product or service.

While calling on employers, Kellee recently was offered a $75,000-a-year "regular job" as a marketing vice president but turned it down, suggesting instead that the company pay her a retainer to market the product plus stock options.

Kellee Harris might easily be an archetype for the postmodern era. She models the personal traits that are needed for occupational and economic survival in today's world: determination and resolve, the wisdom to establish clearly defined occupational goals, and the ability to seek advice and support from others to make progress toward those goals.

Like Kellee Harris, you can decide to accept the responsibility for pursuing your dreams, taking thoughtfully chosen risks when needed. Allow yourself to entertain the possibility that change is not the enemy but can become your friend.

IX

What You Need to Know to Prepare for Your Next Job

*When the student is ready
the teacher appears.*

—ASIAN SAYING

Eric Greenberg of the American Management Association has said, "If your model for normal is the 1960s, '70s or '80s, we will never get back to normal because 'normal' is based on a whole set of global economic conditions that no longer apply."[1] Technology is changing work and virtually everything else about our lives. Citing novelist Thomas Wolfe's book *You Can't Go Home Again,* writer George Church of *Time* eloquently describes the job market of the future as being so different from the past that returning isn't possible "because home isn't there anymore."[2]

Even society's most traditional institutions—in education, health services, and small business—are undergoing transformations with respect to how employees are hired, retained, and rewarded. Being able to cope with change is as important for teachers, academic administrators, and medical personnel as for workers and managers in businesses, corporations, and factories.

The College Professor: How *Not* to Approach Job Search

A man I know lost his full-time job at the four-year college where he was a philosophy professor. At age forty, he found himself in the unenviable position of being an unemployed Ph.D. at a time when many colleges and universities were making cutbacks. He and his wife had three young children and another on the way.

Philosophy isn't a popular field of study in many colleges today and hasn't been for many years. As a white, middle-aged male—unless he was unusually talented—this man probably would have been lucky to find a full-time permanent job in philosophy anywhere. Preference might well be given to a young minority person who would apply for one of the few available full-time jobs, or to someone just out of graduate school who would be low on the pay scale.

Despite these realities of the job market, the professor was being very particular about which of several invitations to interview he would even accept. He let it be known that he wanted to work only in what he considered an academically respected, four-year institution, one traditionally known for providing faculty with the opportunity to conduct research and to publish. He was said to be thumbing his nose at a possible community college professorship, because he felt it was somehow beneath him intellectually. Clearly he was sabotaging himself, thinking about his situation without an awareness of how the workplace had changed.

A more realistic person might have considered alternative ways to make himself feel challenged. In a growing two-year college there might exist a better chance at longevity than he had seen elsewhere. Establishing himself in a setting that wasn't exactly what he had in mind might still have given the professor the opportunity to do the research and writing in which he was interested. After acquiring the job, he could persuade others of the value of such work if it was truly worthwhile.

Thinking creatively about where certain types of work can be done and how one's special interests can be pursued is the way lots of people make themselves happy today. "If you believe something is valuable and find you live in a world that doesn't value it," says

Dr. Gardner Pond, a college administrator in Maryland, "then present yourself as a capable person and, over time, convince the people you work with to go along with it." Such an entrepreneurial spirit leads to success in virtually every field.

The philosophy professor might also have asked himself whether he was qualified to teach courses other than philosophy or willing to take additional courses himself to become more diversely qualified. Could he imagine himself teaching or doing research somewhere other than in a college and, if so, in what areas of study? Might a new career direction spin off from his interest and experience in publishing? What has he done for a living at some other point in his life? What are his other talents and interests? What else has he ever considered as an occupational pursuit? If a part-time position—doing what he wants to do in his special area—is all that seems available, how might such work be combined with other talents in a second job to help support his family and provide stimulation and reward?

Flexibility is essential for most people to secure employment and remain employed. A decade ago, people could hold out for the perfect employer-employee fit, but not today. Those who compete and succeed in the new workplace learn to keep an open mind: They consider lots of different work settings and examine numerous career options.

It's not easy to move beyond the understandable desire to live and work in a world like the one you've always known, a world you've diligently prepared yourself for with education, training, and lots of effort. Grieving over losing the workplace as it was, feeling bitter for a time, and resisting change are all natural reactions. But those who succeed in putting together a satisfying work life learn to transfer into new areas their special knowledge or expertise, problem-solving or mechanical skills, and teaching or technical experience. Often they turn hobbies, recreational activities, or other personal interests into ways to make a living. Such vendor-minded persons ask themselves: What do I have to offer, to whom and how can I best offer it, convincing others of its value?

THE IMPORTANCE OF "SKILL SETS," "PEOPLE SKILLS," AND BALANCE IN YOUR LIFE

When hiring new employees, 3M human resources manager Elton Perry says that he considers the applicant's education as counting for only about 10 percent of the decision to hire. Skill sets—the skills needed to accomplish what the employer wants done—account for 40 percent of the decision. But it is the ability to work productively with others that is the applicant's most important attribute, accounting for 50 percent of Perry's decision that a person belongs with the company. In addition, as organizations flatten their hierarchical structures, retaining fewer managers and supervisors, workers are left to figure out what needs to be done without being told to do this or that. "You can be bright and educated," Perry told me, "but what companies are looking for are people who can use their education to initiate projects and inspire, lead, teach, or in other ways work well with others."

People who aren't individualists—concerned only about getting recognition for themselves—but who get as much satisfaction in seeing someone else succeed, are also sought as new hires. "Fifteen years ago," explained Perry, "graduates came out of school declaring, 'I'm going to be the best engineer I can be and make a name for myself.'" Today most schools are emphasizing the importance of teamwork and influencing skills so you can work together in groups to accomplish something for the company. "You also can't go to the boss or a customer and say something must be a certain way," says Perry. "You have to be able to use influencing skills."[3]

"There also has been a marked shift in performance evaluations away from comparisons between people toward an evaluation against a set of personal objectives, negotiated individually with each employee," says Blake Wattenbarger, a technical manager with AT&T. "The shift away from individualism is real," he continues. "This emphasis on teamwork amounts to Americans adopting a Japanese approach to work."[4]

Often those in a position to hire look for balance in a person's life. A supervisor from a large company in the Southwest told me that he wants more employees who can both work hard and make time for their personal lives with family, friends, hobbies, and other interests. Citing the case of a man who lost his marriage and children because of workaholism in a previous job, the supervisor said that some people overcorrect an imbalance in the past by going too far the other way: For example, this man comes to work late because he is having breakfast with his second marriage family and leaves early to be with his young children. Now his life is out of balance to the opposite extreme.

THE IMPORTANCE OF SELF-KNOWLEDGE

Getting to know yourself better is an excellent way to prepare for your next interview or your next job. You'll want to remember, however, that a person doesn't marry a job, says America's leading management consultant, Peter Drucker. A job can become how you find out what you want to do and that's all. In such a case, "You owe no loyalty to your employer other than not betraying secrets," he says. Be intent on finding out where or whether you belong. Other important advice from this author of twenty-seven books involves thoughtful self-examination. I recommend that you help yourself clarify some important issues Drucker identifies by jotting down in a journal your answers to the following questions:

- Can you cope with working under a lot of pressure?
- Do you belong in a big organization where you can enjoy telling people you work for a big company or institution but where you don't see results because you're too far away from them?
- Do you find it satisfying to surmount a daily crisis or feel it's more satisfying to anticipate and prevent problems?
- Is your manner of perception and problem solving more feeling-oriented or analytical?
- Do you want to sit down at work and pore over stacks of information and plot figures or go around and get input from others?
- Do you prefer working alone or being a member of a team?
- What are the key elements of your basic personality? Are you a self-starter, a timid person, an overplanner, a charmer, a conventional type, a follower, or a leader?[5]

After you ask the above questions of yourself and answer them, examine these same issues as you consider various employment

options. You need to find a match between your personality and
your next job or the job after that. Suppose, answering these questions, you like working with a lot of pressure and working with a
big organization. You like having to surmount a daily crisis and
you're a feeling-oriented person. You like getting input from others
but you prefer working alone. And suppose the job you're considering requires you to work in teams but otherwise the job offers a
match with your personality. The teamwork requirement is a mis-
match but is an opportunity for you to grow as a person and to expand what you offer as an employee. If you master this challenge,
in the future you can work alone or in teams. On the other hand, if
not one but several of these items are not a match, it could be a
"job from hell" and you should stay away from it. Work needs to be
a place where you can grow, learn something of value, have opportunities for advancement, or simply survive for a while or have fun
for a couple of years.[6] What do you want to accomplish?

THE HIGH-PERFORMANCE WORKPLACE

What you need to know about your next job is that you must constantly add value to the company or institution that you work for,
explains technical manager Blake Wattenbarger. "While no one is ir-
replaceable, you should strive for people to respect the contributions you make," he says.

For most people—both blue- and white-collar workers—developing new skills and learning how to anticipate and solve the kinds of
problems your employer needs you to handle make you a hot com-
modity. "What is rather new in the American workplace is that more
and more blue-collar workers are being treated as intelligent people
who are expected to identify problems and suggest improvements
for the processes they use to do their work," agrees Wattenbarger.[7]
Today it is important for all workers to become adept at recognizing
and solving problems.

You can also benefit from looking for ways to improve your ability to relate to others—co-workers, bosses, and your clients, students, patients, or customers.

Never stop learning or acquiring new insights. Look ahead to the
kinds of skills and knowledge that will be needed next year or five
years from now and seek out the training or retraining that will pre-

pare you for the future. Take advantage of every opportunity to better yourself. Most employers will be supportive of any commitment to excellence you demonstrate as a "core" employee and may financially assist you with advanced schooling or retraining. However, if you are a contingent worker, it will be up to you to take charge of planning and financing your own continuing development.

Many contingent workers are creating a demand for themselves, marketing their talents and services, and making more money or finding greater satisfaction in their new jobs than in their old ones. You also can turn temporary, part-time, or contractual work into a rewarding career, a challenging fresh start, or a well-spent period of transition that prepares you for the next chapters of your life.

Especially if you work full-time, expect to work longer, harder hours when you become reemployed. You will need routine outlets for stress just as you have needed a self-care plan to sustain you during the ordeal of job search. Build personal relationships and set aside time for people, meaningful hobbies, music, and exercise as part of your daily life. Promise yourself you'll continue this healthier lifestyle after you return to work.

At a 1993 Workforce Development Summit Conference in Oregon attended by Rick Lamplugh, employers repeatedly said they want front line employees who can problem solve, make decisions, prepare and monitor budgets, set performance standards, hire co-workers, resolve conflicts, review co-workers' performance, communicate, and above all, *deal with change*. These skills—ordinarily associated with those expected of managers—are now being sought in blue-collar employees, too.[8]

Bob Johnson, head of personnel at a Hewlett-Packard plant in Corvallis, Oregon, summed up the new workplace best when he described the evolution of jobs. He said that five years ago Hewlett-Packard employees felt they had a job for the rest of their lives, came in on weekdays, and worked eight-hour shifts. Every ten or twelve workers had one supervisor, work was broken into simple tasks, and employees needed mostly to get there every day and follow directions. Today, shifts are twelve hours long and weekend work is often required. Workers are in fifty-person self-directing teams with no supervisor and are expected to troubleshoot processes, maintain machines, and commit to learning new skills.

The changed and changing job scene—for both blue- and white-collar workers today—is a high-performance workplace, one that can compete in a world environment. In both large and small companies, employers want people who can thrive in teams and yet think for themselves and work on their own when necessary. It is clear that if you want to work for a prosperous employer instead of a business or institution that is just hanging on or dying, you must develop your own skills. You can't wait for a government program or a high-performance employer to pay your way. You have to invest in yourself.

Experts say that thriving employers spend about 5 percent of payroll on training employees. It is wise to invest in your own development in the form of continuing education and training, an amount equivalent to 5 percent of the time you ordinarily would spend at work. That would be two hours a week set aside for improving your work skills. Possibly no single decision you make would enhance your workplace value to a greater extent.

Vocational consultant Lamplugh recommends that you start by identifying an area of weakness such as communicating, problem solving, decision making, or working on a team. Then figure out how to learn more and improve yourself in that area. After that, move on to another area of weakness. High-performance employees are constantly growing and changing, just like the organizations they will work for.

REDEFINING THE CONCEPT OF HAVING A JOB AND JOB SECURITY

The whole idea of what it means to be employed is being transformed in the changing workplace, says Bill Bridges, who helps organizations and individuals in transition. Usually we associate a job with having a certain set of duties, a predetermined wage or salary, and a clear spot on the organizational chart, but this description is becoming obsolete. Many employees today have no permanent job description but instead are assigned to shifting project teams. Workers may be on several teams at once, and on each they're apt to be reporting to a different person. "And realistically, you can't say they have a job. They have full employment, but they don't have what we ever used to call a job," says Bridges.[9]

Current changes in the job market are at least as revolutionary for

Western civilization as was the Industrial Revolution. The first thing an employee has to do, suggests Bridges, is to stop looking at the organization as a structure of jobs, bosses, and hierarchy and start looking at it as a market. Even one's concept of who the employer is needs to change. It is important to start looking at potential bosses as customers, to start thinking about what their unmet needs are. In thinking of yourself as an independent business person looking for customers with unmet needs, ask yourself what you have to offer and how you can use your unique skills and knowledge to meet the needs of customers, those people you once thought of as bosses or co-workers. In other words, create a niche for yourself.

Bridges likens this new employer-employee relationship to the way a movie producer assembles cast and crew to produce a movie: Actors don't go to work with the idea that they have a lifetime career. They go to work saying, "This is a great project, and I really want to do this one." When the project is over, some of the workers disappear, others move on with the coordinator to the next project. It's a very fluid situation in which insiders and outsiders collaborate.

Taking Bridges's analogy a bit further, the downside of the new workplace is that there are a lot of actors wondering when their next project will come along. Feelings of insecurity can result. But, *over time, workers will begin to feel more secure because they will redefine the meaning of security.*

Security no longer means having a job in a large company or institution, receiving terrific benefits, and working until retirement. Security comes not from some external reality or condition at all but instead from discovering and developing your own constantly changing blend of skills and knowledge so you can demonstrate your usefulness.

Change and new ways of thinking can be scary. But survival in a world that is changing requires that we "give up on the continuation of the present," says Bridges. There is no likelihood that what we have always taken for granted is going to continue.

Each of us must begin to create our own security by looking at what we have to give and where we best can give it. It's time to say goodbye to the concept of job as we have known it, whether we work in the field of education, banking, telecommunications, transportation, health care, law enforcement, manufacturing, sales, publishing, or elsewhere.

PREPARING FOR THE FUTURE

Instead of trying to anticipate what kinds of jobs and which industries are the wave of the future (since experts often disagree on the general trends), it is probably wiser to follow the advice of David Birch, president of Cognetics Inc., a consulting firm in Massachusetts. Birch suggests that job seekers look for small- and medium-sized but growing companies to work for since these are the companies that will be performing the work that the giant companies outsource. New technology, says Birch, enables the "gazelles," the innovative small companies, to compete with giant companies as never before. For example, a small business can now create a sophisticated database marketing system on a $1,400 personal computer that only IBM could have operated a few years ago.[10]

Many managers who had been with a large firm and were accustomed to working with numerous specialists may initially find themselves in a state of shock. In a small company, looking around for their sales force, they may find that *they* are the sales force. Looking for the department that puts out brochures, they may find that that, too, is their job.[11] After a period of adjustment to the idea of not having anyone to delegate to, working in such a setting can be extremely challenging and stimulating. You can feel proud and satisfied as you discover latent talents, handle unfamiliar tasks, and solve problems you've never encountered before.

Whether you are expecting to find a blue- or white-collar position, here is some advice as you're preparing for your future:

- In search of a new job, you need to understand yourself and what is important to you. You need to know that every work setting has a personality and every company or institution a set of values. Look for a job and an employer that offer a good match with your own values.[12]

- If you go to work for a big company or institution, don't expect to spend the rest of your life there.

- Don't be surprised if you find yourself reluctantly changing jobs several times in your career, particularly if you work in a troubled industry.[13]

- Open your mind to the possibility of working overseas or for a foreign company at home.

- Be open to the idea of working for a woman. Women are starting companies at 1.5 times the rate men are. Whereas in 1972, 0 percent of the workforce were employed by women, 10 percent to 12 percent are today.[14]

- Get as much education as you can. The future belongs to the knowledgeable worker, the master of everchanging skills and technology.[15]

- If you are already computer-knowledgeable, consider updating or advancing your expertise. Computer literacy is important to both blue- and white-collar workers in today's competitive workplace, and many jobs require fluency.

- Prepare yourself to work in small groups or on your own. The trend in virtually every workplace is to work in teams, although many will do a great deal of their work at home using personal computers and E-mail,[16] fax machines, and the like.

- Be open to becoming an entrepreneur. Talk over your ideas with someone who knows you well and appreciates your talents and skills. What special services or expertise can you provide? What kind of start-up money would you need and where would it come from? What advice can you get from people who are experienced in this type of business? What are the risks? What do you stand to gain? (See Appendix E for the toll-free numbers of the Small Business Administration and other agencies that offer advice.)

- Open yourself to the idea of telecommuting, as 5 percent of the U.S. workforce was doing by 1993, projected soon to be nearly 7 percent.[17] By substituting phone lines for traffic lanes, workers often enjoy less commuting, more time to do other activities, more time with family, and therefore less stress in general.[18]

- Consider self-employment, especially if you have the following attributes, as described by Sarah Edwards and Paul Edwards, authors of *Working from Home*:: (1) *Basic money management skills*: The ability to pay attention to and make sense of your finances; (2) *A marketing mindset*: The ability to make your business known to those who may need what you sell; (3) *Self-management skills*: The ability to self-start, stick to your work, and know when to stop; (4) *Time management skills*: The ability to recognize what is most important and prioritize accordingly; and (5) *Basic office management skills*: The ability to equip and organize your office so it runs efficiently.[19] Franchising a business, starting a home-based business, or opening up a consulting or subcontracting business might bring the new opportunities you're looking for. By consulting with the Small Business Administration and seeking other advice, you can decide whether such a venture is appropriate for you.

- Consider working for an organization that compensates its employees for receiving fewer traditional benefits by offering work-at-home arrangements, job share, and flexible scheduling to help employees balance work and family demands.[20]

- If you have been working for more than two or three decades, you may want to revamp your résumé to emphasize your most recent experience, says Robert Connor, author of *Cracking the Over-50 Job Market*. You can avoid giving the impression that you've been around forever by omitting mention of your earliest jobs and by never mentioning your age in job interviews, he advises.[21] Although it is illegal for potential employers to ask how old you are, many will still inquire. You can make age a nonissue by presenting yourself as an active, healthy, energetic person, comfortable with change and possessing up-to-date skills. Many customer service and sales jobs are available at older-worker-friendly companies such as Days

Inn of America and Staples, according to *Money* magazine, and promising positions are to be found in smaller companies where the experience that comes with age is often seen as a strength.[22] (See also Appendix F for "Resources for Finding Work" for persons over forty.)

- Make a decision to become more flexible, day by day. Open yourself to considering types of work that previously you may never have dreamed of doing. The people who are the most successful in life and the happiest are not rigid and unchangeable.

- Finally, while it is human to feel you deserve recognition for your hard work, you need to abolish any sense of entitlement, the feeling that anyone "owes you" because of all your education, knowledge, or experience. If you go into the next job feeling you deserve more money, special recognition, or whatever, you'll only be making it difficult for yourself to get along with others and succeed.

"The only security in a world where job security is gone is that your skills are better and your network richer at the end of this year than they were at the beginning," says business expert Tom Peters. It's important to improve your skills and make yourself more marketable, whether you are a teamster or a neurosurgeon.[23]

When a person thinks honestly about the new world of work, one does have to acknowledge that it is personally more satisfying to be rewarded for what one contributes to the organization than for simply showing up and staying with the same employer for many years. The new workplace can offer a wide-open world of opportunity: You will be rewarded for hard work, flexibility, openness to ongoing learning, and a willingness to develop new skills. And you can respect yourself more because you have accepted the challenge of truly contributing.

X

Traits of Those Who Triumph

Crises refine life. In them you discover what you are.

—ALLAN K. CHALMERS

In this chapter, various individuals who have suffered bitter struggles in regard to losing their jobs will show us how they were able not only to survive but to triumph. In more than twenty years of helping and studying grieving people, most recently people like you who have suffered the loss of employment, I've had the chance to learn about men and women who grow stronger in a personal crisis as well as those who are permanently broken. I've spent at least five years of my life interviewing people, teaching, reading, and studying—with the focus on identifying personality traits, attitudes and beliefs, decisions made, and actions taken by the people who triumph. I've worked hard to understand as much as possible about the healing process and those who successfully rebuild their lives, many after suffering anguishing losses.

Those who grow stronger at the broken places are the people I call "triumphant survivors."[1] In whatever way life has thrown them down—a loved one's death, a shattered love relationship or marriage, the loss of a dream, job, or financial security—triumphant survivors find a way to get on their feet again. Over time, they reevaluate and reorganize their lives, learn more about themselves and others, and deepen close relationships. Those who eventually prevail certainly suffer and struggle like everybody else. The grief and healing process doesn't come easily to anyone. But these survivors finally triumph, and in the process their lives usually become more fulfilling or productive.

Triumphant survivors learn to live with contradiction: They can feel disappointed and hopeful, depressed and hopeful, discouraged and hopeful. In fact, they seem to commit themselves to finding or creating something positive for the future even when little or nothing good has yet emerged from their suffering. In this chapter, you will meet a variety of such persons for whom job loss initially was devastating but who eventually prevailed.

PROACTIVE PEOPLE

There was a study of unemployed people who were hurting financially but doing well emotionally, and the conclusion was that unemployment can be a life-enhancing experience rather than a destructive one. Researchers Fryer and Payne found that what made the difference was how these people approached their job loss and whether they were able to use their unemployment time constructively. Those who were using this time in an exceptionally positive and creative way, rather than becoming depressed and alienated, had the following characteristics: (1) They had values that gave direction to their lives; (2) they had a desire to be active, regularly structured time for themselves, and vigorously engaged in purposeful, unpaid activity; (3) they saw unemployment as an opportunity for self-development and a chance to achieve certain desired goals; (4) they were highly motivated and willing to work hard to become reemployed; and (5) even though most had problems in some of their relationships, they found support from other people that helped them cope.[2]

These hardy folks were significantly deprived materially, but they did not fall victim to the severe ill effects of unemployment that have been described in this book. They avoided the problems from which many unemployed people suffer such as a disintegrating time structure, social isolation, identity crisis, purposelessness, and inactivity; instead they were able to perceive opportunities in their situation. What each of these well-functioning individuals possessed was the trait of proactivity: the characteristic of choosing to take the lead to bring about wanted changes. Rather than responding passively and allowing life to impose on them the need to revise their hopes and expectations downward, proactive people show a strong work ethic in unemployment: They establish their own tasks and projects and follow through. These people "are not mere pawns suffering the consequences of unemployment, they are agents causing things to happen."[3]

Proactive people are triumphant survivors. They listen to their own inner knowledge about what is still possible and work hard to get what they want. They also have a realistic view of the negatives of *employment*. They may remember, for example, how difficult it was to balance the arbitrary time structure at work against their personal needs and rhythms. They remember the hierarchical system and the autocratic supervision they had to contend with. They realize that much of their past activity was for unclear or unvalued ends and left them feeling empty. They know specifically how they disliked their job or how it imposed a limiting identity on them. By contrast, they are able to cherish (in unemployment) the opportunity to work for goals they themselves value.[4]

For most people unemployment brings about many psychological problems, but the extent to which you actively decide what your unemployment will mean to you plays a powerful role in determining how much distress you will feel. Despite any significant financial problems, you are the one who interprets your own situation and who decides whether your unemployment will be a waste of time or the opportunity of a lifetime.

You can confide in someone you trust and unburden yourself about how painful job loss is, explaining how betrayed, angry, hurt, or devastated you feel. You can describe in detail the awful tension and conflict at home, for instance, and say how unhappy everyone has been. Such sharing can promote healing. But things probably won't begin to improve until you accept responsibility for making the best of your situation. Keep asking yourself, "How can I use this period of unemployment (or unhappy reemployment) as an opportunity to improve the quality of my life?"

History is full of examples of people who have dramatically altered their lives, rising to a challenge to change with a level of activity and self-direction unlike anything they would have thought themselves capable of. You can create the best life within reach for yourself as well.[5]

OSCAR'S STORY: MOVING AHEAD IN SPITE OF SETBACKS AND FRUSTRATIONS

Perhaps you worry about your problems the way a dog gnaws on a bone. You may toss and turn, grind your teeth, ignore everything else, and hold on to whatever is bothering you—as if your worries were a cherished prize instead of something you'd really like to be rid of. In bed at night maybe you stare at the dark ceiling wanting so much to be able to relax and go back to sleep. You feel the tension in every part of your body.

When awake possibly you are disturbed by the continuing noise of worrisome thoughts and fears. Perhaps you imagine catastrophes and, in dwelling on the worst that could happen, remove yourself further from any feeling of optimism. You want so much to regain an attitude of calm. *Such troubling reactions to stress and feelings of anxiety are extremely common.*

Dealing with anxiety is similar to dealing with an addiction in that you must take one small step at a time, changing things slowly at first; dramatic change comes later.

Oscar, a big, strong man with a handlebar mustache, had a dangerous job in an industry where disabling injuries often occur. He was a "choke setter" for a logging company in Georgia. A choke setter is a guy who climbs on top of 75- or 100-foot pine trees that have just been felled and attaches a huge steel cable so a crane can pull each tree to the hilltop. The enormous felled trees lie helter-skelter, precariously balanced on top of each other like monstrous match sticks with branches. Nobody knows whether the trees have finished rolling down the steep slope—until the courageous choke setter climbs astride. Back, knee, and leg injuries happen frequently on these sharply shaped hillsides, and sometimes fatalities occur.

One day a fallen tree knocked Oscar down a forty-five-degree slope, severely injuring his back. After several surgeries and more than two years of physical therapy, Oscar had to face the fact that he would never again be able to work in the logging industry or in any other physically strenuous occupation. He had a high school diploma and had done nothing but timber work except for brief periods of running his own lawn service. But when Oscar tried to get help from Workers' Compensation, his interviewer wrote up a report saying that Oscar didn't need any services, that he had all the skills he needed to get a job on his own.

Oscar was poorly served by professionals a second time while he was receiving unemployment compensation. A counselor from a federal job-training program gave him poor advice about what to study at a local college. After a year of school, Oscar learned a fact his counselor should have known: He would be required to take another year of training—and the federal agency wouldn't pay for it.

Oscar was angry at having wasted a year in school and was anxious about his increasing financial problems. He began to have episodes of shortness of breath, heart palpitations, sweaty palms, trembling, dizziness, and pressure in his chest. Although he was still a young man—only thirty-eight years old—he was afraid that something was wrong with his heart and that he was going to die.

A family doctor wisely sent Oscar for an EKG, a stress test, and a psychiatric evaluation, which showed that his heart was strong but that Oscar was suffering from Panic Disorder, a highly treatable anxiety problem. He was put on medication and directed to another vocational counselor.

When he first started working with Michael, the new counselor, Oscar was leery of receiving more bad advice. Michael was in the same office building as the counselor who had cost him a year of lost time and federal benefits. It was difficult to walk back into that building every week. Sometimes Oscar felt so uncomfortable during a session with Michael that his anxiety symptoms would return. It took a choke setter's courage to continue, and especially to risk trusting another counselor.

Oscar's new counselor looked carefully at his background and recognized business management and "people contact" skills. The counselor suggested a management training program at a local community college with the goal of becoming a manager at a chain store. Oscar felt apprehensive about his future but helped himself by seeing a psychologist and taking prescribed medication for anxiety. Although it must have been difficult for him to study for a new career while doubting himself and feeling anxious, he did well in the business management program. As he was finishing the two-year course and nearing graduation, Oscar decided that he wanted to work for Wal-Mart. Michael called a dozen stores to find out about specific opportunities. Oscar began to prepare for his first interview.

Oscar didn't own a suit or dress shoes. His scraggly hair down to his shoulders, handlebar mustache, and burly appearance made him look like a Wild West character, somebody not to be tangled with. Michael suggested that Oscar make himself look more like the someday-store-manager he wanted to be, which he did before his first Wal-Mart interview. In fact, Michael didn't recognize him when Oscar dropped by the office unexpectedly. Clean-shaven and wearing a short haircut, dark suit and tie, and black shoes—Oscar looked the part of the manager's job he sought.

He wasn't out of the forest yet, however. Emotional reactions that give us trouble have a way of reappearing when we are facing change or challenge. Just weeks before graduation, with Wal-Mart interviews scheduled, Oscar discovered that he lacked two required courses. Once again he had received poor advice, this time from an ill-informed academic counselor at the college. With sweaty palms and heart palpitations, trembling with anger and worry, Oscar sat in Michael's office and told him of his dilemma. Michael immediately got on the phone to the highest authority he could reach at the college, and within twenty-four hours a college official approved Oscar's graduation. Oscar had done well to trust Michael as his advocate, and his anxiety was calmed.

Some of Oscar's anxiety symptoms returned another time. Relocation was necessary for Wal-Mart management trainees, but at the interview Oscar told the personnel officer that he was close to his grown children and didn't want to move away from Georgia. Under these circumstances, Wal-Mart was not willing to hire him. Michael, realizing that Oscar was about to sabotage an excellent career opportunity, walked him through the apprehension of starting a whole new life in strange-feeling clothes. Oscar then was able to contact Wal-Mart and say that relocation would not be a problem.

Although Oscar had to start with an entry-level position, Wal-Mart soon sent him to various management training schools. He has since been promoted several times. The former logger finally tied a strong, secure cable around the future he wanted, despite the emotional risks of having to develop new strengths and bring out new dimensions of his personality.

Like many people injured on the job and other displaced workers, Oscar was victimized first by the events surrounding his job loss and again by "the system" which initially failed him. Determined to keep on trying regardless of setbacks and frustrations, Oscar helped himself by persisting until he got the professional help he needed. He had the courage to keep searching for solutions. Oscar had good reason to blame others but he was able to move beyond blame. He accepted the responsibility for rebuilding his own life.

ALAN W.: THE HEALING POWER OF MAKING A CONTRIBUTION

Alan W. is one of the many students I've had the pleasure of teaching at Essex Community College in Baltimore. When I first met him he was pretty angry and bitter because he had been forced into early retirement at age fifty-five. In fact, Alan had signed up for a weekend workshop I was presenting on dealing with anger in response to personal crisis. An elementary school teacher for twenty-five years, Alan had had an unresolvable conflict with a principal who was on his first assignment and who seemed arbitrary in his dealings with Alan. The principal had ordered him to reconstruct from memory all of his students' grades from a lost record book, something Alan considered unreasonable and extremely time-consuming. The principal wouldn't budge, so Alan retired. Retiring early cost him about a third of his pension, and he was too young to receive Social Security. He did, fortunately, receive rental income from a property he owned. He also did some substitute teaching at a different school.

Alan suffered the loss of his mother that same year. For the first six months he spent a lot of time alone. After that, however, as he said, "I just began to grow again. I'm a social person and I knew I had to have more time with people."

Divorced, he was the president of a singles group where he met a woman and enjoyed a romance that blossomed for a while. His only child, a daughter from whom he'd been estranged, came back to see him, bringing her husband and a baby, Alan's only grandchild. He rebuilt the relationship with his daughter, got on well with his son-in-law, and loved his grandson. All of these relationships helped to counterbalance the loss of a very important relationship in his life—that of being a teacher to his students.

Another experience that helped Alan was volunteering for a telephone service for troubled people. He trained as a listener and in one year spoke with twelve people who were contemplating suicide. He also listened to others' problems with alcohol, drugs, marriage, and children. Gradually, he said, "I realized how lucky I was in a lot of ways."

One year after being forced to retire, Alan started volunteering at a local hospital. There he worked with patients for ten years, "doing everything but windows," two days a week. His jobs included running errands, picking up specimens, stocking supplies, taking food to patients, and visiting patients. Meanwhile, his own life turned from an inward, downward spiral to a rewarding life that focused outward.

Alan's advice to others facing an unwanted retirement is given without hesitation: "Stay busy. Find something outside of your home and get occupied. Don't stay home and watch television and feel sorry for yourself. Go out. You are needed out there by a lot of different social organizations and there's got to be some place where you would love to be working."

Alan explained with satisfaction that he had received a lapel pin for 4,000 hours of volunteer work at the hospital. Wearing the gold pin with the number 4,000 on it on his white lab coat made him feel "prouder than of anything else I've received." There was as much personal fulfillment in volunteering, he realized, as in his teaching accomplishments, even though his only remuneration was $3 toward his lunch and free parking.

"If you go out there and find something you can help somebody else with, it'll make you feel better about yourself and probably prolong your life," said Alan, describing himself as "one of the happiest people I know."

Studying people who triumph, I have often seen this trait of "finding oneself by losing oneself" in the service of others, to put it biblically. In many persons recovering from job loss, volunteering or mentoring was substantially beneficial: They increased their self-respect and confidence, learned skills, and often found new jobs.

Consider where and how you might contribute something worthwhile by building volunteer time into your weekly schedule. Helping people whose needs are greater than or different from your own can also be an excellent way to work through leftover workplace resentments, as it was for Alan. Life is too short for any of us to waste the precious time that we have.

JANICE GUTHRIE: WANTING OTHERS TO BENEFIT FROM YOUR MISFORTUNE

Suffering is intolerable when it has no meaning or redeeming quality. A theme I have seen repeatedly in many years of working with people in crisis is this psychological necessity to create something good out of troubles and sorrows.

Jan Guthrie was a thirty-nine-year-old administrator at the University of Arkansas at Little Rock when she discovered that she had a rare form of ovarian cancer. Already recovering from one major surgery, she learned that she would need a second surgery. Believing that she couldn't do justice to her job and still take care of her health, Jan resigned her position.[6]

While recuperating, Jan read a manual for job hunters and career changers, Richard Bolles's *What Color Is Your Parachute?* The book provides a lot of good advice, a list of valuable resources, and many helpful exercises. Working through the entire book, Jan realized she now would need a home-based job and that she loved to do research.

Meanwhile, Jan had fully researched her own medical condition. She read everything she could find on her type of cancer, and as a result, along with her husband, she made informed choices about the direction of her treatment. She opted for a second surgery rather than radiation therapy. Jan eventually found that her extensive research had kept her alive and enhanced the quality of her life. She also realized that the time she had to live might be limited and that she wanted the chance to do something to help other people—so why not create a business that would give other victims of disease and injury the chance to play an intelligent role in their own treatment?

In 1984 Jan formed a company which she named The Health Resource, Inc. For a fee of $295 she and her staff conduct individualized, in-depth research on a specific diagnosis of cancer—searching a broad range of databases—and she charges $195 for research on conditions other than cancer. She then issues a report of 50 to 250 pages, depending on the amount of relevant information available. For those who want to learn about alternative treatments as well as conventional medicine, she offers a full rundown on the available therapies.

It was three years before Jan's home-based business kept her busy full-time and broke even financially. A sign above her desk reads "Persistence. Persistence. Persistence." She saw the process of building a successful business as "a numbers game." If she had to call on a hundred physicians to get five to display her brochure, then she did it. It wasn't easy to experience the frequent rejections, but she made a conscious effort to remain goal-oriented and not take rejections personally. When she considered the negative physician responses she was getting in Arkansas, Jan thought about where she might get a better response. She advertised nationally, especially on the West and East Coasts, and the work started coming in.

What kept her going was knowing that she had a good idea, that the research had worked for her, and that her reports had similarly empowered many others. Her husband's good listening skills and emotional support were very important, as was his carrying the breadwinning role. After five years, The Health Resource, Inc., was financially successful, and Jan operated the business alone for two more years. Now she has three full-time and eight part-time employees. Jan's company, according to *Nation's Business* magazine, "is one of a mere handful of organizations devoted to helping patients meet their doctors on something like even terms."[7]

In the ten years that The Health Resource, Inc., has been in business, Jan has seen a major change in physicians' attitudes. Many doctors use her service now and she believes that increasingly they will become more computer literate and make greater use of the databases themselves. Jan knows that an irreversible trend is underway among patients: "They want to be empowered, they want to be participants with their physicians."

Jan helped herself through two major events: a life-threatening illness and the loss of a meaningful job she had held for three years.

Although she has had seven surgeries, each of them requiring about six weeks of recuperation, Jan says, "I have a great quality of life. My research has literally kept me alive." When she speaks to school groups, Jan likes to tell young people to listen to their dreams and find work that they really enjoy doing. She has done that with her own life.

You also can experience the satisfaction of finding new meaning and purpose in life. Instead of constantly feeling that you are reacting to the frustrations and challenges of unemployment, you can reframe your situation and think of it as an opportunity to make a contribution somehow. Ask yourself: "What if I had a limited time to live? How would I want to spend the rest of my life? What have I learned from my problems and struggles, and how can I use this knowledge in a way that will benefit others?"

PAUL BURTON: "I DON'T KNOW WHAT IT'S LIKE TO SIT ALONE"

A former salesman in New Mexico struggled for several months with fantasies of shooting the man who fired him. "It's not the firing that caused those fantasies," reflected Paul Burton. "It's the degradation and belittlement I've had to go through in order to survive." Applying for food stamps, Burton explained, "was probably the most degrading thing I've ever done. When I left there, I was crying." What helped him get through those awful times of depression and anger was literally getting down on his knees in prayer and also talking over with his wife "the lust for revenge," an emotion so foreign to what he believed in.

He decided to move with his family from his small town in New Mexico to start a new life in the state of Washington. Burton told Rick Lamplugh that he got by for a time taking jobs "equivalent to selling apples on the corner in the Great Depression." Just trying to bring in some money, he sold wholesale jewelry and keychains on the street. Now Burton works in a food store as a plainclothes security guard whose job is catching shoplifters. He calls it "thumping people," implying a kind of guilt he feels over getting people arrested for stealing food. Burton earns a minimum wage while looking for a job that will pay more and carry benefits.

Helping out in a Cub Scout group lifts his spirits, as do other service activities he performs for his church. His Mormon faith has taught him to be responsible for others, and Burton finds that when he gets involved in other people's problems, he can forget about his own. Burton also believes that "what goes around comes around" and that something good will come from both his struggles and from helping others.

He and his wife seem to take turns being the person with a positive attitude, encouraging one another. "Someday I'll look back on these hard times," he says, "and be thankful for what has happened. Job loss has taught me some humility."

Burton and his wife are very close and have a good relationship. As soon as he was fired, he went home and said, "Honey, *we're* out of work." This feeling of being in a tough situation but being in it together with loved ones and other helpers is a common theme heard in people who prevail. No matter how bad things get, Burton says that his wife doesn't forget the positives of life, health, family, and food on the shelf. Burton also describes himself as dearly loving his children. "Whenever I sit at home at night," he says, "I always have kids on my lap or at my side. I don't know what it's like to sit alone."

His Mormon church family, too, provides a support network. "Wherever you go [as a church member] you have immediate friends," Burton explains. Prior to the move from New Mexico to Washington, Burton took a trip to the new location and spoke with several Mormon "brothers." Weeks later, when the family arrived with all of their belongings, six people were waiting to help them unload their truck. The Mormon church also helped the family pay for the move. "It's the church's philosophy," says Burton, "that we look out for and help each other."

Whether you connect yourself to positive thinking family members or surrogate family in the form of friends, caring people at your church or synagogue, a support group like Alcoholics Anonymous or Parents Anonymous, a family counselor, or an individual therapist—that feeling of being supported by a family of some kind is essential to healing.

ANGIE ROBERTS: HUMOR, FAMILY SUPPORT, AND "MOXIE"

By the age of twenty-nine, only eight years after starting out as a nurse, Angie Roberts had an M.B.A., an expensive sports car, a corner office, and the position of marketing vice-president reporting to the chief executive officer of a hospital system in Reno, Nevada. She assumed she would always have a job in health care, because people would always get sick. Then a layoff from her fast-track position in Reno, followed by another layoff from a similar position in Portland, Oregon, shattered such assumptions. "I crashed and burned at age thirty-nine," said Angie. "The American Dream wasn't there for me anymore."

Four weeks before losing the second job, Angie was operated on for a herniated disc and a tumor which had wrapped itself around two vertebrae and her spine. She was recuperating at home in a full-body cast and still unable to drive when she was called in for a meeting at work. It was awkward trying to get around, but she went. "Let me guess, you're not promoting me," Angie quipped, minutes before being told that she and about 200 others would lose their jobs. Angie's sense of humor—which has played an important and constant role in maintaining her survival and sustaining her courage—was amazingly present even on that day.

Life had already been hitting her hard. The tumor on Angie's spine was found much later than it should have been. Although she had had the best possible health insurance and a professional knowledge of how the health care system works, she was poorly served by a series of ill-advised physician referrals and medical misdiagnoses. It was disillusioning for her as a former nurse to experience incompetence in medical management and to be entrusted to nurses whom she saw as having "frightfully inadequate skills." While in much physical pain, she was also facing the likelihood of having some permanent disability.

There was also the problem of Angie's mother, who had come from out of town during Angie's early period of recuperation from surgery. Angie describes her as "a woman who lives her entire life on the basis of 'What will the neighbors think?'" Explained Angie, "My mother, who was not very loving toward me, had jumped on an airplane just to be able to tell the people back home that she rushed to my side in a time of great need."

Angie, who is in a permanent love relationship with another woman and had carefully kept her private life a secret from her mother for many years, took privacy precautions before her mother's arrival. Unfortunately, her mother searched her home and eventually found a loving get-well card from Susan. She didn't say anything until the day she went home. "You've delivered me a blow that even I can't handle," said Angie's mother. "Let's just say it's out of the closet, and those are words you should understand!"

It hurts Angie that she has not heard from her mother in two years. Her relationship with her mother had been tumultuous for a long time, but the rejection was still difficult to bear. Sadly, a relationship with a sister who was previously close also became strained.

"I don't know what I'd have done without Susan," says Angie, recalling how she coped. Fate had inflicted a series of devastating blows—a disabling illness, surgery, job loss, family rejection, and chronic pain. "The mind does all sorts of things and you're sure you're going to be in that same awful place of suffering all your life," Angie told me. A person needs someone who will say, "This will all pass. Everything changes." Fortunately for Angie, her companion Susan, a psychotherapist, provided that perspective and was warmly supportive.

Susan's parents, too, were kind and gracious with Angie. They included her in family activities and holiday gatherings, and when they telephoned Susan, it meant a lot that they always took time to speak to Angie too. Their warmth and acts of kindness helped offset the rejection of her own mother and sister and did much to strengthen Angie.

Although Susan had a demanding full-time job, she helped Angie while the latter was incapacitated. "I can't recall a time when Susan got angry with me," Angie says. "I needed someone to help me with the basic things of life: I couldn't get up from a chair alone; I couldn't bend. Susan was a lifesaver."

Unlike so many partners or family members who "catch" the unemployed person's depression and other symptoms, Susan didn't pick up any of Angie's symptoms. She dealt with the demands of work and Angie's temporary dependency by continuing to take good care of herself. An insulin-dependent diabetic, Susan had to develop good health habits, including exercise and diet. While helping to care for Angie, she did not deviate from her own regimen. It's an important lesson: You can maintain greater patience and sustain the ability to be giving when you take the time to care well for yourself.

A recovering alcoholic for more than three years, Angie was also an active Alcoholics Anonymous member. There is a tremendous mutual support between members at AA that enables them to think of people other than themselves.

Another outlet for Angie was her sense of humor. "If you can laugh at something, at its absurdity," she says, "that's a way of knowing that the pain it's causing you will end." Angie made a point of speaking daily with her seventy-year-old AA sponsor, a woman with a wonderful sense of humor who had been sober for many years. The sponsor had the ability to give Angie those good belly laughs that provide the same release as crying. Angie also watched funny movies as a way to lighten up. And she told jokes to Susan and made an effort to see how silly some things are in life.

The most strengthening family support she received was from Susan. As in many nontraditional relationships (heterosexual and homosexual), Angie and Susan had an egalitarian approach to solving problems, each with an equal say in the discussions and decisions. When there are no rigidly defined roles in a relationship, basic choices can be made without tension and the burden of responsibility is not placed on the shoulders of one partner.

Angie and Susan discussed their various options and what each was willing to do to accommodate the other. Each was willing to relocate, if necessary. Partners who respect each other usually fare pretty well when facing the crisis of one partner's unemployment. Ultimately, the two decided to stay in Portland where Susan's career was well established and where the couple had the financial connections to undertake an entrepreneurial venture together.

At this turning point in her life, Angie kept focusing on an idea she wanted to pursue. Angie had read my last book, *Coming Back* and found herself almost crying as she read about people who had rebuilt their lives after crisis or loss. Angie was inspired whenever she recognized resilience in a person, the ability to endure, and an absolute refusal to give up—a wisdom about life emphasized also at AA meetings.

Angie decided to open a business where people recovering from physical or emotional injury could gain courage, find inspiration, and receive support, and where loved ones could learn how best to provide help. The store would offer reading materials, greeting cards, instructional and musical tapes and CDs, and works of art. It would also consign artists whose works portrayed courage and hope. As bespeaks her ongoing sense of humor, Angie named the store Comebacks R Us.

To Angie, Comebacks R Us is more than the name of a "books and gifts" store; it is the story of her own job loss and healing. Because of the caring support of Susan, Susan's parents, and her friends at AA, and because of knowledge gained through inspirational readings, Angie is moving forward again and finding her life rewarding.

In making a comeback, you also may need to broaden your concept of family support so the persons willing and able to offer encouragement or assistance become the people you think of as family. Some of your own close relatives simply may be unable to do anything but hurt you with unkind comments or value judgments in your time of vulnerability. In almost every family there lives at least one person who has perfected the ability to blame, belittle, ignore, or otherwise inflict injury. In such cases, make every effort to avoid those family members who would make your healing process more difficult, or at least significantly control the amount of time you spend with them. While the wounds heal in any personal crisis, you can draw strength—as Angie did—from those who know how to take care of themselves yet are compassionate, tolerant, and kind in their dealings with you.

Sabrina Nickerson: "You Have to Convince Yourself That You Can Do Anything"

Sabrina Nickerson is thirty-seven years old. She has been a prelaw student, a secretary, a cashier, a successful laborer in the decidedly male occupation of copper mining, a self-employed landscaper, and after attending truck-driving school, she spent several years driving eighty-foot double trailers across the country between Los Angeles and New York.

She is five feet tall and weighs just 105 pounds, but she has a lot of spirit and spunk. A few years ago, after a truck-driving business partnership had dissolved, she found herself out of work again. When a male friend with a tow truck told her that a person could always put bread on the table if he owned a tow truck, she decided to start her own business—All Ways Towing and Repair, in Tucson, Arizona.

"I've never been motivated by women's lib," she told *Parade* magazine. "I do this for survival. Men's jobs pay better. And I don't feel happy working indoors."[8]

After Sabrina used her savings to buy a tow truck, she was self-employed again but without any business. Initially she had a hard time trying to compete in an industry dominated by men. "It was really kind of humiliating," she recalled. When she went around to talk to people about getting towing work, they would answer her questions, but with a smirk. For about a year, the only work she found was at the bottom of the towing barrel, which was moving wrecks for salvage yards.

Somewhere along the way Sabrina had learned a coping technique that in psychology we call "reframing events," an approach to teasing, rejection, and frustration that has come in handy. Instead of getting angry at those who would smirk and refuse to offer a woman work, she realized that they might have an ego problem. "We're all in this life together," she explained, "and if some men weren't so threatened, they could have a woman who could help them."

Instead of focusing on what others think of a lady tow truck operator, she remembers that the real issue is to keep the truck going. Hence, when a man remarks about what a cute little thing she is and says that she ought to quit towing and get married, Sabrina has learned to joke back.

Her mother encouraged Sabrina years ago to believe that she could do anything she set her mind to. "She had a hard, hard life," says Sabrina of her mother, "but she stood up for herself and lived a nonconventional life in a time when it was much more unacceptable to be an independent-thinking and -acting woman."

When business is tough, Sabrina imagines the way she wants things to be. Thinking positively instead of negatively is a key aspect of survival. She helps herself in this regard by associating with friends and relatives who approach life constructively and who encourage her. She keeps away from people who are not supportive and those with "bad habits," such as drugs, excessive alcohol, and fighting. Sabrina has at least five long-term close friends. She has a warm relationship with her mother and with an aunt who has helped her financially and provided good business advice and encouragement.

"I've learned that you never quit," she says, looking at a successful business that is expanding. She has a second truck and has carefully chosen two more drivers. "I quit college before I made it to law school and regret it. I left the truck-driving partnership when we were just starting to make some decent money. Now I've learned not to quit this business."

Sabrina has an attitude of cooperation and an openness to support from others. Yet it is mostly her independent spirit that keeps her going.

There's a certain mental toughness required of men and women alike, people who are learning to convince themselves of what is possible. What you can learn from Sabrina Nickerson as you work to rebuild your life is how to stay focused. It's important, for example, to reframe events so that the negative individuals in your life will not have the power to defeat you. Look behind the words of those who would disparage or discourage you, and become aware of their psychological problems, vulnerabilities, or blinders. Remember that their words of criticism and negativity say much about themselves and little about you.

Stay focused on your goals. As Sabrina Nickerson would say, "You must never give up!" Even if you are small or gentle, you can be strong. Find the supportive people you need to associate with to further the quality of life that you yearn for, and methodically avoid those who are negative or self-destructive. Take pride in whatever work you do and pursue it with dignity and integrity.

TRAITS OF THOSE WHO TRIUMPH

Survivors of job loss have a lot of characteristics in common that are described throughout this book in addition to those mentioned here. You may want to record in a journal the traits that appear in this chapter and elsewhere. Although no single person is blessed with all of these personal characteristics or is capable of every positive attitude, triumphant survivors have many of these qualities:

- They work through the pain. They don't try to bury their troublesome feelings, but rather they acknowledge their anger, sadness, regret, and any sense of betrayal. They find emotional release by writing in a journal, talking with a confidant, or engaging in creative or physical activity.
- They can embrace life's opposites, know both joy and sorrow, and hold fast to hope even while experiencing devastating circumstances.
- They try to make sense of the events that have occurred, asking: "Why did this happen?" or "What changes in society and

at work do I need to understand?" even if there are no easy answers.

- Over time, after working through feelings and explanations, they clarify how the loss has permanently changed their life, how they view themselves, and what opportunities or benefits might result.
- They stay busy, through purposeful activity and meaningful daily routine. They do not allow their time structure to disintegrate, but rather assign themselves tasks and complete them, often enjoying unemployment as much as or more than being employed.
- They are "proactive": They *make* things happen rather than wait for things to happen.
- They have the courage to ask for help from family, friends, professionals, support groups, and agencies.
- They establish realistic goals and take small attainable steps each day to reach those goals.
- They live one day at a time, focusing primarily on that day's tasks and concerns, neither idealizing the past nor catastrophizing the future.
- While not discounting their own pain or personal problems, they repeatedly make an effort to place events into perspective: Job loss and its accompanying ills are difficult to deal with, but they know that many other people suffer in far greater ways.
- They are thankful for all that is still good in their lives.
- They find encouragement wherever it may be found: people, books, events, anything that can teach them something of value. They open themselves to serendipitous encounters. They expect good things to happen and remain receptive.
- They shift gears and change the direction in which they're moving as they get reliable new information regarding the best destination.
- They recognize and seize an opportunity that presents itself even if it's not the opportunity they were seeking.
- They listen to advice and act on it when it's wise.
- They are willing to put time and effort into activities that many people avoid—such as working through personal and family problems, becoming healthier through physical activity, ag-

gressively pursuing their job search, and obtaining additional education or developing new skills.

- They imagine the future in positive ways. They look ahead six months, a year, five, ten, and vividly imagine where they want to be then.
- They believe in hard work and personal integrity and usually commit themselves to higher values such as a belief in God or to humanitarian concerns.
- They have the courage to change. As frightening as it may be to try new things, they are willing to learn new skills and attitudes for a new work environment.
- They search for meaning in adversity, looking for ways to turn suffering and struggle into something of lasting benefit to themselves and others.
- They find ways to "lighten up" by sharing in fun or silly activities with children or grandchildren, watching humorous movies, collecting and sharing funny stories, clowning around, seeing the absurdities in serious events and learning to laugh at them.
- They have developed a self-care plan that gives them the energy and persistence necessary to search for a new job.
- They *want* to see their job loss as an opportunity to develop a better life and a brighter future. They associate themselves with optimistic, positive people and avoid the doomsayers.
- When circumstances assume crisis proportions, they develop strategies for coping with the stress and solving specific problems. They are proud that they can prevail in adversity.
- They are grateful to the people who help and the new opportunities that emerge. They come to appreciate the resilience of the human spirit and often are among those to whom it comes very naturally to be thankful for healing.

The bottom line is that while acknowledging that life is often unfair, people who triumph in the aftermath of job loss and other difficulties accept responsibility for making themselves happy. As Jesse Jackson has said: "It may not be your fault that you've been knocked down, but it's your fault if you don't get up again."[9]

XI

Reevaluating Your Life

Until you make peace with who you are,
you'll never be content with what you have.

—DORIS MORTMAN

For many people the ordeal of job loss becomes a blessing in disguise. Even if you loved your last job, your present situation can become an opportunity to reevaluate your life and make important changes while there is still time. You can set a chain of circumstances into play that will improve the rest of your life.

Often work conditions at the lost job were anything but satisfying. You may have grown accustomed to insufficient challenge, boring or tedious tasks, overdemanding bosses, unreasonable production expectations, low pay, high stress, or other unpleasant or even dangerous conditions. You may have been forced to compromise your integrity or go against your values in the last job just to survive. Prejudice, acts of discrimination or harassment because of sex, race, age, religion, disability, or sexual orientation may have been apparent, yet difficult to combat. Perhaps the job you left was emotionally uncomfortable because of personality conflicts, deadlines, or inadequate personal time. Maybe the job was physically uncomfortable because of long hours, poor lighting, inappropriate temperature, loud noise, or too much time on your feet. Quite possibly you wouldn't have left this job on your own initiative but, having been forced to leave, you feel relieved.

Crisis experiences have a way of breaking up patterns of behavior that have been limiting a person's development. Often new opportunities are presented that lead many survivors of job loss, illness, and other disruptive events to reorganize their lives in a constructive way, grow in self-understanding and empathy for others, and deepen their relationships.[1]

The time that has been made available to you right now can provide a rich opportunity for reevaluating your life. Surely this book can help you deal with the immediate problems of coping with unemployment, grieving, and finding successful reemployment. But even more important is the rest of your life and the choices you may need to make in order to be happier.

ED DREXEL: "I KNEW I WASN'T SMELLING THE FLOWERS"

Ed Drexel's story is like that of millions of others who have personified the American Dream: A person without a college degree works hard for years and eventually makes a good living, acquires a house and a couple of cars, proudly counts himself as an industrious and prosperous member of the middle class—all so that he and his wife can send their own children to college.

Ed had worked ten years in car sales when he was promoted into management. As business manager, he was in charge of the bank loan process and also sold insurance on customer contracts. It bothered him that the interest rate was negotiable, that the knowledgeable person would receive a better rate than somebody with less education and a lower income. "It went against my nature," he remembered,. "to take advantage of people." He went back to sales, taking a sales manager's position at another dealership. He gave up a job with three weeks of vacation only to lose the new position four months later. After he had trained a family member of the owner, the boss said, "You're not fired—I just don't need you anymore."

Four days later Ed had another sales manager's job. He was thirty-four years old, making $25,000 a year, but he felt he should be making more. So he went to a different dealer as a salesman, and a few years later he was a manager again. Soon he was making $60,000 to $90,000 a year selling luxury cars and driving one home every night.

There were constant financial pressures and temptations not to be ethical. "For so many years people sold cars by bargaining and negotiating—like horse trading—because the auto business came out of the horse and carriage business," Ed explained. He tried to be fair as a negotiator—trying to get the best price but not cheating the customers. What bothered his conscience was something else. He was almost never home. He was making very good money but working fifty to sixty hours a week. He had to beg and bargain for his two weeks of vacation every year, and he was allowed only three holidays. He was almost never able to attend his children's school functions or share in family gatherings. Labor Day, Fourth of July, and Memorial Day were big days for auto sales. Still, he had three children and a wife working part-time, and there was a lot of money to be saved for twelve years of college.

A turning point came a few years before Ed was finally fired for the last time. In the showroom one day a local radio station was playing "Cat's in the Cradle," a soulful tune by Harry Chapin about a father and an estranged son. Ed started crying. He left the building for some fresh air, thinking about the time he had already missed with his two teenage daughters and the time he was missing now with his young son.

There was something else that made him wonder how long he wanted to stay in the auto business. In a field where a salesman had to be a topnotch producer to get respect, he had seen how the older men were often disparaged by the younger, sharper managers. Ed, in his early forties, began to ask himself what else he could do for a living.

Like a raccoon taking an untimely stroll on a suddenly warm December day, soon to return to her den, sometimes our human yearnings creep out and rather quickly go back into hiding. Carrying the human part of the analogy a bit further, it's awfully hard to walk away from a nice warm haven, safe and secure, when there's plenty of money coming in to keep things cozy.

But in 1991 when he was abruptly fired and replaced with a manager ten years younger who would be making $10,000 a year less, Ed knew that he was ready for a major change. With all of his experience, he knew he could get a managerial job elsewhere, but he realized that after nineteen years in the auto business, he was getting burned out. Also gnawing on him was the time he wasn't spending with his family. He just didn't want to do that anymore. "I knew I wasn't smelling the flowers," Ed told me.

The Drexels had wisely put away some "rainy day" money over the years. In two decades the couple had seen a lot of car salesmen, managers, and their families go into financial free-fall; hence they hadn't bought a more expensive house when they could have done so. And Mrs. Drexel immediately got a full-time job with family medical benefits.

The grief process is virtually inevitable in response to job loss regardless of an individual's or family's ability to absorb the blow financially. As would be expected, Ed felt depressed and angry, doubted himself, worried about making money again, and lost sleep over the impending expense of two daughters going to college. There were numerous conflicts within the family as everyone tried in his or her own way to handle the many changes wrought by the stress.

Fortunately for everyone, there was a voice in Ed's head that embraced the change. "I knew the Lord wouldn't let me down," Ed told me. "This was going to work out for the best in some shape or form. Father-son, husband-wife, father-daughters—I knew that somehow our lives would improve."

After several detours and travels over some rugged terrain, the family got into counseling with a certified social worker who had a sliding fee scale and charged them only $20 per session. The Drexels found these therapy sessions extremely helpful. Ed successfully resisted both his own internal and many external pressures to get a "quick fix" next job. He did a great deal of soul-searching and investigating and decided on the new career path of becoming a financial consultant with a large, well-known, national insurance company. He took a training course and completed a series of self-study programs. Ed was working sixty-hour weeks again to do the necessary studying, but he did a lot of it late at night because right after the job loss he had started sharing more activities with his son. They played ball, watched TV and ate popcorn together, and Ed drove his son to school every day.

After passing some challenging exams, Ed felt knowledgeable enough to call on potential clients. "They tell you in the insurance business to call 100 people you know and sell to them," Ed explained, "but I didn't want to expose my friends and relatives to someone who wasn't an expert, so I had to become an expert." He is currently working forty-five hours a week but says it feels like a part-time job because now he has the pleasure of coaching his son's basketball and baseball teams, escorting him to sports events, and having many more dinners with the family.

What Ed cherishes most about his new life is being able to take off virtually whenever he feels like it, since he controls his own schedule. With a stronger presence at home and a greater role as a decision maker, he also has more self-respect, although there is still more conflict among family members than when he was often absent and everyone was accustomed to his wife making all the decisions.

Ed knew that it would be tough starting out in a new career, and it was, but in the second year all his studying and other hard work paid off and his income rose significantly. His income is comparable now to what he was making before. "I just want to be successful without being greedy," he says. "I earn these dollars for financial security; I'm not into making money for show."

His goals are eventually to complete the requirements for becoming a certified financial planner and to get his wife back to running the house. Being more present in the family as a loving father and husband is something he continues to care about and work on, but I think he sees himself as light years from where he was when working in the automobile industry.

Ed also has gained a wonderful perspective on his years in the auto industry. He feels no animosity toward the automobile business but rather is thankful that, given his level of formal education—only two years of college—it provided the level of income over the years that it did.

You also can feel good about your work in fulfillment of your own version of the American Dream, especially if you've tried to live in an ethical way as Ed has described. Despite the fact that your livelihood was taken from you prematurely or regardless of whether you were treated poorly when laid off or fired—if it fed your family or was a ticket into prosperity, you can be thankful that you had that job and income for as long as you did.

Now that you are unemployed or temporarily employed, you can use this time to reevaluate your personal values, the relationships that matter most to you, and your priorities and dreams.

In particular, look carefully at your close family relationships, as Ed did, and ask yourself what regrets you may be burdened with for the rest of your life unless you change some things now. Are you yearning for more time with loved ones or wanting to compensate for certain mistakes in the past?

IMBALANCED LIVES

There is a strong undercurrent in North America today of people being unhappy with their work life. In a recent Roper Organization survey, only 18 percent of Americans said they felt their careers were personally and financially rewarding. In another survey, half of the respondents said they would sacrifice a day's pay for an extra day off each week. Among those earning $30,000 a year or more, 70 percent said they would be willing to exchange one-fifth of their income for more time with family and friends.[2]

While you are out of work, you have the perfect opportunity to think about how to pursue a career that would be more rewarding and one that would give you the time away from work which so many workers say they want.

Many of us find that our lives are out of balance. Sometimes it takes a crisis to force us into new realizations and a redirection of our lives. Therapist Robert Pasick says that men, especially, often drift along through life, out of touch with their inner feelings. Pasick says that men frequently "drive themselves like cars without tune-ups or tire changes until they start using beer for oil or need a major valve job performed by a highly paid cardiologist."[3]

If you are a man, one of the most beneficial mental exercises you can do is to write a paragraph in a journal about the relationship that you had (or lacked) with your father, and then write a second paragraph about how you want things to be the same or different with your own children. Also examine in a paragraph what was positive and negative about your parents' marriage and how you want to be similar or different from your father in your love relationship or marriage. What was your father's approach to the often competing best interests of career and family? How might you resolve such conflicts in a more satisfying way?

Peter Drucker, speaking of a need to create second careers, describes three men who started life all over again: a forty-five-year-old market researcher, a college professor, and an officer in the armed forces for twenty years. Initially the men felt spent, despite the fact that mentally, biologically, and physically they were sound. Scared out of their wits when they began their new jobs, six months later they were working in new ways and feeling twenty years younger. Each of these men had recovered their enthusiasm, were growing, and had new ideas. Their wives were enchanted and the men were excited about life again.[4]

Whether you are male or female, married or single, have children, grandchildren, or no children, you probably can benefit from asking yourself what would make you feel younger and more excited about life as eventually you settle in with a new job. Try to be patient with yourself when you feel anxious or fatigued, and focus on the goal of finding a way to have a satisfying personal life while making a living. Reflecting on the life your parents had, be clear in your mind about how you want your own life to be by comparison and in contrast.

DOUG SWEENY: "YOU HAVE TO MAKE IT POSSIBLE FOR YOURSELF TO THINK IN NEW WAYS"

For a long time, Doug was a gardener for a wealthy family. Then he worked awhile with retarded children. After that, he spent ten years working at a high school for troubled youth, trying to keep high-risk teenagers in school, in part-time jobs, and out of jail. This was a tough assignment, since many of Doug's clients and their parents were former felons and ex-drug abusers, but he was excellent at working with these families.

Unfortunately, there was a great deal of paperwork to his job, something he hated, but documentation was important to Doug's bosses because they constantly had to justify the monies they were getting from the school system and the state. Doug's supervisor said his paperwork was never up to speed, a "nightmare," and finally got exasperated with him when he made no significant effort to change. Doug was forty-eight years old and was also going through a divorce when he was fired.

"But I was burned out long before I lost my job," Doug told Rick Lamplugh. With many people who are fired or laid off, a reevaluation process has already been going on, either consciously or unconsciously, by the time the change is forced upon them. Perhaps Doug had passingly considered the consequences of not getting his files in order. Perhaps not. At any rate, even though he was extremely talented at working with young people nobody else could work with, there are many failure experiences in such an occupation and Doug was ready to leave.

Doug said goodbye to his own children for a while, leaving them with their mother in his hometown of Corvallis, Oregon, and he drove out to the coast to take some time for reflection. He took some books, a stack of self-stick note pads, some pens to write with, and his station wagon to sleep in—not because he had no other place to sleep but because this was where he did his best thinking. The central Oregon coast has sandy beaches and sandstone cliffs, rocky tide pools with driftwood everywhere, and wonderful sea life. It's a setting that a contented person would find to be a great place of beauty, and where a person who is hurting would go to heal. Doug planned to spend three days there but ended up staying three weeks.[5]

Ordinarily a physically strong man, a multisport athlete accustomed to taking ten-mile hikes with a seventy-pound backpack, Doug found that walking along the coast for fifteen minutes carrying a paperback exhausted him. His grief was affecting him physically. Even if he was ready for a change, it was hard to leave people he had cared about and served well. He had a bachelor's degree and not a clue as to what he would do next to make a living. At night, lying in his station wagon, Doug would get an idea, write it down on a "Post-It," and slap it up onto the inside roof of the wagon. "I wonder if I would like to be a ———," he would write, filling in one type of job after another. Work with computers? Become an Outward Bound counselor? A store manager—he had done that before—how about running a retail store?

When there were "Post-Its" all over the inside ceiling of his station wagon, Doug knew that it was time to return home.

Back in Corvallis, Doug was emotionally ready to take the next step in considering what he wanted to do. He had listed the occupations that interested him. Now he started calling people to set up interviews to talk to them—not about getting a job but about what the job entailed, the skills or training he would need, the type of work it would be, and so on.

Doug was very practical in his approach, doing informational interviewing to find out whether this or that job was something he would want to do. For a man burned out on work he had been doing for ten years, this was a valuable and healing way to begin his job search.

After finishing the hard work of gathering a lot of new informa-

tion to consider, Doug went on a fishing trip with a couple of bud-
dies, an Alaskan adventure that had been planned before he was
fired. While catching hundreds of pounds of fish and flying it back
to Oregon, Doug had more good time to reflect. The out-of-doors
that he always loved is the setting that he uses best for making important decisions.

At this point Doug thinks that he will probably choose gardening
again and that perhaps he won't go back to work full-time for a
while. He is financially and emotionally responsible to his children
and former wife. He bought his wife out of a real estate investment
they shared by refinancing at a lower interest rate and drawing out
some cash. In this way he has financed time for himself to decide
his new life direction.

When he and his wife separated, they had their young children
stay in the house and the two of them take turns being at home
with them. He has his own simple apartment and she lives with her
mother when not with the children. This arrangement, along with
his ex-wife's employment, gives his children stability while Doug
works out his occupational plan.

"Unemployment," writes researcher Ian Miles, "confronts people
with empty time, which is often experienced as a desert in which it
is difficult to construct new goals and find new routes."[6] People in a
time of major change need to think about life in a comprehensive
way. In order to do so, most people have to get some physical and
mental distance from their familiar surroundings and usual obligations. You don't have to take an expensive vacation, as Doug has
demonstrated by sleeping in his station wagon, but you do need to
get away to a quiet and peaceful setting, someplace comfortable to
you. Don't try to push yourself or attempt to decide in one long
weekend—or even two weeks away from home—everything that
needs to be decided for the rest of your life. As the famous psychotherapist Fritz Perls was fond of saying, "Don't push the river, it
flows by itself."

Experiences of beauty in nature aid healing and allow the mind
the freedom to think in new ways. If you prepare the way by giving
yourself these opportunities to meditate and reflect on your life—
through getaway trips, daily walks, visits with old friends you can
talk with about matters of substance, prayer, or whatever works for

you—little by little you will know the message of your heart and the wisdom of your mind.

THE SEARCH FOR PURPOSE AND MEANING

The wise and wonderful Dr. Viktor Frankl, age ninety-one, lecturing recently in Hamburg, Germany, said something of relevance here that won him a fifteen-minute standing ovation from 5,000 mental health professionals from around the world. America is an example of how material wealth does not bring happiness, Dr. Frankl said. A Nazi concentration camp survivor, Frankl pointed to the high rates of adolescent suicide, drug and alcohol addiction, and the prevalence of violence in the United States. Human beings are sustained by *meaning* in their lives, not by material acquisitions, Dr. Frankl proclaimed.[7]

When you take the time to think honestly about your life, you know within yourself that money, possessions, position, and status do not bring happiness, however seductive such things are. Meaning in life, on the other hand, is something we all need.

The reason that 5,000 psychologists, psychiatrists, mental health counselors, and clergy stood to cheer Dr. Frankl is that they (and we) know from experience that the single-minded pursuit of material prosperity still leaves us feeling impoverished, both spiritually and emotionally. Happiness requires something else—or at least something additional.

You can live well with yourself and others whether you have a job or not, have a lot of money or a little, as long as your life has purpose. "Yes," you may say, "but my purpose is to provide for my family, and I can't do that without enough money." Of course we must have food and shelter, but beyond that, providing for the family is more emotional than material. We've all been brainwashed by advertising to want *more* than that, and we've become accustomed to having and spending a lot of money. But providing for a family has to do really with the way people are cared about, heard, and accepted in a household and with the values being taught or demonstrated. Is everyone in the family getting the hugs and verbal encouragement they need to build self-esteem and feel secure? Or are society's materialistic values being overemphasized so people (adults included) are focusing on the presence or absence of things instead of time spent together in meaningful ways?

We all need to ask ourselves regularly: Where and what is my meaning in life and how do I see the purpose of my existence? After I'm gone, what do I want people to say about me and the life that I lived? Do I want people to say that I worked hard and could afford to buy myself a nice car and my children some expensive tennis shoes? I don't think so. That I had a lot of education and an impressive, five-page résumé? Not really. That I was a loving person and knew how to listen to my children so they would talk to me? You bet. That in our family we treated each other with respect? That we had fun together? That we all knew that our home was a place where we would be cared about when we were hurting, making mistakes, or needing help? And that I helped our home to be that kind of a place? Absolutely. I would die a happy person if—in the end—I knew that I had provided in *this* way.

People who live with intentionality are more likely to live fully and die at peace. Those who turn job loss into a blessing in disguise think about the kind of people they want to be and the quality of relationships they want to have—and then set about to reach those goals.

XII

Building Your Future

My interest is in the future because
I am going to spend the rest of my life there.

—CHARLES F. KETTERING

"Life is a teacher in the art of relinquishment," said Socrates. And so it is. Many of us spend years learning how to let go of the past and move ahead into the future. Whether recovering from job loss or other losses, it isn't easy to acquire the wisdom to release hurts and disappointments. But by doing so, you will free yourself to live without bitterness or regret—to master your losses and to regain confidence and hope. What Socrates might have added is that life's first lesson in relinquishment is not to deny the pain. A second lesson is the futility of blame: It helps no one to inflict pain on someone else or to harbor resentment. Your problems will only multiply if you don't find some way to make peace with the past.

What to do with any anger you're still carrying because of the losses or mistreatment you've suffered? If you're still holding some anger toward a former employer, supervisor, or co-worker, or toward a family member, try to look honestly at how much trouble these resentments are causing. Accept that only you are being hurt by them. Speak with yourself truthfully about how releasing the old grudges would benefit your health and relationships and increase your chances of success in a new job. Forgiveness almost always does more for the forgiver than for the person being forgiven. Let it go. Unencumber yourself so you can freely move on.

THE "OKLAHOMA SYNDROME": THE PROBLEM WITH SEEING YOURSELF AS SELF-SUFFICIENT

A couple of years ago a family counselor in a radio interview said something about Oklahoma that grabbed my attention: Oklahoma—where I was born and reared—has the highest divorce rate of any state in the United States. Since about half of American marriages end in divorce, those statistics sounded pretty grim. I wondered why Oklahoma would have such a high rate. As I listened further, I recognized from personal experience that the counselor's explanation was right on target: Oklahomans, perhaps more than any other Americans, have taken to heart the "frontier mentality." Generally speaking, Oklahomans believe in independence and self-sufficiency: Unless facing a disaster of tragic proportions, one should keep quiet about and then solve one's own problems. With that attitude, however, most of life's everyday difficulties keep getting worse. For example, if a couple waits until their relationship is so near disintegration that it's too late to set it right again, marital counseling is of no avail. Furthermore, with the "frontier mentality" solidly in place, mental health facilities in Oklahoma are often inadequately funded and understaffed. Those who finally do seek professional help may face long waiting lists. Can you imagine having a marriage in crisis or a youngster with a drug problem and having to wait months for an appointment?

All North Americans know the stories about the brave and resourceful pioneers who traveled far, battled adversity, and built a life for themselves in the American and Canadian frontiers. In Oklahoma these stories have assumed the power and status of mythology—in part because we lived on the land where the buffalo once roamed, where both Native Americans and settlers struggled to survive.

The mythology, however, fails to acknowledge that the people who journeyed west survived because they relied heavily on fellow travelers, other settlers, friendly Native Americans, and their religious faith. These were hardy individuals, but few were self-sustaining. Likewise, Native Americans and those who came to America as slaves survived not only because of their strength and determination but also by reason of their spirituality, reliance on one another, and support from some decent people here and there who treated them like human beings. Even the bravest of us seldom prevail in adverse circumstances without support from someone.

In times of profound crisis, such as when the terrorist bombing occurred in Oklahoma City in 1995, the people of Oklahoma demonstrate for all the world to see the power of coming together and of relying on their religious faith and on one another for strength. But Oklahomans, like many other people, can fail to recognize the importance of reaching for help in confronting life's day-to-day crises.

After one of my job loss seminars in which I talked about this "Oklahoma Syndrome," as I have termed it, an unemployed man in his middle thirties passed me a note. "Thanks for giving me a name for what I'm doing to myself," he said. "I hadn't realized that what I've been putting up with is a case of 'Oklahoma-itis'!" Many problems are common in the aftermath of job loss. Like this unemployed man, you don't have to suffer silently or wait so long to get help that your difficulties multiply.

In the past when a loss or crisis occurred, you could go to your job, get your mind off your troubles, and feel that you were contributing something. There were people there who cared about you. Your activity, daily routines, and responsibilities aided healing. Since going to work is how you survived previous losses, no wonder it's sometimes difficult to cope with life's changes now. You have to manage your present situation without the support that work has always provided.

Find the support you need. Just talk to someone you trust about your family problems or other concerns. Say how you are feeling and express your desire to get a new life started. Try to identify specific emotions and problems that are especially troublesome so you and the person you confide in can generate ideas about ways to feel better. It's always easier for two people to find practical solutions to problems.

Think about the stress you're living with, and come up with some thoughts about how to reduce these burdens. What concrete actions or decisions would give you and your loved ones more opportunity for healing?

If you can't find someone to confide in or your distress feels unmanageable at times, seek professional help. Healing will come as you ventilate your emotions, especially self-doubt, hurt, and anger.

Then you will be ready to ask: What specific decisions do I need to make or steps do I need to take to alleviate financial pressure, improve my mental attitude, and relieve family tension?

A certified professional—social worker, psychologist, marriage or family counselor, or pastoral counselor—can help you and your family move beyond this crisis.

"All growth," writes psychiatrist Harold Bloomfield, "is a combination of both insight and behavior change." To break free of old self-defeating patterns, "you may have to give up feeling sorry for yourself, straining to be someone you're not, hiding the parts of yourself you fear are unacceptable, and worrying about what others might think. You may have to forgive yourself and others for not being perfect and stop expecting superhuman feats from your loved ones."[1] Such changes never come easily and almost never happen at all when one is trying to maintain the illusion of self-sufficiency.

KEN STACK: "I'VE LEARNED I'M STRONG"

For the fourteen years he was a designer making house calls for a large furniture company in Baltimore, Ken Stack enjoyed working with people and selling carpeting, draperies, and home furnishings. He was good at his trade, having taken design courses at the Maryland Institute College of Art and the University of Houston. Feeling stuck at the level of assistant manager, however, Stack left the company to become a store manager elsewhere, then later returned to the original company as a senior manager. In each instance, he raised the annual sales of the store he managed by $1 million in just a few years. Yet both companies eventually fired him. He lost the first position after being moved up to operations manager, where he was resented by the owner's sons, who had been making some decisions that their father would not have agreed with, had he known. He lost the second job because the company wanted to exchange his $60,000 a year manager's salary for that of a cheaper employee.

Throughout his adult life, Ken Stack dreamed of having his own furniture business, and he had nearly taken the plunge a decade earlier. It was fortunate for him, as well as his wife and children, that he hadn't taken the risk then and put his house up for collateral: The furniture market plummeted during the 1981 recession. "I was in my early thirties and thought I knew everything," Stack told me. "But I would have been stuck with a disaster."

Stack is now in his midforties, his children are grown, and his wife is working outside the home. It is the ideal time, he feels, to be in business for himself and do what his own father never adequately did, which is to think of the future. "My father had opportunities but never took them," Stack said sadly. "He always decided, Don't make any changes. This is the way it is.'" His father didn't plan ahead—and he also didn't have life insurance to protect his family when he died.

"As a youngster I had a dream to be different from my father, although when I grew up I was just like him," Stack lamented. "I never took any risks. If it was a good restaurant, I always went back to the same one." Until recently. Finally, a metamorphosis began with introspection: "Ken," he asked, as if into a mirror, "what do you want for yourself in life?"

Listening to an inner yearning and summoning the courage to risk making a change, Stack got start-up money from a home equity loan plus a gift from his mother, and he opened his own small furniture store. He buys from dealers whose price for an item is the same whether he purchases one or fifty, so he can compete with the big companies. In partnership with a friend who provides 50 percent of the financial backing but leaves the management decisions to Stack, he is happy with his newfound adventure and independence.

Departing finally from the pattern of reticence and fear he inherited from his father, Stack is able to benefit now from the positive aspects of his father's conservative approach to life. "It takes the pressure off not to borrow money," he says; "I'm not going to guarantee a loan with my house because it's all that I have." He has a month-to-month lease at a downscale mall where the rent is affordable, and he pays up front for all the furniture he orders in order to receive a discount. By keeping his expenses down—including doing his own painting and carpet cleaning—Stack can offer low prices to his customers.

"I always thought I was capable, but I've proved to myself that I am," he says proudly. "I always was so afraid to make a change. Now I can't say I have any fear."

After he was fired the first time, Stack and his wife went for marriage counseling when family problems arose. They now enjoy an increased feeling of closeness, and he speaks of his wife as "my best friend." They work out at a gym, walk regularly together at the mall where his store is located, and he also plays racquetball for fun and fitness. Through adversity, Stack also has deepened his sense of being spiritually grounded. "God was showing me the way," he says, looking back on the prayerful decision he made to take the risk of going on his own. He and Mrs. Stack decided jointly to live happily although more simply in the ways they spend money on clothes and entertainment.

"I'm definitely a lot more comfortable, not as hyper, much more low-key," Stack concludes. "I've learned I'm strong. I was able to face the unknown. Now if I have to face more uncertainty, I know I can do it because I already have."

You may also want to listen carefully to the yearnings of your inner voice. Don't come to the end of your life some day and wonder why you never had the courage to acknowledge hidden hopes and dreams. You wouldn't want to face the misery of a life-shortening illness or despairing old age characterized by regret. The words "I should have . . . " or "Why didn't I?" and "If only . . . " are bitter-tasting when too much time has gone by to make the changes one has yearned to make. Risks taken in the service of your dreams, on the other hand, will allow you to live in peace with yourself.

BUILDING A LIFE

Once or twice a year at AT&T, Technical Manager Blake Watten-barger and many other managers offer career planning for their employees. They help professionals and support staff determine what their aspirations are, what they might want to do next, whether they are ready for a new challenge, or if they are getting tired of what they have been doing. Wattenbarger always starts by asking the men and women to examine their personal values, what they want out of work, what needs are met by their work life, and how much energy and time they're willing to put into work. "If your job is mostly a paycheck," he tells them, "you may want to invest a minimum amount of energy in it and save the rest for your true love," whether it's family, sailing, or another sport or allegiance. "On the other hand," he continues, "if you want to get your main satisfaction from your work, then you need to expect to put a lot of your energy into it."

According to Wattenbarger, the old model for advancing a career was to envision your job as a ladder and see how far up the rungs you could climb. "That's not how it works today," he says. Building a career and a future is not necessarily about looking for another promotion, Wattenbarger emphasizes. "Career development now involves learning how to make yourself happier at work, moving around within a company or area of expertise, making lateral moves, and taking on new challenges."[2]

GOING FORWARD WITH RENEWED ENERGY AND EMPOWERMENT

Hope for the Best and Buffer Your Stress

People to whom good things happen often have learned not to expect the worst but to hope for the best; they recognize good fortune and decent fellow human beings when such events and individuals present themselves and are able to respond in kind.

One of my students—a middle-aged woman who almost simultaneously became unemployed and embroiled in an ugly divorce—told me that she makes a habit of expecting good fortune to come her way. Charlotte symbolizes this expectation by looking for a lucky penny every day. Sometimes she finds a dime or a quarter and thinks of it as ten or twenty-five days' worth of serendipity. Although she never counts the money until after a new year has begun, every year her lucky "pennies" add up to considerably more than $3.65. Looking for lucky coins is a metaphor in her life for anticipating solutions to problems and finding ways to be happy again after experiencing misfortune. Since what one "gets" in life is often what one expects, it's a good idea for all of us routinely to examine our expectations.

Rebuilding a life takes a lot of energy, and the more stress you can eliminate the more energy you'll have. Limit the time you spend with negative people and release your troubles and clarify your aspirations by writing to a "paper psychologist" in the form of a journal.

Take control of your "self-talk": You can stop badgering yourself, second-guessing, and self-criticizing. You can quit blaming yourself for the past, putting yourself down in the present, and catastrophizing about the future. It takes practically everyone a long time to learn to cope with change and get a new show on the road. Treat yourself like a cherished and cherishable loved one, show more respect for yourself, and cut yourself some slack.

In a state of relaxation and meditation, you can make good use of positive imaging techniques. Vividly imagine that in six months, a year, and five years you are feeling much better. You no longer carry the unhappy emotional baggage surrounding the circumstances of your lost job. See yourself feeling productive again, successfully reemployed, and increasingly satisfied with your responsibilities and relationships. Doing deep breathing exercises in a quiet place and in a relaxed frame of mind, allow these pictures of a positive future to permeate your thinking like water dispersing itself through wine. So much of going forward and having a positive future comes from deeply believing that good things will happen to you, trusting that your hard work and integrity will *cause* many good things to occur. There are no guarantees, of course, but as one writer in *Working Woman* magazine has said, "The positive attitude of resilient people is their most potent survival skill."[3]

As I was walking with an old friend along the winding streets in my neighborhood last March, my friend suddenly stopped and declared, "Look! This is what I love about spring!" There at our feet, growing out of the asphalt, literally breaking away a piece of the street, was a tulip. I remember thinking that's how strong the life forces are within nature and within us. New life is always breaking through one incredible obstacle or another. Nature provides all living things with a great deal of resilience and strength.

Strategies for Survival and Triumph

- Job loss involves a major adjustment. You probably need more time to recover and rebuild your life than you thought necessary when you first picked up this book. Try to remember the intense but natural emotions described here: powerful feelings of loss, disillusionment, betrayal, anger, and self-doubt, as well as worry, depression, and fatigue. You've lost something important, a job that in many ways defined you, gave you self-respect, and added meaning to your life. Be patient with yourself and grant yourself the time required for healing.

- Remember that continuing to ruminate about the past makes successful reemployment more difficult. Focus your energy on your present relationships, tasks, and goals.

- You can return needed structure to your life by establishing a daily routine, posting a schedule, taking specific break times, and accomplishing self-assigned tasks.

- Seek quality financial advice and make the decisions that you need to make as a family to get your financial house in order.

- Keep in mind the importance of exercise and additional ways you can enhance your physical and emotional health. Reduce or eliminate your alcohol intake, stay clear of any street drugs, reduce your caffeine consumption, and consume in moderation foods high in fat or sugar. These things can affect your mood, motivation, and energy level.

- You may find spiritual strength in a support group, daily meditation or prayer, church or synagogue attendance, nature's beauty or music, or volunteer work. Journal writing can also be empowering if you record your thoughts and feelings, and your personal goals and actions to take toward realizing them. Write down the names of loved ones, how to spend more time with them, and also the people and activities that discourage you and how to avoid or cope with them.

- If you feel overwhelmed by a depression that doesn't seem to be getting any better, get the professional help you need. Recognize the symptoms of Major Depression, a highly treatable mood disorder. These include irregular sleep, change in appetite, loss of interest in activities once pleasurable, difficulty concentrating or making decisions, and feelings of fatigue, worthlessness, or hopelessness. Recurrent thoughts of suicide or death always must be taken seriously. If you experience such symptoms nearly every day for at least two weeks, you need to be evaluated by a medical doctor (preferably a psychiatrist). Most people with Major Depression start to feel better in just a few weeks when taking medication. (See Appendix D for the numbers to call "For Help with Severe Depression," including referral sources for well-qualified psychiatrists and support groups.)

- How your employment situation affects your family depends considerably on you. If you can become more flexible, egalitarian, and accepting of changing roles, family tension can be reduced. Improve communication with your spouse or children by holding regular family meetings, reading one of the books recommended in chapter 7, taking a family relations or parenting course, or getting counseling.

- Redefine your personal values and the meaning of your life. Instead of predicating your worthiness on a certain job or income level, focus on living a productive life according to new perspectives: sustaining meaningful relationships, living a more balanced life, and making a contribution to the betterment of someone else's life.

- Accept the new realities of the changing workplace with honesty and courage: Expand your skills, learn about relevant technologies, and make yourself more nimble. Prepare yourself to become part of a company's core permanent workforce or to become an entrepreneur, independent contractor, or consultant. Or choose a part-time or temporary job simply to earn a paycheck, and find your satisfaction in life apart from work.

- If redeveloping or advancing a career is a primary goal, you'll need routine outlets for stress to sustain you, first during the demanding job of work search and then during long hours of work. Set aside time for loved ones and self-care, and also some time every week or month for improving your work skills after becoming reemployed.

- Recognize that present circumstances—however difficult or unpleasant—can be translated into a valuable opportunity to learn and grow. You can become a wiser, happier person: Reevaluate your priorities, identify your strengths and blessings, and resolve to live a more fulfilling life.

Hold Your Head Up

September 26, 1994—the day that baseball manager Johnny Oates of the Baltimore Orioles was fired—immediately became his "Family Day." After he got the news and issued a brief written statement to the press, Oates spent the day with those closest to him. With his wife and two daughters—one an elementary teacher and the other a high school sophomore—and his eighteen-year-old son, who stayed in touch by telephone, Oates was able to set his healing process into motion. He picked up only a couple of the forty calls that came to the house, Oates explained, "because I felt it was important to spend time with my family—to make sure they were comfortable and tell them there were worse things that could've happened to me. I didn't want them going to school feeling depressed."[4]

"This being fired is a thunderstorm in my life," Oates said. "After it rains, the roots grow deeper and stronger—and that's what's taking place here right now."

The message clearly was heard by Oates's children. When daughter Jenny, age fifteen, went back to school the next day, she wore every piece of Oriole clothing she could find. "It was her way of breaking the ice with her friends so they wouldn't feel uncomfortable—and to say that we're proud of the job we did in Baltimore," said Oates, whose team had a winning record of .563 at the end of the strike-shortened season when he was fired.

Johnny Oates—who only the year before was named by his fellow managers the American League Manager of the Year—felt disappointment and hurt but didn't weep, and he was determined not to be bitter. He went out of his way not to blame the owner who fired him or the manner in which the firing was handled, which many fans felt was unfair. He was thankful, he said, that the Orioles had given him his first chance to manage at the major-league level. "The first chance is always the toughest to get and a lot of guys never get that opportunity. . . . Now it's up to me," he concluded, "to get another opportunity."

"Hold your head up," go the words to a rock song popular many years ago, ironically a song played these days over loudspeakers in Baltimore when the home team pitcher has gotten into trouble and is being thrown out of the game. "Hold your head up, hold your head up, hold your head high. . . . "5

Like Johnny Oates, you also can decide to go on with your life in a classy manner. Whether you've justifiably shed tears or been bitter over your lost job, you can decide how you want to manage things now. Whether you've handled well or poorly with your family the awful changes you've had to cope with thus far, there is still time for a class act finale. You can respect yourself more and teach your loved ones an important lesson about going forward in life without bitterness by focusing on what you have to be thankful for, what that last job gave you that was good or beneficial. You can accept with graciousness all of the opportunities that have come your way in the past and accept responsibility now for creating your own future opportunities. The finest players in baseball history have been thrown out of the game. You too can decide that it's no big deal. Move forward with your head held high.

The "Freeze Frame" Perspective

Perhaps because I was in my late thirties when I first became a mother and in my early forties when the second child came, usually I don't take the joys of having children for granted. There are periods, though, when I'm preoccupied with my responsibilities as sole provider, when I'm working on an extremely demanding project or dealing with some personal problem—and, temporarily, my perspective blurs.

Thankfully, what I call "freeze frame experiences" keep happening to me, prompting a refocus. We've all seen the "freeze frame" technique used in movies: At an especially important moment, a still shot suspends movement, enabling us to study a moment in time and savor it. My similar experiences occur at various places, but especially at home. A happy little kid bounces through the kitchen in tennis shoes that literally light up when she goes by, all excited about starting a new school year—and for the flash of a moment everything stops. An almost-sixth-grader tenderly pats and pets her beloved hamster, grooming him gently with a tooth-brush—and time is suspended. From the desk in my office at home, I look through a large glass window into the next room where these same two girls are having a snack at the kitchen table. My daughters are less than twelve feet away and my brain takes a photograph and holds it in place. I see the profile of Amanda's cherishable, pretty face and the long black braid that runs the length of her back. I ponder dear Ashley's pretty little smile and face, blue-rimmed glasses matching mine. These are the most wonderful days of my life, I realize, and these dear children a precious gift.

I'm so glad that time stops in this way—when we allow it to—and that God grants us these occasional opportunities to have a freeze-frame perspective. There are many such precious moments in life, but we all need to give ourselves more time and space to ponder, more moments to cherish the good life that exists right in front of us.

Personal crisis with the accompanying turmoil is real, demands our attention, is often unavoidable. In order to heal and go forward, usually there's no getting around the pain, depression, frustrations, and disappointments. Generally, all that miserable stuff simply has to be sorted through. But it's also utterly necessary for each of us to stop and look at all that's still cherishable about life, despite the ad-versity.

A few feet from you or in the next room, down the street or next door, a telephone call away, or at a nearby church, synagogue, or therapist's office is somebody who cares about you. There are loved ones, too, who have passed on but whose influence, encourage-ment, love, and inspiration belong to you always and can be called upon now.

Coming through the ordeal of your job loss, try to stay aware of these positive people in your life and the simple pleasures and joys. You can be thankful for your good health or the healing power of music and nature's beauty. Become more aware of the resilience of the human spirit.

As you build your future, it will help you also to remember the opportunities and advantages you've had and your skills, talents, and other personal strengths. Write them down. You'll surprise yourself at the resources for strength that already have become a part of your life. Allow yourself to celebrate life even while you're going through difficult times.

Freeze frame those special moments. As you cherish the goodness in the life that you presently have, you'll grow stronger in the ability to seize other moments and thus to create the future you yearn to have.

For Further Reading

Beyer, Cathy, Doris Pike, and Loretta McGovern. *Surviving Unemployment: A Family Handbook for Weathering Hard Times* (New York: Henry Holt and Company, 1993).

Birsner, E. Patricia. *Mid-Career Job Hunting: The Official Handbook of the 40 Plus Club* (New York: Facts on File Publications, 1991).

Bloomfield, Harold H. *The Achilles Syndrome—Transforming Your Weaknesses into Strengths* (New York: Random House, 1985).

Bolles, Richard Nelson. *The 1994 What Color Is Your Parachute? A Practical Manual for Job-Hunters and Career-Changers* (Berkeley, California: Ten Speed Press, 1994).

Borysenko, Joan. *Minding the Body, Mending the Mind* (New York: Bantam Books, 1987).

Brunette, William Kent. *Conquer Your Debt: How to Solve Your Credit Problems* (New Jersey: Prentice Hall, 1990).

Connor, Robert. *Cracking the Over-50 Job Market* (New York: Dutton, 1992).

DePaulo, J. Raymond, Jr., and Keith Russell Ablow. *How to Cope With Depression* (New York: Ballantine Books, 1991).

Dowling, Colette. *You Mean I Don't Have to Feel This Way?* (New York: Charles Scribner's Sons, 1991).

Edwards, Paul, and Sarah Edwards. *Working from Your Home: Everything You Need to Know About Living and Working Under the Same Roof* (Los Angeles: J. P. Tarcher, 1990).

Edwards, Paul, and Sarah Edwards. *The Best Home Businesses for the '90s* (Los Angeles: J. P. Tarcher, 1991).

Faber, Adele, and Elaine Mazlish. *How to Talk So Kids Will Listen and Listen So Kids Will Talk* (New York: Avon, 1991). (Also available from Nightingale-Conant Audio, 7300 North Lehigh Avenue, Chicago, Illinois 60648.)

Hadley, Joyce. *Part-Time Careers for Anyone Who Wants More Than Just a Job—But Less Than a Forty-Hour Week* (Hawthorn, New Jersey: Career Press, 1993).

Hom, Tony, and Edward Claflin. *Smart, Successful and Broke: The Six-Step Action Plan for Getting Out of Debt and Into the Money* (New York: Dell, 1991).

Jukes, Jill, and Ruthan Rosenberg. *Surviving Your Partner's Job Loss* (Washington, DC: National Press Books, 1993).

Lamplugh, Rick. *Job Search That Works* (Los Altos, California: Crisp Publications, 1991).

Metcalf, C. W. *Lighten Up: Survival Skills for People Under Pressure* (Reading, Massachusetts: Addison Wesley, 1992).

Myers, David G. *The Pursuit of Happiness* (New York: Avon Books, 1993).

The Occupational Outlook Handbook (published every year by the U.S. Department of Labor, Washington, D.C.). This book is an extremely useful resource and is available at your local library.

O'Connell, Peggy. *The Temp Track: Make One of the Hottest Job Trends of the 90s Work for You* (Princeton, New Jersey: Peterson's Guides, 1994).

Pennebaker, James W. *Opening Up—The Healing Power of Confiding in Others* (New York: Avon Books, 1990).

Resnick, R. Linda. *A Big Splash in a Small Pond: Finding a Great Job in a Small Company* (New York: Simon and Schuster, 1994).

Sher, Barbara. *Wish Craft* (New York: Ballantine, 1979).

Sinetar, Marsha. *Do What You Love, The Money Will Follow* (New York: Paulist Press, 1987).

Stearns, Ann Kaiser. *Living Through Personal Crisis* (New York: Ballantine Books, 1985).

Stearns, Ann Kaiser. *Coming Back—Rebuilding Lives After Crisis and Loss* (New York: Ballantine Books, 1989).

Tavris, Carol. *Anger: The Misunderstood Emotion* (New York: Simon and Schuster, 1989).

Vantura, John. *Fresh Start* (Dearborn, Michigan: Financial Publications, 1992).

Yate, Martin. *Knock 'Em Dead: The Ultimate Job-Seeker's Handbook* (Holbrook, Massachusetts: Bob Adams, 1994).

APPENDIX A

Who to Call If You Believe You Have Been Discriminated Against

WHEN TRYING TO GET THE JOB

Federal law protects workers from discrimination in the **job-seeking process** by prohibiting discrimination in recruitment, testing, referrals, and hiring.

Discrimination on the basis of sex, race, color, religion, or national origin in hiring or firing; wages; fringe benefits; classifying; . . . among other things: Title VII of the Civil Rights Act of 1964 is the principal law that protects workers from discrimination in employment. If you think you've been treated unfairly, call the Equal Employment Opportunity Commission at 800-669-EEOC.

Discrimination based on age: The Age Discrimination in Employment Act of 1967 (ADEA), as amended, generally prohibits employers from using age as a basis for employment decisions for persons forty or older. If you think you've been discriminated against on the basis of age, call the Equal Employment Opportunity Commission at 800-669-EEOC.

Discrimination based on disability: The Americans with Disabilities Act (ADA) prohibits discrimination against individuals with disabilities. If you think you've been discriminated against on the basis of disability, call the Equal Employment Opportunity Commission at 800-669-EEOC.

DISCRIMINATION ON THE JOB

If you think you're not being paid the minimum wage or required overtime pay: Look in the blue pages of the phone book under U.S. Government, Department of Labor, Wage and Hour Division. Call to inquire whether you are being paid according to the law.

If you think you're not being paid equal pay for equal work: Call the Equal Employment Opportunity Commission at 800-669-EEOC, which enforces the Equal Pay Act.

Discrimination on the job on the basis of sex, race, color, religion, or national origin in hiring or firing; wages; fringe benefits; classifying; . . . among other things: Title VII of the Civil Rights Act of 1964 is the principal law that protects workers from discrimination in employment. If you think you've been treated unfairly, call the Equal Employment Opportunity Commission at 800-669-EEOC.

Discrimination on the job based on age: The Age Discrimination in Employment Act of 1967 (ADEA), as amended, generally prohibits employers from using age as a basis for employment decisions for persons forty or older. If you think you've been discriminated against on the basis of age, call the Equal Employment Opportunity Commission at 800-669-EEOC.

Discrimination on the job based on disability: The Americans with Disabilities Act (ADA) prohibits discrimination against individuals with disabilities. If you think you've been discriminated against on the basis of disability, call the Equal Employment Opportunity Commission at 800-669-EEOC.

Pregnancy discrimination: Title VII of the Civil Rights Act of 1964, as amended in 1978, prohibits this discrimination. If you think you've been discriminated against on the basis of pregnancy, call the Equal Employment Opportunity Commission at 800-669-EEOC.

Sexual harassment: Title VII of the Civil Rights Act of 1964, as amended in 1978, prohibits this discrimination. If you think you're being sexually harassed, call the Equal Employment Opportunity Commission at 800-669-EEOC.

Unsafe working conditions: The Occupational Safety and Health Act of 1970 is designed to ensure safe and healthful working conditions throughout the nation. If you think unsafe or unhealthful conditions exist in your workplace, file a complaint with the agency listed on the poster about state or federal health and safety law that's required to be posted at every workplace. If there's no poster, contact OSHA.

Employee access to personnel files: There is no federal law which requires employers to allow employees to examine their own personnel files. However, at least twenty states have laws which require some or all employers to allow employees such access.*

*U.S. Department of Labor, Office of the Secretary, Women's Bureau, "A Working Woman's Guide to Her Job Rights," August 1992 (leaflet #55).

APPENDIX B

Financial Counseling

Obtain free budget counseling and other valuable help from the National Consumer Credit Service. For more information about this nonprofit group, and to locate offices in your region, call 800-388-CCCS.

Protection from Abuse from Debt Collectors

To file a complaint, call the Federal Trade Commission in Washington, D.C.: 202-326-3758.

APPENDIX C

Directory of Share-USA Programs

The Self-Help and Resource Exchange (SHARE) program enables individuals and families to trade volunteer time in the community for the opportunity to purchase food packages significantly reduced in price. You can save 60 percent on food and help your community, too.

ComeSHARE (IL)
1222 Bunn Avenue
Springfield, IL 62703
217-529-2500

Fare SHARE (MN)
807 Hampden Avenue
St. Paul, MN 55114
612-644-6003

Heartland SHARE
215 S.E. Quincy
Topeka, KS 66603
913-234-6208

SHARE-Baltimore
808 Barkwood Court
Linthicum, MD 21090
410-636-9615

SHARE-Central Florida
3854 S. Orange Avenue
Orlando, FL 32806
407-858-0333/800-726-7427

SHARE-Central Illinois
1825 N.E. Adams Street
Peoria, IL 61603
309-637-0282/88

SHARE-Colorado
9360 Federal Boulevard
Denver, CO 80221
303-428-0400/800-933-7427

SHARE-Food Program, Inc.
2901 W. Hunting Park Avenue
Philadelphia, PA 19129
215-223-2220

SHARE-Georgia
710 Ashby Street, N.W.
Atlanta, GA 30318
404-873-2322

SHARE-Hampton Roads
1115 Tabb Avenue
Norfolk, VA 23504
804-627-6599/800-253-7842

SHARE-Heart of the Carolinas
P.O. Box 2009
Fayetteville, NC 28302-2009
919-485-6923/800-758-6923

SHARE-Iowa
1102 S. 7th Street
Oskaloosa, IA 52577
515-673-4000

SHARE-Mid-Michigan
2010 S. Washington Avenue
Lansing, MI 48910
517-482-8900

SHARE-New England
146 Will Road
Canton, MA 02021
617-828-5151/800-8-SHARE-0

SHARE-New Jersey
436 Ferry Street
Newark, NJ 07105
201-344-2400

SHARE-New York
1601 Bronxdale Avenue
Bronx, NY 10462
718-518-1513

SHARE-Northern California
4075 Lakeside Drive
Richmond, CA 94806
510-222-2506/800-499-2506

SHARE-Northern Ohio
250 Opportunity Parkway
Akron, OH 44307
216-253-8806

SHARE-Rockford
320 S. Avon
Rockford, IL 61102
815-961-7328

SHARE-S.E. Wisconsin, Inc.
13111 W. Silver Spring Drive
Butler, WI 53007
414-783-2500

SHARE-Southern California
3350 "E" Street
San Diego, CA 92102
619-525-2200

SHARE-Tampa Bay
1405 E. Second Avenue
Tampa, FL 33605
813-248-3379

SHARE-Virginia
106-B S. Franklin Street
Christiansburg, VA 24073
703-381-1185

SHARE-Wash., D.C.-Metro
5170 Lawrence Place
Hyattsville, MD 20781
301-864-3115

Tri-State SHARE
415 Eleventh Street
Ambridge, PA 15003-0428
412-266-0470

APPENDIX D

FOR HELP WITH SEVERE DEPRESSION

To receive a newsletter and other written or oral information regarding psychiatric referral sources, support groups, and workshops or seminars on depression, write to the Depression and Related Affective Disorders Association (DRADA) at Meyer 3-181, 600 N. Wolfe Street, Baltimore, Maryland 21287-7381 or call 410-955-4647. The DRADA office in Baltimore can connect you with support groups and well-qualified psychiatrists throughout the United States and in the District of Columbia.

In addition, the following groups are available by phone and offer information and support: (1) The National Depression and Manic Depression Association (NDMDA)—for persons suffering with depression and other mood disorders: 800-826-3632; (2) The Depression Awareness Recognition and Treatment (D/ART) Program: 800-421-4211; (3) The Anxiety Disorders Association of America: 301-234-9350; and (4) offering support to family members, The National Alliance for the Mentally Ill (NAMI): 800-950-6264.

If you are struggling with thoughts of suicide, get help immediately. Please call the American Association of Suicidology (during business hours in Colorado) at 303-692-0985 and ask for the crisis hotline phone number in your area. Or call information (411) and ask for your local suicide or crisis intervention hotline number.

FOR HELP WITH A DRINKING PROBLEM

Call Alcoholics Anonymous (the phone number is listed in your local or area telephone directory). It is also important to know that a problem with alcohol or another substance is often symptomatic of severe depression. Call 410-955-4647 if you need the name of a professional well qualified to evaluate and treat depression.

FOR ENCOURAGEMENT AND INSPIRATION

"Beyond Crisis with Ann Kaiser Stearns" is an audiocassette tape produced by New Dimensions Radio and is available by writing P.O. Box 410510, San Francisco, CA 94141-0510 (phone 415-563-8899). Ask for tape number 2089.

APPENDIX E

Entrepreneurial Advice

Here is how you can get information, advice, and assistance on starting your own business and keeping it going:

1. The U. S. Small Business Administration (SBA) provides inexpensive management assistance to small businesses. For more information, call 800-827-5722.
2. The SBA's Small Business Development Centers are affiliated with universities and offer training and counseling to owners of new and established businesses in forty-two states. To locate the Development Center nearest you, call 800-827-5722.
3. The SBA's Business Information Centers, in the ten regional SBA offices, provide information of interest to small businesses through the use of computer modems. To locate an Information Center, call 800-827-5722.
4. The SBA's Service Corps of Retired Executives (SCORE), through about 13,000 volunteers, offers free advice and assistance. For more information, call 202-205-6762.*

*Meg Whittemore, "Beginning at the Beginning," *Nation's Business,* February 1994, 70.

APPENDIX F

Resources for Finding Work—Age Forty Plus

Forty Plus is a nonprofit outplacement organization for professionals age forty or older, with twenty chapters in thirteen states and Washington, D.C. Services and costs vary by chapter, but most offer the use of computers, telephones, and fax machines. (Call 202-387-1582 for more information.)

The *American Association of Retired Persons* (AARP) conducts a low-cost, eight-session job-hunting program called AARP Works. (Call 202-434-2100 for more information.)

Notes

I. JOB LOSS: A PERSONAL CRISIS

1. Italics mine. Leonard Greenhalgh, "Maintaining Organizational Effectiveness During Organizational Retrenchment," *Journal of Applied Behavioral Science,* 18, no. 2 (1982), 156.
2. Mary Jo Purcell, "Really I'm Fine—Just Ask Me," *Newsweek,* November 30, 1992.
3. Ibid.
4. Stephen Fineman, *White Collar Unemployment and Stress* (New York: John Wiley and Sons, 1983), p. 19.
5. Ibid.
6. Ibid.
7. Ibid.
8. Ibid.
9. Leonard Fagin and Martin Little, *The Forsaken Families* (London: Penguin Books, 1984), p. 28.
10. Richard Smith, "What's the Point. I'm No Use to Anybody: The Psychological Consequences of Unemployment," *British Medical Journal,* 291 (November 9, 1985), 1338.
11. Bruce Nussbaum, Ann Therese Palmer, Alice Z. Cuneo, and Barbara Carlson, "Downward Mobility," *Business Week,* March 23, 1992, 56–63.
12. Nick Kates, Barrie S. Greiff, and Duane Q. Hagen, *The Psychosocial Impact of Job Loss* (Washington, DC: American Psychiatric Press, 1990), p. 62. Kates et al. quote E. Stafford, P. Jackson, and M. Banks: "Employment, Work Involvement and Mental Health in Less Qualified Young People," *Journal of Occupational Psychology,* 53 (1980), 291–304.
13. Ramsay Liem and Joan Huser Liem, "Psychological Effects of Unemployment on Workers and Their Families," *Journal of Social Issues,* 44, no. 4 (1988), 87–105. Professors Liem and Liem write that "workers in even the most alienating jobs face critical losses as a consequence of forced dislocation. Rather than emancipation from marginal jobs, unemployment creates a no-win situation." The authors refer to Jacobson's (1987) work proposing "that the strain of

unemployment is actually related directly to the effects of alienating work. According to [Jacobson], workers who experience minimal control on the job, who see themselves as compromised in their place of work, are the most vulnerable to the strain of unemployment. Job loss for them serves as a final insult and confirmation of their status as a mere object."

14. K. Moser et al., "Stress and Heart Disease: Evidence of Associations between Unemployment and Heart Disease from the OPCS Longitudinal Study," *Postgraduate Medical Journal,* 62 (1986), 797–99. Moser and colleagues analyzed the results of a longitudinal study of British men seeking work in 1971. They found an abnormally high mortality rate in 1971–1981. There was an excess mortality from heart disease among younger unemployed men (aged fifteen to forty-four at death) and among wives of unemployed men. Also M. Harvey Brenner, *Mental Illness and the Economy* (Boston: Harvard University Press, 1973); "Mortality and the National Economy: A Review, and the Experience of England and Wales, 1936–76," *The Lancet,* September 15, 1979, 568–73; and "Economic Change, Alcohol Consumption and Heart Disease Mortality in Nine Industrialized Countries," *Social Science Medicine,* 25 (1987), 119–32.

15. Elaine (Hilberman) Carmen, Nancy Felipe Russo, and Jean Baker Miller, "Inequality and Women's Mental Health: An Overview," *American Journal of Psychiatry,* 138, no. 10 (October 1981), 1319–30.

16. Ibid.

17. W. R. Gove and M. D. Geerken, "The Effects of Children and Employment on the Mental Health of Married Men and Women," *Social Forces,* 56 (1977), 66–76.

18. Carmen, Russo, and Miller, "Inequality and Women's Mental Health: An Overview," 1323. The authors cite G. Brown, M. Bhrolchain, and T. Harris, "Social Class and Psychiatric Disturbance among Women in an Urban Population," *Sociology,* 9 (1975), 225–54.

19. Carmen, Russo, and Miller, "Inequality and Women's Mental Health: An Overview," 1323.

20. Sten-Olof Brenner and Lennart Levi, "Long-Term Unemployment among Women in Sweden," *Social Science Medicine,* 25, no. 2 (Great Britain: Pergamon Journals, 1987), 153–61. (Also Bengt B. Arnetz et al., "Neuroendocrine and Immunologic Effects of Unemployment and Job Insecurity," *Psychotherapy and Psychosomatics,* 55 (1991), 76–80.

21. H. G. Kaufman, *Professionals in Search of Work* (New York: John Wiley and Sons, 1982), p. 74.
22. Ibid., p. 75.

II. STRUGGLING WITH ANGER AND FATIGUE

1. Guy Toscano and Janice Windau, "Fatal Work Injuries: Results from the 1992 National Census," *Monthly Labor Review,* October 1993, 43.
2. A useful book on this topic has been written by Rabbi Harold S. Kushner entitled, *When Bad Things Happen to Good People* (New York: Schocken Books, 1981).
3. *New York Times* News Service, February 28, 1993.
4. "Tragic Layoff," *USA Today,* March 26, 1993.
5. Ibid.
6. Blair Justice and David F. Duncan, "Child Abuse as a Work-Related Problem," a paper presented at the American Public Health Association's 103rd Annual Meeting, "Health and Work in America," Child Abuse Session, Chicago, November 20, 1975. Laurence D. Steinberg, Ralph Catalano, and David Dooley, "Economic Antecedents of Child Abuse and Neglect," *Child Development,* 52 (1981), 975–85. Richard D. Krugman et al., "The Relationship between Unemployment and Physical Abuse," *Child Abuse and Neglect,* 10 (1986), 415–18. David G. Gil, "Violence Against Children," *Journal of Marriage and the Family,* November 1971, 637–48. Also Loring Jones, "Unemployment and Child Abuse," *Families in Society: The Journal of Contemporary Human Services,* December 1990, 579–84.
7. B. Nichols, "The Abused Wife Problem," *Social Casework,* 57 (1976), 27–32.
8. Redford Williams, "The Trusting Heart," *New Age Journal,* May–June 1989, 26–30, 101. Adapted from *The Trusting Heart* (New York: Random House, 1989).
9. Ibid.
10. Ibid.
11. Ibid.
12. Nick Kates, Barrie S. Greiff, and Duane Q. Hagen, *The Psychosocial Impact of Job Loss* (Washington, DC: American Psychiatric Press, 1990), p. 51.
13. Ibid.
14. Williams, "The Trusting Heart."
15. William J. Morin and James C. Cabrera, *Parting Company: How to Survive the Loss of a Job and Find Another Successfully* (New York: Harcourt Brace Jovanovich, 1991).

16. Theodore Isaac Rubin, *The Angry Book* (New York: The Macmillan Company, 1969).

17. "Workplace Violence Killed 750 Last Year, Report Shows," *The Sunday Oklahoman,* September 5, 1993.

18. "Marketplace," from American Public Radio, October 18, 1993.

19. "Weekend Edition," National Public Radio, April 17, 1993.

20. "Women, Children and Work," editorial in the *New York Times,* January 12, 1993. According to an item in the *Baltimore Sun* on February 4, 1993, about 150,000 American workers each year lost their jobs because they needed time off for family emergencies. President Bill Clinton changed that when he signed the Family and Medical Leave Act in 1993; however, tens of thousands who work for small companies not covered by the law may still lose their jobs in any given year. Taking time off to care for a loved one can be costly to those who are vulnerable because of where they work.

21. Michelle Morris, "On the Wrong Side of the Mommy Track," *Baltimore Sun,* April 12, 1993.

22. Ibid.

23. Ibid.

24. Ibid.

25. Ibid.

26. Ibid.

27. Carrie R. Leana and Daniel C. Feldman, *Coping with Job Loss* (New York: Lexington Books, 1992). The authors found that "individuals engaged in the most community activism had the worst reemployment."

28. Karen Astrid Larson, "Should You Sue?" *Working Mother*, February 1993.

29. John Archer and Valerie Rhodes, "Bereavement and Reactions to Job Loss: A Comparative Review," *British Journal of Social Psychology,* 26 (1987), 217.

30. Timothy J. Mullaney, "Recovery Comes But Slowly, for Architects," *Baltimore Sun,* December 19, 1993.

31. Gary Scheiner, "Rx Exercise," *Diabetes Forecast,* June 1993, 25–28.

32. Ibid., 27.

33. "First Steps," *Health,* May–June 1993, 64.

34. Scheiner, "Rx Exercise," 28. People with a chronic illness such as diabetes should have a physical exam after age thirty-five before beginning an exercise program, Scheiner says.

35. Rita Rubin, "Body of Evidence Stresses Fitness, Not Fatness," *Los Angeles Times Syndicate,* May 31, 1994.

36. Carol Tavris, *Anger: The Misunderstood Emotion* (New York: Simon and Schuster, 1989).
37. Archer and Rhodes, "Bereavement and Reactions to Job Loss: A Comparative Review," 215. (Here the authors draw from the wisdom of C. M. Parkes and R. S. Weiss in *Recovery from Bereavement* [New York: Basic Books, 1983]).
38. "Health Update," *Better Homes and Gardens,* April 1993, 52.
39. Ibid.
40. James Pennebaker, *Opening Up: The Healing Power of Confiding in Others* (New York: Avon Books, 1990).
41. Gayle Brown, "The Healing Power of the Journal," *Arthritis Today,* January–February 1993.
42. Ibid.
43. Pennebaker, "Opening Up: The Healing Power of Confiding in Others," 100–106.
44. Tom Hallman, Jr., "Harrington: I Had to Start a New Life," *The Sunday Oregonian,* May 2, 1993.
45. Ibid.
46. Ibid.
47. Ibid.
48. Much of this story is based on my interview with Penny Harrington on January 24, 1994.
49. Penny Harrington, quoted in "Harrington: I Had to Start a New Life," by Tom Hallman, Jr.
50. Ibid.
51. *Monthly Labor Review,* February 1994, 65, and *Maclean's Magazine,* January 1, 1994, 35. Also "Democrats Unveil Job Transition Plan for Defense Workers," *The Oregonian,* May 22, 1992. Also "Marketplace," from American Public Radio, March 4, 1994.
52. Barbara Koeppel, "For Airline Workers the Crash Can Be Fatal," *Washington Post,* September 5, 1993.
53. Stephen Barr, "Gore Report Targets 252,000 Federal Jobs," *Washington Post,* September 5, 1993.
54. "Marketplace," from American Public Radio, broadcasts on December 6, 7, and 8, 1993 and January 26, 1994. Also "Boeing Announces Cutbacks, Layoffs," *The Oregonian,* January 27, 1993. Also "U.S. Aircraft Makers Join the List of Corporate Giants Eliminating Jobs," *Time,* February 8, 1993, 21. Also "McDonnell Douglas Cuts 1,650 More Jobs," *The Oregonian,* June 21, 1992. Also "Aetna Plans to Lay Off 10% of Work Force," *The Oregonian,* June 30, 1992. Also "Boeing Announces Cutbacks, Lay Offs," *The Oregonian,* January 27, 1993. Also "American Express Takes Huge Charge; 4,800 Jobs

Cut," *Eugene Register-Guard,* October 27, 1992. Also "1,000 Goodyear Jobs Cut; Roofing Business for Sale," *The Oregonian,* January 27, 1993. Also "When Downsizing Becomes 'Dumbsizing,'" *Time,* March 15, 1993, 55. Also "Kodak Will Trim About 2,000 Jobs to Slice $2 million," *The Oregonian,* January 20, 1993. Also "Sears Plans to Eliminate 50,000 Jobs," *The Oregonian,* January 26, 1993. Also "BankAmerica Plans to Cut Thousands After Merger," *The Oregonian,* March 20, 1992. Also Cable News Network, January 11, 1994. Also "DuPont Will Trim 4,500 Jobs," *Baltimore Sun,* September 14, 1993. Also "ABC World News Tonight," January 26, 1994. Also "Ameritech Phone Firm to Cut 6,000 Jobs by End of '95," *Baltimore Sun,* March 26, 1994.

55. "MacNeil/Lehrer News Hour," August 15, 1994.

56. "Marketplace," from American Public Radio, broadcasts on November 4, 1993, January 4, 1994, and January 11, 1994. Also "American Airlines Will Lay Off 350 Pilots Beginning in August," *The Oregonian,* June 1, 1993. Also "Alaska Airlines to Cut 98 Jobs in Latest Round of Reductions," *Eugene Register-Guard,* January 6, 1993. Also "Delta to Lay Off Up to 200 Pilots," *Eugene Register-Guard,* October 21, 1992. Also "Northwest Airlines Announces It Will Lay Off 1,000 Workers," *The Oregonian,* January 5, 1993. Also "Procter and Gamble Cleans House," *Time,* July 26, 1993, 20. Also "Dun and Bradstreet to Cut Jobs," *Baltimore Sun,* October 30, 1993. Also "MacNeil/Lehrer News Hour," The Public Broadcasting System, February 10, 1994. Also "USAir Prepares to Slash 9,000 Jobs," *The Oregonian,* September 18, 1993.

57. "Nynex to Eliminate 16,000 Jobs," *Baltimore Sun,* January 25, 1994.

58. "General Mills Inc. Announces Plans to Close 31 Restaurants," *The Oregonian,* May 25, 1993. Also "Alcoa to Lay Off Workers," *The Oregonian,* June 29, 1993. Also "John Hancock Cuts 700 Jobs," *The Oregonian,* January 10, 1993. Also "When Downsizing Becomes 'Dumbsizing,'" *Time,* March 15, 1993, 55. Also "Tektronix Sales Up, But Layoff Notices Still Coming to Employees," *The Oregonian,* September 17, 1992. Also "Marketplace," from American Public Radio, January 11, 1994 broadcast.

III. OVERCOMING DIMINISHED SELF-ESTEEM

1. Nick Kates, Barrie S. Greiff, and Duane Q. Hagen, *The Psychosocial Impact of Job Loss* (Washington, DC: The American Psychiatric Press, 1990), p. 18.

2. John Archer and Valerie Rhodes. "Bereavement and Reactions to

Job Loss: A Comparative Review," *British Journal of Social Psychology*, 26 (1987), 217. The authors cite: C. M. Parkes, *Bereavement: Studies of Grief in Adult Life* (London: Tavistock, 1972); J. Hill, "The Psychological Impact of Unemployment," *New Society*, 43 (1978), 118–20; K. H. Briar, "The Effect of Long Term Unemployment on Workers and Their Families," Doctor of Social Work Thesis, University of California, Berkeley, 1977; and P. Swinburne, "The Psychological Impact of Unemployment on Managers and Professional Staff," *Journal of Occupational Psychology*, 54 (1981), 47–64.

3. Leonard Fagin and Martin Little, *The Forsaken Families* (London: Penguin, 1984), p. 169.

4. Archer and Rhodes, "Bereavement and Reactions to Job Loss: A Comparative Review," 211.

5. Ted Shelsby, "Firm Thrives on Layoffs," *Baltimore Sun*, February 21, 1994.

6. Ibid.

7. David Jacobson, "Models of Stress and Meanings of Unemployment: Reactions to Job Loss among Technical Professionals," *Social Science Medicine*, 24, no. 1 (1987), 13.

IV. REDUCING FINANCIAL WORRY

1. Christopher Ruhm, formerly of Boston University, Visiting Professor of Economics, University of North Carolina-Charlotte, in a telephone interview, October 21, 1993.

2. Peter B. Doeringer, *Turbulence in the American Workplace* (New York: Oxford University Press, 1991). The author cites Christopher J. Ruhm, "The Economic Consequences of Labor Mobility," *Industrial and Labor Relations Review*, 41 (1987), 30–42; and Michael Podgursky and Paul Swaim, "Job Displacement and Earnings Loss: Evidence from the Displaced Worker Survey," *Industrial and Labor Relations Review*, 41 (1987), 17–29.

3. Jane Bryant Quinn, "The Good-Job Market: R.I.P.," *Newsweek*, November 30, 1992, 64.

4. W. Hugh Missildine, *Your Inner Child of the Past* (New York: Pocket Books, 1982), pp. 54–55.

5. Kim C. Flodin, "Giving Credit to the Family," *Baltimore Sun*, October 6, 1993.

6. Katherine S. Newman, *Falling from Grace: The Experience of Downward Mobility in the American Middle Class* (New York: Vintage Books, 1989), p. 125.

7. Ibid., 128.

8. Ibid.
9. Jane Bryant Quinn, *Making the Most of Your Money* (New York: Simon and Schuster, 1991).
10. Dorian Burden, "Filing for Unemployment," *Executive Female,* March–April 1992, 57. Italics mine.
11. Dan Moreau, "If You Lose Your Job," *Changing Times,* March 1991, 62–63.
12. Ibid.
13. Lani Luciano, "How to Cut Your Expenses 20 Percent (and Live Better, Too)," *Money,* December 1991, 70–75.
14. Brad Edmondson, "Remaking a Living," *Utne Reader,* July–August 1991, 72.
15. Jane Bryant Quinn, "Managing Money without a Paycheck," *Executive Female,* March–April, 1992, 35.
16. Luciano, "How to Cut Your Expenses 20 Percent (and Live Better, Too)."
17. Elizabeth Fenner, "Fourteen Terrific Moves That Can Save Plenty," *Money,* December 1991.
18. *Tips for Tough Times,* Consumer Protection Division, Maryland Attorney General's Office, Issue 7.
19. Ibid.
20. Moreau, "If You Lose Your Job," 62.
21. Quinn, "Managing Money without a Paycheck," 35.
22. Ibid.
23. Dawn M. Baskerville, "When You're In Over Your Head," *Black Enterprise,* January 1992, 64–66.
24. Moreau, "If You Lose Your Job," 63.
25. Luciano, "How to Cut Your Expenses 20 Percent (and Live Better, Too)."
26. Ibid.
27. Ellen James Martin, "Homebuyers: Look for Ways to Break Decision Deadlock," *Baltimore Sun,* June 27, 1993.
28. Quinn, *Making the Most of Your Money.*
29. Ibid.
30. Lee and Barbara Simmons, *Penny Pinching* (New York: Bantam Books, 1993).
31. Carol Kleiman, "Con Artists in Career Marketing Have Foe in Rado," *Chicago Tribune,* July 21, 1985.
32. Paul Anderson, "Australia to U.S. Job Seekers: We Really Don't Need You," *Miami Herald,* May 11, 1991.
33. Gene Tharpe, "Scam Promised Good Job, High Pay in Exotic Locale," *Atlanta Journal/Atlanta Constitution,* July 27, 1992.

34. Carol Kleiman, "Odd Jobs," *Washington Post,* September 5, 1993. Also Betty Joyce Nash, "Job Seekers Disappointed by Promise of High Pay Overseas," *Greensboro News and Record,* August 14, 1991.
35. Julia Lawlor, "Job-Scam Artists Work Overtime," *USA Today,* July 9, 1992.
36. Ibid.
37. Ibid. Also Cable News Network reported on September 2, 1993, that phony executive search firms are charging $2,000 to $3,000, and urged job seekers never to pay up-front fees.
38. *Tips for Tough Times,* Consumer Protection Division, Maryland Attorney General's Office, 1992, Issue 3.
39. Ibid.
40. *Tips for Tough Times,* Consumer Protection Division, Maryland Attorney General's Office, 1992, Issues 4 and 6.
41. Ibid.
42. "48 Hours," CBS Television, February 3, 1993.
43. H. Jackson Brown, Jr., *Live and Learn and Pass It On,* (Nashville, Tennessee: Rutledge Hill Press, 1991).
44. Bill Moyers, "Minimum Wages," Public Television Videocassette Service, 1320 Braddock Place, Alexandria, VA 22314-1698, (703-739-5380).
45. Larry Reibstein and David L. Gonzalez, "Employment-Agency Scams," *Newsweek,* February 20, 1989, 40.
46. Lawlor, "Job-Scam Artists Work Overtime."
47. Ibid.
48. Elizabeth Fenner, "A Bomb Blast Hero Picks Up the Pieces," *Money,* May 1993, 145–52.
49. Ibid.
50. Ibid.
51. Ibid.
52. D. Jacobson, "Models of Stress and Meanings of Unemployment: Reactions to Job Loss among Technical Professionals," *Social Science Medicine,* 24 (1987), 13–21.
53. Nick Kates, Barrie S. Greiff, and Duane Q. Hagen, *The Psychosocial Impact of Job Loss* (Washington, DC: American Psychiatric Press, 1990).

V. JOB LOSS CAN BE HARMFUL TO YOUR HEALTH

1. Sara Arber, "Social Class, Non-Employment, and Chronic Illness: Continuing the Inequities in Health Debate," *British Medical Journal,* 294 (April 25, 1987), 1069.

2. Carl D'Arcy, "Unemployment and Health: Data and Implications," *Canadian Journal of Public Health,* 77, supplement 1 (1986), 124–31.
3. Richard Smith, "'What's the Point; I'm No Use to Anybody': The Psychological Consequences of Unemployment," *British Medical Journal,* 291 (November 9, 1985), 1338–41. Also Ramsay Liem and Paula Rayman, "Health and Social Costs of Unemployment," *American Psychologist,* 37, no. 10 (October 1982), 1116–23. Also P. Warr, "Work, Jobs and Unemployment," *Bulletin of the British Psychological Society,* 36 (1983), 305–11. Also P. R. Jackson and P. B. Warr, "Unemployment and Psychological Ill Health: The Moderating Role of Duration and Age," *Psychological Medicine,* 14 (1984), 605–14.
4. Smith, "'What's the Point; I'm No Use to Anybody': The Psychological Consequences of Unemployment." Also J. Paul Grayson, "The Closure of a Factory and Its Impact on Health," *International Journal of Health Services,* 15, no. 1 (1985), 69–93. Also Leonard Fagin and Martin Little, *The Forsaken Families* (London: Penguin, 1984), p. 202. And Liem and Rayman, "Health and Social Costs of Unemployment," 1120. Also Sten-Olof Brenner and Lennart Levi, "Long-Term Unemployment among Women in Sweden," *Social Science Medicine,* 25, no. 2 (Great Britain: Pergamon Journals, 1987), 153–61. That job loss can affect the immune system is a conclusion reached by numerous experts, including Brenner and Levi (1987) and also B. Arnetz et al., "Immune Function in Unemployed Women," *Psychosomatic Medicine,* 49, no. 1 (January–February 1987). Brenner and Levi (1987), in their study of unemployed women in Sweden, found no significant changes in the tobacco and alcohol consumption of women who suffered job loss. Peck and Plant (1986) found no association between unemployment and alcohol use among young people in Scotland and Denmark, and D'Arcy (1986) found similarly in Canada. However, many other studies, including the United Kingdom General Household Survey in 1982, Crawford et al. in 1985, and Smart's study in Canada published in 1979, clearly show an increase in alcohol abuse. (An increased use of tobacco, and to a much lesser extent, an increase in illicit drug use has been reported, too.)
5. Bengt B. Arnetz et al., "Neuroendocrine and Immunologic Effects of Unemployment and Job Insecurity," *Psychotherapy and Psychosomatics,* 55, no. 2–4 (1991), 76–80. Arnetz found that the symptoms of stress were highest during the phase when an individual knows a job is about to be lost. Stress decreased after the actual job loss, and increased again at the one year of unemployment

mark. Carrie Leana and Daniel Feldman in *Coping with Job Loss* (New York: Lexington Books, 1992, p. 61), observed a rather different pattern of adjustment on the part of the blue-collar steelworkers in Pennsylvania and white-collar Florida Space Coast workers they studied. Data from these groups showed the greatest levels of depression, apathy, and listlessness in the first six months of unemployment. From seven through nine months there was a decrease in symptoms of stress, "while for those unemployed over nine months, depression rose once again." Leana and Feldman theorized that depression, apathy, and listlessness increase with time, after unemployment compensation runs out and following a concerted but unsuccessful effort to become reemployed. After the unemployed person tries hard to reestablish personal control by finding a new job, he or she may "sink into the depression and apathy that characterize helplessness."

6. M. Studnicka et al., "Psychological Health, Self-Reported Physical Health and Health Service Use," *Social Psychiatry and Psychiatric Epidemiology* 26 (1991), 86–91.

7. Leonard Fagin and Martin Little, *The Forsaken Families* (London: Penguin, 1984) p. 117.

8. Arnetz, "Neuroendocrine and Immunologic Effects of Unemployment and Job Insecurity." It is worth saying that 75 percent of the subjects in this study were women, since so many similar studies have addressed the health implications of unemployment on men. "Results showed marked effects during the anticipatory and early unemployment phase on mental well-being, serum cortisol, prolactin, total cholesterol, HDL cholesterol, and phytohemagglutinin reactivity of lymphocytes. Most of these changes appear to be of short-term duration," Arnetz continued. "However, changes in cardiovascular risk factors are observed at least two years following the loss of one's job."

9. Carl D'Arcy, "Unemployment and Health: Data and Implications," *Canadian Journal of Public Health,* 77, supplement 1 (May–June 1986), 124–31. D'Arcy used a sampling system designed to eliminate those who lost their jobs because they were already ill.

10. Ibid., 127–28 and figures 1a and 2c.

11. K. A. Moser, A. J. Fox, P. O. Goldblatt, and D. R. Jones, "Stress and Heart Disease: Evidence of Associations between Unemployment and Heart Disease from the OPCS Longitudinal Study," *Postgraduate Medical Journal,* 62 (1986), 797–99. Also Nick Kates, Barrie S. Greiff, and Duane Q. Hagen, *The Psychosocial Impact of Job Loss* (Washington, D.C.: American Psychiatric Press, 1990), p. 52. From

an initial sample of more than 500,000, Moser followed for a decade 6,000 unemployed men and nearly 8,000 women married to or living with such men. Excluding men who were out of work because of sickness, and controlling for certain socioeconomic factors that could account for increased mortality rates, Moser and associates saw a 20 percent to 30 percent increase in mortality due to the stress of unemployment.

12. M. Harvey Brenner, "Relation of Economic Change to Swedish Health and Social Well-Being, 1950–1980," *Social Science Medicine,* 25, no. 2 (1987), 183–95. Usually there is a time lag—of two or three to eleven years—between the increased unemployment rate and increased death rate, explains Brenner. However, men aged forty to seventy and women forty to fifty-nine also have an increased risk of heart disease mortality within the first two years, and men aged fifty to fifty-nine have the highest immediate risk.

For a brief review of the argument that increases in the unemployment rate do *not* result in significant increases in the death rate, see Joseph Eyer, "Does Unemployment Cause the Death Rate to Peak in Each Business Cycle?" *International Journal of Health Services,* 7, no. 4 (1977), 625–26. Eyer argues that the variation in housing and nutrition, alcohol and cigarette consumption, and social relationship changes account for the greatest part (72 percent) of the business cycle variation of the death rate, and he asserts that there are greater sources of stress during economic booms than increased health risks during business cycle depressions. Richard Smith, in his 1985 article in the *British Medical Journal,* "'What's the Point. I'm No Use to Anybody': The Psychological Consequences of Unemployment" (November 9, 1985), 1341, concedes that "Brenner has warned that we may miss large effects on health by comparing the employed with the unemployed because both may be experiencing the effects." Smith goes on to conclude that while Brenner's studies are controversial because, in his opinion, Brenner's methods are suspect, Smith does believe that Brenner's broad conclusions are correct. Smith further states, "The case has been made that unemployment leads to a deterioration in mental health."

13. Lorraine Branham, "Peril to Jobless Goes Beyond Livelihood," *Baltimore Sun,* January 29, 1982.

14. Barbara Koeppel, "For Airline Workers the Crash Can Be Fatal," *Washington Post,* September 5, 1993.

15. Ibid.

16. The Richard Brooks story is taken from the Koeppel article.

17. Arnetz et al., "Neuroendocrine and Immunologic Effects of Unemployment and Job Insecurity." Also, according to researcher Loring Jones of San Diego State University, most longitudinal studies of unemployment reveal that the psychological and health problems of the unemployed person and spouse recede with reemployment, but only if the new job provides a comparable status and income to the job that was lost. This is a finding of great importance in the late 1990s and early part of the new century, since increasing numbers of blue- and white-collar workers end up having to take jobs at lower pay and status. Healthy lifestyles that promote physical health and coping strategies that promote psychological health become all the more important when economic downsizing is the reality that so many North Americans and Europeans have to live with. (Loring Jones, "Unemployment and Child Abuse," *Families in Society: The Journal of Contemporary Human Services,* Family Service America, 1990, 579–84. Jones cites the following studies: Liem and Rayman, 1982; Stephen Fineman, *White Collar Unemployment and Stress* [New York: John Wiley and Sons, 1983]; and Warr and Jackson, 1985.)

18. Joan Borysenko, *Minding the Body, Mending the Mind* (New York: Bantam Books, 1988), pp. 25–26.

19. Ibid.

20. Gerald Caplan, "Stress Reactions: New Concepts and Opportunities" and "Practical Applications of Support Systems Theory: Interventions in Child and Adult Stress Reactions," lectures presented at the International Hotel, Baltimore-Washington International Airport, for the Health and Education Council, May 19, 1981.

21. K. B. Nuckolls, J. Cassell, and B. H. Kaplan, "Psychosocial Assets, Life Crisis and the Prognosis of Pregnancy," *American Journal of Epidemiology,* 95 (1972), 431–41.

22. Susan Gore, "The Effect of Social Support in Moderating the Health Consequences of Unemployment," *Journal of Health and Social Behavior,* 19 (1978), 157–65.

23. Gordon E. Moss, *Illness, Immunity and Social Interaction* (New York: John Wiley, 1973).

24. Ibid.

25. Gore, "The Effect of Social Support in Moderating the Health Consequences of Unemployment," 158. Also J. Blake Turner, Ronald C. Kessler, and James S. House, "Factors Facilitating Adjustment to Unemployment: Implications for Intervention," *American Journal of Community Psychiatry,* 19, no. 4 (August 1991), 532. In this study, unmarried women and men who had a confidant and a

strong social support network also had less likelihood of depression, anxiety, and physical illness.

26. Maya Pines quotes Suzanne Kobasa in "Psychological Hardiness: The Role of Challenge in Health," *Psychology Today*, 4, no. 7 (December 1980), 39.

27. Borysenko, *Minding the Body, Mending the Mind*, pp. 24, 25. Borysenko cites the work of Harvard psychologist George Vaillant, who for thirty years followed a group of Harvard alumni. He found that those who had an immature coping style became ill four times more often than those who had a hardier style.

28. Stephen Fineman, *White Collar Unemployment and Stress* (New York: John Wiley and Sons, 1983).

29. "Psychotherapy and Melanoma," *The Harvard Mental Health Letter*, 10, no. 10 (April 1994).

30. Ibid. Also Fawzy I. Fawzy et al., "Malignant Melanoma: Effects of an Early Structured Psychiatric Intervention, Coping, and Affective State on Recurrence and Survival Six Years Later," *Archives of General Psychiatry*, 50 (September 1993), 681–89.

31. Richard Smith, *British Medical Journal*, 1338. Smith cites M. Colledge and R. Bartholomew, *A Study of the Long-Term Unemployed* (London: Manpower Services Commission, 1980).

32. Fagin and Little, *The Forsaken Families*.

33. David Jacobson, "Models of Stress and Meanings of Unemployment: Reactions to Job Loss among Technical Professionals," *Social Science Medicine*, 24 (1987), 13–21.

VI. Danger Signs: Severe Depression and Suicidal Thoughts

1. A University of Southampton professor, C. Pritchard, wrote in 1990 that the greater the rise in unemployment, the stronger is the association between suicide death rates and unemployment. Throughout most of the 1980s Pritchard saw that in the Western world "critical levels" of unemployment were positively correlated with male suicide. This correlation, according to World Health Organization statistics, was less strong for females. (C. Pritchard, "Suicide, Unemployment and Gender Variations in the Western World 1964–1986: Are Women in Anglo-phone Countries Protected from Suicide?" *Social Psychiatry and Psychiatric Epidemiology*, 25, no. 2 [1990], 73–80.) Also M. Boor, "Relationships between Unemployment Rates and Suicide in Eight Countries, 1962–1976," *Psychology Report*, 47 [1980], 1095–1101. Boor found a positive association in

the unemployment and suicide rates in six of the eight countries he studied—the United States, Canada, France, West Germany, Japan, and Sweden. However, his work covered only 1962–1976, years of relatively low unemployment. And M. Harvey Brenner, "Economic Change, Alcohol Consumption and Heart Disease Mortality in Nine Industrialized Countries," *Social Science Medicine,* 25 [1987], 119–32. Brenner, of Johns Hopkins University, also reported a clear relationship between increased unemployment and an increased relative risk of suicide.

In a study of Japanese suicide, researcher Michael Snyder found a strong correlation between suicide and unemployment in Japanese males between the ages of thirty-five and fifty-four (Michael L. Snyder, "Japanese Male Suicide Before and After Retirement," *Psychology, A Journal of Human Behavior,* 27, no. 2 [1990], 47–52.) In France, Alain Philippe found that unemployment increases the suicide risk of the more vulnerable segments of the population, such as those in lower income groups and those who have had psychiatric problems. (Alain Philippe, *"Suicide et Chomage/*Suicide and Unemployment," *Psychologie-Medicale,* 20, no. 3 [March 1988], 380–82.)

In Italy, Florenzano and Crepet, who studied the decade between the mid-1970s through the mid-1980s, saw a positive correlation for both sexes between unemployment and suicide (including suicide attempts). (Francesco Florenzano and Paolo Crepet, *"Suicidio e disoccupazione: Analisi del rischio attribuibile e delle correlazioni/*Suicide and Unemployment: Analysis of the Attributable Risk and of the Correlations," *Rivista Sperimentale di Freniatria e Medicina Legale delle Alienazioni Mentali,* 111, no. 1 [February 1987], 7–20.)

In Brazil, Galdino Loreto reported that economic changes, and especially a rise in the unemployment rate, are significantly related to depressed mood and to an increase in the suicide rate, at least in urban areas. Those who had learned good coping skills and had access to social resources, said Loreto, were less vulnerable to the stressful life event of economic change. (Galdino Loreto, *"Depressao, Crise e Recessao Economica/*Depression, Crisis and Economical Recession," *Neurobiologia,* 50, no. 1 [January–March 1987], 1–12.)

Sri Lanka's suicide rate, according to a recent article in *The Economist,* is one of the highest in the world. While there are said to be many reasons why more than 8,000 people took their life in this small country in 1991, "some suicides, or attempted suicides, are said to be the result of Sri Lanka's many well-educated but un-employed people. Their ambitions stretch beyond their rural back-ground and traditional upbringing, and it is their frustrations which have played a role in various insurrections." Most are under age thirty. ("Sri Lanka's Other Killing Ground," *The Economist,* November 28, 1992.)

Unemployment and poverty are "definite causes" of suicide and suicide attempts in India, according to A. V. Rao. The author writes of a wave of suicide "among the goldsmiths of India when they found themselves suddenly unemployed as a result of the promulgation of the Gold Control Order by the Government of India." (A. V. Rao, *Suicide in India* [Baltimore: University Park Press, 1975]). A Scottish study found that in 1982 unemployed men in Edinburgh were 11.8 times more likely to attempt suicide than employed men. Women who had lost their jobs were at least seven times more likely to attempt suicide than those who were employed. Workers unemployed for more than a year had the highest rates of attempted suicide. (Keith Hawton, Joan Fagg, and Susan Simkin, "Female Unemployment and Attempted Suicide," *British Journal of Psychiatry,* 152 [1988], 632–37.)

2. Stephen Platt, "Parasuicide and Unemployment," *British Journal of Psychiatry,* 49 (1986), 401–5.
3. Olle Hagnell and Birgitta Rorsman, "Suicide Rates in the Lundby Study: A Controlled Prospective Investigation of Stressful Life Events," *Neuropsychobiology,* 6 (1980), 319–32. (The suicide group and two control groups were drawn from a twenty-five-year prospective study of 3,563 persons. All of the persons who later committed suicide had been examined by psychiatrists on one or two occasions at a "normal" period in their lives. After the suicides, more information was gathered from persons intimately knowledgeable about the lives and stressful circumstances of those who died.)
4. Ibid.
5. Hawton, Fagg, and Simkin, "Female Unemployment and Attempted Suicide."
6. Platt, "Parasuicide and Unemployment."
7. Carrie R. Leana and Daniel C. Feldman, *Coping with Job Loss* (New York: Lexington Books, 1992), p. 7. Also Leana and Feldman, "Individual Responses to Job Loss: Perception, Reactions, and Coping Behaviors," *Journal of Management,* 14 (1988), 375–89. Also P. Ullah, M. H. Banks, and P. B. Warr, "Social Support, Social Pressures, and Psychological Distress during Unemployment," and Warr, Jack-

son, and Banks, "Unemployment and Mental Health," both in *Psychological Medicine,* 15 (1985), 283–95.

8. Leana and Feldman, *Coping with Job Loss.*

9. Robert I. Yufit, "American Association of Suicidology Presidential Address: Suicide Assessment in the 1990's," *Suicide and Life-Threatening Behavior,* 21, no. 2 (Summer 1991), 152–63.

10. American Psychiatric Association: Diagnostic and Statistical Manual of Mental Disorders, 4th ed. Washington, DC, American Psychiatric Association, 1994.

11. The emphasis in this discussion on the relevance of the Lundby Study findings in understanding the problem of job loss and suicide comes from Dr. J. Raymond DePaulo, director of the Center for Affective Disorders at the Johns Hopkins Hospital. Dr. DePaulo is a respected friend and colleague whose conversations with me in this regard have been most valuable. In the Lundby Study, men with moderate depression had a suicide rate of 220 per 100,000 people each year. Severely depressed men showed the startlingly high rate of 3,900 per 100,000 each year (nearly 4 percent)! (Hagnell and Rorsman, "Suicide Rates in the Lundby Study.")

12. J. Raymond DePaulo, Jr., and Keith Russell Ablow, *How to Cope with Depression* (New York: Fawcett Crest, 1991). Also Janet Farrar Worthington, "A Taint of Blood," *Hopkins Medical News,* Winter 1995, 35–41.

13. William W. Dressler, "Unemployment's Depressive Symptoms in a Southern Black Community," *Journal of Nervous and Mental Disease,* 174, no. 11 (November 1986), 639–45.

14. S. D. Platt and J.A.J. Dyer, "Psychological Correlates of Unemployment among Male Parasuicides in Edinburgh," *British Journal of Psychiatry,* 151 (1987), 27–32.

15. Yufit, "Presidential Address."

16. Norman Kreitman, Vera Carstairs, and John Duffy, "Association of Age and Social Class with Suicide among Men in Great Britain," *Journal of Epidemiology and Community Health,* 45 (1991), 195–202.

17. DePaulo and Ablow, *How to Cope with Depression.*

VII. FAMILY PROBLEMS: FINDING SOLUTIONS

1. Leonard Fagin and Martin Little, *The Forsaken Families* (London: Penguin Books, 1984), p. 171.

2. R. Liem and J. Liem, "Social Class and Mental Illness Reconsidered: The Role of Economic Stress and Social Support," *Journal of Health and Social Behavior,* 19 (1978), 139–56.

3. Raymond Cochrane and Mary Stopes-Roe, "Women, Marriage, Employment and Mental Health," *British Journal of Psychiatry,* 139 (1981), 373–81.
4. Mary Amanda Dew, Evelyn J. Bromet, and Herbert C. Schulberg, "A Comparative Analysis of Two Community Stressors' Long-Term Mental Health Effects," *American Journal of Community Psychology,* 15, no. 2 (1987), 167–84. Professor Dew and her colleagues used demographically comparable samples of women and followed for three years both the wives of the unemployed men and the women who experienced the stress of the nuclear accident. For the T. M. I. sample, the index of the accident's stressfulness was the distance of residence from the plant. The index of the personal stressfulness of unemployment was created from data on the husband's employment history during the interval between each interview. The unemployed subjects were studied for three and a half years. This remarkable study was possible because the authors were two and a half years into their longitudinal study of the mental health effects of the nuclear accident when T. M. I.'s comparison site experienced massive unemployment in the local steel industry owing to a severe economic depression. Data were collected from 361 married women who delivered a child between January 1978 and March 1979 (the month of the T. M. I. accident). Of these, 257 lived within ten miles of the T. M. I. facility in Middletown, PA, and 104 lived near the Beaver Valley-Shipping port (BV-S) nuclear plants in western Pennsylvania. Subjects were interviewed nine, twelve, thirty, and forty-two months after the T. M. I. accident, and the BV-S layoffs began immediately after the thirty-month interview. The BV-S women were interviewed a fifth time fifty-four months after the accident.
5. Dew, "A Comparative Analysis of Two Community Stressors' Long-Term Mental Health Effects," 167, 181.
6. Fagin and Little, *The Forsaken Families.* Also L. Margolis and D. Farrau, "Unemployment: The Health Consequences," *North Carolina Medical Journal,* 42 (1981), 849–50.
7. Nicola Madge, "Unemployment and Its Effects on Children," *Journal of Child Psychology and Psychiatry,* 24, no. 2 (1983), 311–19. Madge cites M. Brennan and B. Stoten, "Children, Poverty and Illness," *New Society,* 36 (1976), 681–82. Also Loring Jones, "Unemployment and Child Abuse," *Families in Society: The Journal of Contemporary Human Services,* (1990), 583.
8. Madge, "Unemployment and Its Effects on Children."
9. J. Paul Grayson, "The Closure of a Factory and Its Impact on Health,"

International Journal of Health Services, 15, no. 1 (1985), 78.

10. Fagin and Little, *The Forsaken Families.*

11. Katherine S. Newman, *Falling from Grace: The Experience of Downward Mobility in the American Middle Class* (New York: Vintage Books, 1989), p. 56.

12. Quoted in J. Blotzer, "When the Fire Dies: A Special Report on Pittsburgh's Laid-Off Workers," *Pittsburgh Post-Gazette,* supplement, December 30, 1985.

13. Quoted in Thomas J. Cottle, *Commonweal,* June 19, 1992, 17. (The author is a sociologist and clinical psychologist with fifteen years of experience in meeting men unemployed for at least six months and usually longer.)

14. Ibid.

15. The family is described in Fagin and Little, *The Forsaken Families,* p. 73.

16. Jeffry H. Larson, "The Effect of Husband's Unemployment on Marital and Family Relations in Blue-Collar Families," *Family Relations,* 33 (1984), 505, 509. In the Liems' study of Boston area families, the midyear of unemployment was said to be an especially crucial period. Some couples had adapted to the stress by then. But reemployment itself was particularly stressful at this time, disrupting the couple's pattern of accommodation. At six months, the wives of white-collar workers who were still unemployed even showed an improvement in their emotional well-being, evidencing accommodation. (Ramsay Liem and Joan Huser Liem, "Psychological Effects of Unemployment on Workers and Their Families," *Journal of Social Issues,* 44, no. 4 [1988], 87–105.)

17. Newman, *Falling from Grace,* p. 56.

18. Ibid.

19. Jeffrey K. Liker and Glen H. Elder, Jr., "Economic Hardship and Marital Relationships in the 1930s," *American Sociological Review,* 48 (June 1983), 343–59.

20. Richard Smith, "'We Get on Each Other's Nerves': Unemployment and the Family," *British Medical Journal,* 291 (1985), 1707–10.

21. Ibid. Smith cites J. Burgoyne, "Unemployment and Married Life," *Unemployment Unit Bulletin,* November 1985, 7–10 and the Central Statistical Office, *Social Trends,* 15 (1985), 39. Also K. Windschuttle, *Unemployment: A Social and Political Analysis of the Economic Crisis in Australia* (Victoria: Penguin, 1980). Also J. J. Grayford, "Wife Battering: A Preliminary Survey of 100 Cases," *British Medical Journal,* ii (1975), 388–91.

22. Ellen Goodman, "Why Didn't Anybody Say Something?" *Baltimore*

Sun, June 22, 1994, 11A. Also CNN, "Headline News," June 22, 1994.

23. Mark Thompson, "The Living Room War," *Time,* May 23, 1994, 48–51.

24. Jill Jukes and Ruthan Rosenberg, *Surviving Your Partner's Job Loss* (Washington, DC: National Press Books, 1993).

25. M. Segal, "Economic Deprivation and the Quality of Parent-Child Relations: A Trickle Down Framework," *Journal of Applied Developmental Psychology,* 5 (1984), 127–44. Also L. Steinberg, R. Catalano, and D. Dooley, "Economic Antecedents of Child Abuse and Neglect," *Child Development,* 52 (1981), 975–86. Also David G. Gil, *Violence Against Children—Physical Child Abuse in the United States* (Cambridge, MA: Harvard University Press, 1970), p. 111. Gil's national survey showed that 47.5 percent of the fathers of abused children were out of work during the year before the child was abused and 11.8 percent were unemployed at the time of the abusive act.

26. Loring Jones, "Unemployment and Child Abuse," *Families in Society: The Journal of Contemporary Human Services,* December 1990, 579–84. Jones cites Madge (1983), who reviewed British studies, and Margolis and Farrau (1983).

27. Richard D. Krugman, Marilyn Lenherr, Lynn Betz, and George Edward Fryer, "The Relationship between Unemployment and the Physical Abuse of Children," *Child Abuse and Neglect,* 10 (1986), 415–18. Also E. C. Weeks and S. Drencacz, "Rocking in a Small Boat: The Consequences of Economic Change in Rural Communities," *International Journal of Mental Health,* 12 (1983), 62–75.

28. Jones, "Unemployment and Child Abuse."

29. Blair Justice and David F. Duncan, "Child Abuse as a Work-Related Problem," a paper presented at the American Public Health Association's 103rd Annual Meeting, "Health and Work in America," Child Abuse Session, Chicago, November 20, 1975. Frequent pregnancy in mothers with excessive workloads or an overload of work and domestic obligations can lead certain women to abuse their children. Justice, of the University of Texas Health Science Center, and Duncan, of the State University of New York at Brockport, explain that a woman may be overworked and struggling to cope with too many young children "when the extra demand of a sick, crying or disobedient child" prompts the susceptible mother to "strike out against this further excessive demand." They explain the overworking husband problem thus: "As working late, business trips and work brought home from the office intrude more and more

between husband and wife, an isolated wife with a desperate need to be comforted and cared for may turn to her child for satisfaction. Finding her need frustrated . . . , she may strike out in anger at her offspring."

30. Laurence D. Steinberg, Ralph Catalano, and David Dooley, "Economic Antecedents of Child Abuse and Neglect," *Child Development,* 52 (1981), 975–85.

31. Jones, "Unemployment and Child Abuse." Citing a study released by The National Center on Child Abuse in 1988, Jones reports that families with an income less than $15,000 a year in 1986 were four times as likely to commit all forms of abuse as those earning more than that amount. Another important factor says researcher Jones, is that job loss causes the breadwinner's status to diminish within the family, especially in families with traditional role orientations. Often abuse grows out of the father's attempts to reassert his status. (Loring Jones, "Unemployment and Child Abuse," *Families in Society: The Journal of Contemporary Human Services,* [1990], 581.) Several other researchers have written that unemployed men show a stronger tendency to overassert their power with their children than with their wives. (Ibid. Jones cites Madge [1983], Elder [1974], Komarovsky [1940], and Lewis [1987].) Although unemployed men are also at a greater risk of abusing their wives than men who are employed, the abusive behavior may be directed toward children because the unemployed man feels more vulnerable in regard to his wife. When the man has a full-time job, unequal division of labor in a marriage can be justified, but once the man's provider role is disturbed, the balance between spouses is disturbed too. Thus, needing her support, he is more likely to take his frustrations out on the children. (Ibid. Jones cites Cutright [1971].)

A person's sense of self can get quite a battering, says psychologist Stephen Fineman, in his book *White Collar Unemployment and Stress.* Various expressions of this include feelings of inferiority, loss of self-respect, reduced self-confidence, and damaged ego. (Stephen Fineman, *White Collar Unemployment and Stress* [New York: John Wiley and Sons, 1983], p. 31.)

I am convinced that persons with low self-esteem are far more likely to strike out in physical violence or brutal words. Therefore, the more progress an individual makes in truly enhancing self-esteem, the more that person can overcome any abusive tendencies. A person who grows in feelings of genuine self-regard gets more control over various emotions and improves the quality of his or her relationships with loved ones. Regaining control of one's own life enables the person to grow in self-respect as well.

32. Justice and Duncan, "Child Abuse as a Work-Related Problem."
33. Steinberg, Catalano, and Dooley, "Economic Antecedents of Child Abuse and Neglect."
34. Ibid.
35. Ibid.
36. Loring Jones, "Unemployment and Child Abuse," 584.
37. Ibid.
38. Paul L. Lerner, "When the Family Loses a Job," *Amtrak Express,* September–October 1993, 13.
39. Harold Bloomfield, *The Achilles Syndrome* (New York: Random House, 1985), p. 76.
40. Lerner, "When a Family Loses a Job," 10–13.
41. Lewis P. Lipsitt, "Lee Salk (1926–1992)," *American Psychologist,* 48, no. 8 (August 1993), 908. Psychologist Lewis P. Lipsitt wrote this paraphrase of Lee Salk's words in Salk's obituary in the *American Psychologist,* August 1993.
42. Jukes and Rosenberg, *Surviving Your Partner's Job Loss,* pp. 93–96.
43. Ibid., pp. 114, 115.
44. E. Wethington and R. C. Kessler, "Perceived Support, Received Support, and Adjustment to Stressful Life Events," *Journal of Health and Social Behavior,* 27 (1986), 78–89.
45. From a lecture in Baltimore in the early 1970s. The concepts Dr. Haim Ginott discussed in that lecture are also presented in *Between Parent and Child* (New York: Avon Books, 1976).
46. Fagin and Little, *The Forsaken Families.*

VIII. SURVIVING IN A CHANGED AND CHANGING WORKPLACE

1. Barbara Tuchman, *The Guns of August* (New York: Ballantine Books, 1994).
2. E. J. Dionne, Jr., "Job Summit Deserved More Than a Back Seat to Scandal," *Seattle Times,* March 17, 1994.
3. Brad Edmondson, "Remaking a Living," *Utne Reader,* July–August 1991.
4. Ibid.
5. Katherine S. Newman, *Falling from Grace: The Experience of Downward Mobility in the American Middle Class* (New York: Vintage Books, 1989), p. 25.
6. Ibid. (Newman cites the *New York Times,* December 14, 1986.)

Newman points to Robert Lawrence (1983) as a critic of the dein-dustrialization thesis. According to Lawrence's perspective, "it is in Europe rather than in the United States that employment is under-going absolute deindustrialization." He says that manufacturing productivity in the United States has risen more rapidly than in any other sector (including service industries), increasing indus-trial output but with a significant decrease in the size of the work-force, capital investments, and dollars devoted to manufacturing research and development."

It is difficult for anyone who understands the principles of capi-talism "to explain why a manufacturer of, say, refrigerators would make them in Texas rather than on the other side of the Rio Grande if 'Made in Mexico' costs significantly less than 'Made in U.S.A.'" Actually, "if the capitalist's company has shareholders, it is more or less against the law not to maximize profits and the value of their shares." Richard Reeves points out that, in fact, Mexico more resembles the United States than China, and that the manu-facturing of products soon is going to pass right through Mexico to cheaper labor in Vietnam and China. It is unlikely that America will again lead the world in manufacturing during our lifetime. In many fields, "the work produced will always be divided by the cost—and the number that pops out determines who is the best. And that final number is rarely going to be produced after divid-ing by $10 or $20 or $30 an hour." (Richard Reeves, "Unthinkable Thoughts About Jobs," *Baltimore Sun,* March 24, 1993.)

7. In a 1986 *Wall Street Journal* article it was reported that 600,000 middle managers lost their jobs in 1985 alone. Newman, however, cites Bureau of Labor Statistics findings (1986) indicating that 487,000 managers were displaced over a four-year period, a figure both she and I consider more accurate.

8. George J. Church, "The White Collar Layoffs That We're Seeing Are Permanent and Structural. These Jobs Are Gone Forever," *Time,* November 22, 1993, 34–39.

9. John Greenwald, "The Job Freeze," *Time,* February 1, 1993, 51–53.

10. U.S. Department of Labor, news release, May 5, 1995.

11. Newman, *Falling from Grace: The Experience of Downward Mobil-ity in the American Middle Class.*

12. Tom Peters, "Thriving in Chaos," *Working Woman,* September 1993, 43–45, 100–102.

13. "Risk of Layoffs Grows for Middle-Aged Men," *Baltimore Sun,* May 21, 1994.

14. Kevin G. Salwen, *Wall Street Journal,* March 16, 1994.

15. Ibid. It is President Bill Clinton who has often estimated that Americans will change jobs seven or eight times in their lifetimes.
16. According to the *Baltimore Sun,* "In the 33 months after the recession [that] ended in 1991, only 2.7 million jobs were created," raising the national payroll 2.5 percent. These figures are in striking contrast to the same period after the previous *three* major recessions, when the national payroll increased by an average of 10 percent. (Gilbert A. Lewthwaite, "Now Hiring," *Baltimore Sun,* Sunday, January 23, 1994, 1, 3D. Also Business Digest, "Layoffs at U.S. Firms Hit High," *Baltimore Sun,* February 7, 1994, 16D. The figures cited were tracked by Challenger, Gray and Christmas, a Chicago-based consulting firm.)
17. Wal-Mart created more jobs in the early 1990s period of economic recovery than any other employer, but they generally paid only $5 to $9 an hour. "One study found that of 2,000-odd workers let go by RJR Nabisco, 72 percent found jobs—but at wages that averaged only 47 percent of their previous pay." There are similar reports from a wide variety of blue- and white-collar settings in a vast array of institutions and industries. (George S. Church, "The White Collar Layoffs That We're Seeing Are Permanent and Structural. These Jobs Are Gone Forever," *Time,* February 1, 1993, 51–53. Also Barbara Koeppel, "For Airline Workers the Crash Can Be Fatal," *Washington Post,* September 5, 1993. Also Carrie Leana and Daniel C. Feldman, *Coping with Job Loss* [New York: Lexington Books, 1992]. Also Boston University assistant professor of economics, Christopher Ruhm, in a 1993 telephone interview with Ann Kaiser Stearns.)

   Robert Reno writes: "If you're a wage earner or a salaried worker . . . [America] is not exactly the promised land. . . . [T]his butchery of the corporate work force . . . is proceeding at a faster pace" in a time when the nation's businesses are experiencing rising productivity, increased profits, improvements in global competitiveness, and technological advancement. "Job security is a concept that is disappearing. Wages are still stagnant. . . . Incomes are far more unevenly distributed than they were a decade ago. Part-time or temporary workers are the fastest-growing segment of the work force." Robert Reno, "A Great Economy, Except for Workers," *Baltimore Sun,* May 5, 1994. Also Thomas J. Cottle, "When You Stop You Die," *Commonweal,* June 19, 1992, 18.
18. "New Jobs in the 90s Pay Well," *Baltimore Sun,* October 17, 1994, from the *New York Times* News Service.
19. George J. Church, "Recovery for Whom?" *Time,* April 25, 1994.

20. Janice Castro, "Disposable Workers," *Time,* March 29, 1993, 43–47.
21. Frank Swoboda, "For Growing Ranks of Part-Time Workers, More Burdens and Fewer Benefits," *Washington Post,* September 5, 1993, H2.
22. Ibid.
23. Quoted in Alan Durning, "How Much Is Enough?" *World Watch,* November–December 1990.
24. David G. Myers, *The Pursuit of Happiness* (New York: Avon Books, 1992), p. 150.
25. Consultant Judith Bardwick is quoted by Jane Bryant Quinn in "Survivors of Downsizing are 'Topping Out' Younger," *Baltimore Sun,* October 10, 1993.
26. Rick Lamplugh interviewed Dr. Al Siebert on June 16, 1993, which is when we heard this story of the Tektronics manager.
27. Lance Morrow, "The Temping of America," *Time,* March 29, 1993, 40–41. Also Janice Castro, "Disposable Workers," *Time,* March 29, 1993, 43–47.
28. Morrow, "The Temping of America."
29. Michael Barrier, "Now You Hire Them, Now You Don't," *Nation's Business,* January 1994, 30–32.
30. Castro, "Disposable Workers," 47.
31. Ibid.
32. Meg Whittemore, "Beginning at the Beginning," *Nation's Business,* February 1994, 70.
    Also consulted in the writing of this chapter:
    Peter B. Doeringer, *Turbulence in the American Workplace* (New York: Oxford University Press, 1991). Consultations with managers Elton Perry of 3M Company, Eleanor Fink of AT&T, Marian Wattenbarger of Riverview Medical Center in Red Bank, NJ, and freelance editor Ilene McGrath of Leonia, NJ, contributed to the chapter, too.

IX. What You Need to Know to Prepare for Your Next Job

1. George J. Church, "The White Collar Layoffs That We're Seeing Are Permanent and Structural. These Jobs Are Gone Forever," *Time,* November 22, 1993, 34–39.
2. Ibid.
3. This discussion is based on conversations between Elton Perry and Ann Kaiser Stearns which took place in Baltimore on September 6, 1994.
4. The insights from Blake Wattenbarger, a psychologist and technical manager with AT&T's Bell Labs in Holmdel, New Jersey, are

quoted from conversations with Ann Kaiser Stearns over a period of several days in October 1994.

5. Peter Drucker, "Career Moves for Ages 20–70," *Psychology Today,* November–December 1992, 54–57, 74–76. (This article, amazingly, is a reprint from 1968 and illustrates Drucker's insight on jobs, life paths, and maturity.)

6. This discussion grew out of conversations between Blake Wattenbarger and Ann Kaiser Stearns, as cited in note 4.

7. Ibid.

8. "High Performance Employees" was the topic of Rick Lamplugh's radio program on November 3, 1993. Some of the discussion that follows and certain quotes in this section are taken from that broadcast on KLCC, Eugene, Oregon.

9. Vocational consultant Rick Lamplugh interviewed Bill Bridges for his weekly radio series, "Work in Oregon," which was broadcast by KLCC, Eugene, Oregon on April 28, 1993. Some of the ideas discussed in that program are reviewed, with a good deal of Lamplugh's commentary interspersed.

10. Quoted in Church, "The White Collar Layoffs That We're Seeing Are Permanent and Structural."

11. David Birch, quoted in *Time,* November 22, 1993.

12. These ideas come from conversations with 3M human resources manager Elton Perry, September 6, 1994.

13. Sarah Mahoney, "Fired Again," *Working Woman,* April 1994. Of the 21 million people who found themselves out of work in 1992 (latest available data), 5.7 million had weathered previous spells of unemployment, accordingly to the Bureau of Labor Statistics.

14. David Birch, quoted in Church, "The White Collar Layoffs That We're Seeing Are Permanent and Structural."

15. Church, "The White Collar Layoffs That We're Seeing Are Permanent and Structural."

16. David Birch, quoted in ibid.

17. Ripley Hotch, "Managing from a Distance," *Nation's Business,* February 1993, 24.

18. Ibid., 25, and Maureen Quaid and Brian Lagerberg, "Puget Sound Telecommuting Demonstration (Executive Summary)," Washington State Energy Office, Olympia, Washington. This study was launched in 1990 to explore the environmental, organizational, and personal sides of telecommuting at twenty-five public and private organizations.

19. John Hartnett, "What You Need to Succeed," *Changes,* April 1993, 33. Hartnett quotes from Edwards and Edwards's book as cited in the text.

20. Patricia Braus, "American Workers Want More from Their Jobs Than Ever Before," *Oregonian,* August 30, 1992.
21. Robert Connor, *Cracking the Over-50 Job Market* (New York: Dutton, 1992).
22. Elizabeth Fenner, "How to Find Work When You're Over 50," *Money,* March 1994, 88.
23. Tom Peters, "Thriving in Chaos," *Working Woman,* September 1993, 102.

X. Traits of Those Who Triumph

1. Ann Kaiser Stearns, *Coming Back—Rebuilding Lives after Crisis and Loss* (New York: Random House, 1988, Ballantine Books, 1989).
2. David Fryer and Roy Payne, "Proactive Behaviour in Unemployment: Findings and Implications," *Leisure Studies* 3 (1984), 273–95. Unfortunately, there were only eleven people in this study of the self-actualizing unemployed. The study, however, is a qualitative empirical examination of these individuals, and Fryer and Payne's findings are consistent with other studies, especially the scores of interviews we conducted in writing this book. Interestingly, the study of the eleven shares some common themes with findings from the study of 11,500 air traffic controllers fired by President Ronald Reagan, as reported by anthropologist Katharine S. Newman in *Falling from Grace* (New York: Random House, 1988). Most of the controllers suffered enormous and long-term financial losses and yet fared well psychologically: They had a sense of purpose, had a strong support community, and tended to have a proactive approach to job loss as well as a strong work ethic and a realistic view of the negatives of their previous employment.
3. Ibid., 290.
4. Ibid., 289–90. Italics my own.
5. Ibid., 292. Also Stearns, *Coming Back—Rebuilding Lives after Crisis and Loss.*
6. Rick Lamplugh interviewed Janice Guthrie on June 9, 1993. Some information for this segment was also taken from Michael Barrier's article, "Patient Know Thy Illness," in *Nation's Business,* May 1993, 14–16.
7. Michael Barrier, "Patient Know Thy Illness," 14.
8. Al Santoli, "I'd Rather Drive a Tow Truck," *Parade* Magazine, Janu-

ary 10, 1993, 8. While a few facts and quotes are from *Parade,* most of the information in this story came from Nickerson's interview with Rick Lamplugh in 1993 and her August 20, 1994, interview with Ann Kaiser Stearns.

9. Jesse Jackson was quoted by syndicated columnist Clarence Page in a 1994 article that appeared in the *Baltimore Sun.*

XI. REEVALUATING YOUR LIFE

1. Ann Kaiser Stearns, *Coming Back—Rebuilding Lives After Crisis and Loss* (New York: Random House, 1988). Also P. Watzlawick, J. H. Weakland, and R. Fisch, *Change: Principles of Problem Formation and Problem Resolution* (New York: Norton, 1974). Also T. Boydell and M. Pedlar, *Management Self-Development* (Farnborough: Gower, 1981). Also N. L. Magos and G. A. Mendelsohn, "The Effects of Cancer on Patients' Lives: A Personological Approach," in *Health Psychology,* ed. by G. A. Stone, F. Cohen, and N. E. Adler (San Francisco: Jossey-Bass, 1979).

2. Jim Schutze, "Corporate Dropouts," *Home Office Computing,* February 1993, 46–53.

3. Robert Pasick, *Awakening from a Deep Sleep: A Powerful Guide for Courageous Men* (San Francisco: Harper, 1992). Also Charles Honey, "Midlife: Lives Often Out of Balance," *The Oregonian,* March 5, 1993.

4. Peter Drucker, "Career Moves for Ages 20–70," *Psychology Today,* November–December 1992, 75. The manner in which Drucker spoke of the three men described here made it unclear whether he was speaking hypothetically or describing actual men.

5. The poetic language here describing the Oregon coast is in Rick Lamplugh's words, as it's a place he cherishes, too.

6. Ian Miles, "Some Observations on Unemployment and Health Research," *Social Science Medicine,* 25, no. 2 (1987), 223–25.

7. Viktor Frankl, Keynote Address, International Conference on "The Evolution of Psychotherapy," Hamburg, Germany, July 29, 1994.

XII. BUILDING YOUR FUTURE

1. Harold H. Bloomfield, *The Achilles Syndrome* (New York: Random House, 1985), pp. 17–18.

2. Telephone interview with AT&T psychologist and technical manager Dr. Blake Wattenbarger, October 12, 1994.

3. Ronni Sandroff, "The Psychology of Change," *Working Woman,* July 1993, 52–56.
4. Jim Henneman, "Oates Manages Fine Thanks to Family, Friends," *Baltimore Sun,* September 28, 1994.
5. The rock group Argent sang "Hold Your Head Up," a 1976 Epic Recording, on their album entitled *Anthology.* The song was a best-seller in 1972, and the words and music were written by Rod Argent and Chris White.

Index

Author

A psychology professor and former counselor, Ann Kaiser Stearns is the best-selling author of *Living Through Personal Crisis,* which was described by syndicated columnist Ann Landers as "the best all-purpose self-help book I have seen in years." The book is also published in British, Braille, Spanish, Portuguese, Italian, Chinese, and German editions, as well as in Recordings for the Blind. Dr. Stearns's second book, *Coming Back—Rebuilding Lives After Crisis and Loss,* has been described in the media as "a soul stirring affirmation of human love that sustains and nourishes." She has also written "Counseling the Grieving Person," in *Pastoral Counseling,* edited by Estadt, Compton, and Blanchette.

Now Dr. Stearns has written a timely third book, *Living Through Job Loss.* With the help of consultant Rick Lamplugh, she has studied the dramatically changing American workplace, interviewed scores of blue- and white-collar unemployed people and their families, and interviewed successfully reemployed workers. Dr. Stearns has also done extensive research related to the health, family, financial, and other problems of those who suffer job loss.

She has a bachelor of arts degree from Oklahoma City University, a master of divinity degree from Duke University, and a Ph.D. in psychology from the Union Institute. She was a chaplain at Michigan State University, was for many years on the faculty of the Family Practice Residency Program at Franklin Square Hospital in Baltimore and an adjunct professor at Loyola College, and is a long-time professor of psychology at Essex Community College. Dr. Stearns has appeared on several hundred radio and television stations nationwide, lectures widely around the country, and is the mother of two young daughters.

CONSULTANT

Rick Lamplugh is a certified vocational consultant in Oregon. He has been a business owner and manager, has trained and supervised vocational consultants and job developers, and has written training manuals and staff development material. Lamplugh is the author of *Job Search That Works* (Los Altos, California: Crisp Publications, 1991; Asker, Norway: Kompetansesenteretas, 1994) and produced a weekly public-radio series entitled "Work in Oregon." He has served as a valued consultant on this project.